CONTENTS

*Front cover: A summer picnic
beside the Tea House Bridge
in the gardens at Audley End.*

Copyright © English Heritage 1997
Designed by Collins & Brown Limited
Reproduction by Dot Gradations, Chelmsford, Essex
Printed by Jarrolds, Norwich
ISBN 1 85074 655 9

FOREWORD

I would like to invite you to visit some of the most important historic buildings and ancient monuments in England. You will find splendid diversity representing every aspect of the history of England, expressed in earthworks, dolmen, henges, stone circles, magnificent Roman remains, medieval castles, abbeys, houses and gardens.

I can promise you that no matter what the fabric or location, each visit will provide a fascinating glimpse of England's heritage. Nearly 10.5 million people visited our properties last year.

Besides being responsible for the care of 408 historic properties, we are the leading conservation organisation in England, and offer grants, advice and expertise whenever and wherever England's heritage is at risk, in partnership with a whole host of organisations to ensure that our built heritage is conserved for future generations.

This year we are particularly proud to be celebrating the 1400th anniversary of St Augustine's arrival in England. At St Augustine's Abbey, one of our World Heritage Sites, we have chosen 1997 to celebrate the Christian Heritage of England, whose buildings are the glory of England.

I am also delighted to announce the opening in July of Down House in Kent, the home and workplace of Charles Darwin for the last forty years of his life, which we acquired for the nation last year and are now restoring to its condition in 1877.

We have a saying at English Heritage and that is 'ENGLAND'S HERITAGE IS YOURS. ENJOY IT!' Don't miss out in 1997.

SIR JOCELYN STEVENS
Chairman

WELCOME TO ENGLISH HERITAGE

At English Heritage we do everything we can to make the most fascinating parts of this country's history accessible to the most important people – you. This handbook provides you with all the information you need to visit the extraordinary array of sites in our care, spread across the whole of England. Each one is different, letting you visit everything from a neolithic

Special Events bring history to life

dolmen in the heart of the countryside to the most fabulous of medieval castles. This year many of our sites will also be opening on New Year's Day for the first time, giving you another opportunity to enjoy the splendours of our common heritage.

Our work in preserving the fabric of our history is only possible with your help. Your contributions through membership and admission fees are vital to the continued maintenance of our country's heritage. Without them we would be unable to back major projects such as the renovation of the Albert Memorial – which we hope in return will heighten the enjoyment of your visits to this country's greatest historical sites.

PLANNING YOUR VISIT

Opening times
- Full details of opening arrangements are shown under each entry.
- Many properties are open daily but this varies in the winter months.
- Where a property can only be visited by prior arrangement, contact details are provided.
- Where a property is described as open 'Any reasonable time', we ask that you visit only during daylight hours for reasons of safety and to avoid disturbance to adjoining properties.
- For reasons of safety, many sites close at 6pm or dusk (whichever is earlier) in October. We define dusk as when the levels of light prevent a safe and enjoyable visit. You may wish to contact the site you intend to visit for advice.
- Where a site is opened and unlocked by a keykeeper, please contact either the keykeeper or the appropriate regional office.

A young visitor to Castle Acre Priory

Admission charges
- All admission prices in this handbook are valid from 22 March 1997 to 31 March 1998.
- Admission to all properties is free to English Heritage members unless otherwise stated. Most special events are also free to members.
- Admission charges for non-members are set out as in follows: *£1.20/90p/60p*.
  – The first figure shown is for adults.
  – The second is for concessions (senior citizens, unemployed people – on production of UB40 – and students – on production of student union card).
  – The third is for children under 16 (under fives are admitted free).
- The new **Family Tickets** available at some of our major sites are a great money saver for a family day out.

Group & school visits

- Discounts of 15% are available at most properties for groups of 11 or more. If you are a group organiser or a tour operator, contact our Customer Services Department (see inside back cover) for a free copy of our Group Visits Guide.
- Student and school groups are admitted free to properties provided they book in advance through the relevant English Heritage regional office (see inside back cover). Our new **Windows on the Past** scheme offers many valuable benefits including free admission for up to 4 teachers – contact Customer Services for further details.

Over 600 historical re-enactments are planned for 1997

Travelling by road, train or bus

- Road directions and public transport details are shown under each entry.
- We are grateful to Barry S Doe for providing the public transport information. Please send any comments to him at 25 Newmorton Road, Moordown, Bournemouth, Dorset BH9 3NU or telephone 01202 528707.

When you visit

- We welcome **families with children** of all ages. However, inside some of our grander properties we regret that babies cannot be carried in back carriers as this increases the risk of damage to house contents. Alternative means of carrying babies are provided free of charge at these sites.
- **Photography** is welcomed in the grounds of all our properties provided it is not for commercial use. We regret that photography is not permitted inside certain properties for conservation reasons. Please enquire on arrival.

- **Smoking** is not permitted inside any of the historic houses listed in this guide.
- We aim to welcome **dogs** at as many sites as possible. Symbols are shown in individual entries where there are restrictions on dogs. Guide dogs and hearing dogs for the deaf are welcome at all our properties.
- Some of our properties, due to remoteness or the sensitive historic fabric of the site, do not have toilets. Custodians will be happy to direct visitors to the nearest conveniences.
- **Unforeseen closures** of our sites are extremely rare. However, to avoid possible disappointment we do advise ringing the site before your visit.

Visitors enjoying a carriage ride at Osborne House

DOWN HOUSE

English Heritage's newest acquisition, Down House – the home for forty years of Charles Darwin – will open to the public this summer.

The purchase, made possible through the generous support of The Wellcome Trust, the Natural History Museum and the Heritage Lottery Fund, marks a new departure for English Heritage as the property's significance lies in its illustrious former owner and the memorabilia on his life and work that it contains.

The study at Down House

Guide books are specially designed to help children learn about our heritage

Children play medieval games at Mount Grace Priory

SPECIAL FEATURES AND FACILITIES

Visitors with disabilities

- English Heritage aims to make our properties open to everyone who wishes to enjoy them. Over 100 sites in this guide are marked as especially suitable for people with disabilities, indicating that much of the site is easily accessible.
- At many properties there are personal stereo guided tours specifically for wheelchair users or visitors with a visual impairment. At some, there are personal stereo tours in basic language for visitors with learning difficulties.
- Staff will be pleased to assist visitors with special needs, if at all possible. We recommend you contact the site's custodian in advance so that preparations can be made to ensure you have a more rewarding visit.
- **Admission is free for the assisting companion** of a visitor with disabilities.
- Our Guide for Visitors with Disabilities (also available in braille, large print and on tape) gives full details. For a free copy contact our Customer Services Department (see inside back cover).

Bring your visits to life

- **Guidebooks**, often illustrated in colour, are on sale at almost all the properties where an entrance fee is charged. If you prefer, you can buy guidebooks before your visit through our postal sales service (telephone 01604 781163).
- **Personal stereo guides**, which combine history with drama and music to add an extra touch of realism to your visit, are now available at nearly 40 sites.
- **Interactive audio tours** at Battle Abbey, Stonehenge, Framlingham Castle and Dover Castle's Secret Wartime Tunnels allow you to control the information you hear as you move around the site.

A warm welcome to families and children

- We welcome families and children to our properties, and at many sites there are special features, exhibitions, or educational facilities to make the visits particularly interesting for children. Look out for the family friendly symbol (◉) and free activity sheets.
- **Baby changing** facilities are now available at some of our larger sites. Look out for the symbol (◉) in the entry.
- From April to October, special events take place at our sites, most of which are especially suitable for children.

Shops and restaurants

- Many of our properties have a shop offering an attractive range of souvenirs, gifts and books. No two English Heritage shops are exactly the same, as our merchandise is selected to suit each type of site from abbey to castle, historic house to prehistoric monument.
- Refreshments are available at many of the properties. At others you can enjoy a sit-down meal in one of our restaurants or tea rooms, which are often located within the historic buildings. Picnics are also welcome in the grounds. See individual entries for details.

The inter-active audio tour at Stonehenge

Displays and exhibitions

- At most properties, display panels explain how the site would have appeared in the past, often with the help of reconstruction drawings or interactive displays.
- There are special exhibitions at many sites highlighting particular aspects of the site's history.
- Other properties host temporary exhibitions of paintings and sculpture.

Computer-generated displays in the Visitor Centre at Carisbrooke Castle

A fire-eater dazzles the crowd during a special event

Special events and concerts

- Our special events programme runs from April to October and ranges from military displays and re-enactments of famous battles to family entertainments and re-creations of life in days gone by. Among this year's highlights are 'Victoria's Glory' – a commemoration of Queen Victoria's Diamond Jubilee 100 years ago – which is being held at Wrest Park, 21–22 June; and 'History in Action II' – a weekend of spectacular displays from the Romans to VE Day – which is being held in the grounds of Kirby Hall, 2–3 August.
- Our summer open-air concerts combine world-class performances with superb surroundings – not forgetting our firework displays which accompany many of the concerts.
- For full details please ask for our free Events and Concert diaries, available from sites, or contact our Customer Services Department (see inside back cover).

Overseas visitors

- Visitors to England will find the Overseas Visitor Pass the convenient way to visit our sites. For further information, contact our Customer Services Department on 0171 973 3434.
- Many of our sites display a wide variety of leaflets in different languages, and translations of souvenir guides and audio tours are also available at many properties.

We're at your service

If you have any queries about the information in this handbook, or any other aspect of English Heritage work, please contact our Customer Services Department (PO Box 9019, London, W1A 0JA. Tel 0171 973 3434). We aim to provide information, answer your questions and to investigate if the service we provide does not reach the very high standards we have set ourselves. In the meantime we hope you enjoy visiting our various sites and share our pride in England's rich history.

MAKE A PRESENT OF OUR PAST

English Heritage gift membership makes an ideal and original present, whatever the occasion. Give your friends a year to remember:

- Days out with friends and family – free entry to over 400 historic attractions throughout England.
- Spectacular entertainment – free entry to our special events.
- Romantic music on a summer evening – enjoy our open air concerts.
- Participation in conservation – *Heritage Today* magazine revealing the stories behind the scenes.

Gift membership comes in a presentation box with handbook, map and special greetings card with a voucher, enabling the new member to start their membership when they please.

It costs just £23 for an adult or £40 for the whole family (with plenty of categories to choose from).

To order your gift of English Heritage membership, call us on 0171 973 3434.

ENGLAND'S CHRISTIAN HERITAGE

1997 is an important year in this country's history. It marks the 1400th anniversary of the arrival of St Augustine in Kent as the emissary of Pope Gregory. English Heritage is celebrating this special year by highlighting the immense influence that Christianity has had on the architectural heritage and history of this country.

St Augustine's Abbey in Canterbury, the cradle of Christianity in England, will

be at the centre of the celebrations in honour of its founder. The Abbey is part of the World Heritage Site complex at Canterbury and one of the most significant and treasured sites in our care. A new visitor centre and displays will open in the Spring.

In 1997 we will be celebrating the fundamental influence of Christianity across the country and bringing to the fore the diversity, wealth and quality of Christian Heritage sites throughout England.

Christianity – the force shaping England's history

Christianity has been central to the history of England for over 1600 years. In the great ecclesiastic sites spread across the country you can see the highpoints of our artistic and architectural heritage as well as the symbols of our historical progress.

Many of the most breath-taking buildings of the Middle Ages were built by the Church. Huge amounts of work and skill created the soaring Gothic cathedrals and abbeys as well as the less extravagant, but equally important, parish churches in every English village.

These sites are central to our history. The Synod of Whitby, held in 664 at the Abbey now under the care of English Heritage, confirmed

The Archbishop of Canterbury

the new dominance of united Christianity in England. 800 years later the Dissolution of the Monasteries left us the romantic ruins that remind us of the bitter religious divisions that spread through the country.

Conserving our Christian Heritage

English Heritage plays a key role in the preservation of our

In 1996 Ely Cathedral (left) received £650,000 from English Heritage to help repair the south side of the Choir

Christian buildings. It cares for many well-known sites across England, including Lindisfarne Priory and Rievaulx Abbey, as well as fascinating reminders of Christian life – from the early Roman chapel at Lullingstone Villa in Kent to the remains of Mistley Towers, an 18th-century church by Adam in Essex.

The restoration of churches and cathedrals across Britain, is a major priority for English Heritage. Grants worth over £20 million have been awarded since 1991, aiding all types of religious buildings from the grand cathedrals at Durham and York Minster, to isolated parish churches and chapels.

Visit historic properties

You can join in the celebrations by visiting the many sites that express our Christian heritage. Return to see the magnificent remains of Lindisfarne or Rievaulx or take the chance to discover the many hidden gems, tucked away throughout England. The properties run by English Heritage encompass every aspect of the Christian history of England. From Mount Grace Priory in North Yorkshire to Cleeve Abbey in Somerset you can take advantage of the

improved visitor and educational facilities to find out more about one of the most fascinating parts of our heritage.

Celebrate with us

English Heritage is arranging and supporting a number of events to commemorate this year of Christian Heritage. Events across England will include lectures, re-enactments and special days out for members and their families.

Remember that when you visit our sites you will be giving your support to the nation's heritage. The income generated from your visits supports the conservation and restoration of England's most significant sites.

Further information

Look out for the Christian Heritage symbol (🔒) on sites

Visitors at Lindisfarne Priory, where new facilities have been created by English Heritage

featured in this handbook. For more details about English Heritage's celebrations see updates in the members' magazine, *Heritage Today*, the special leaflets available or ring Customer Services on 0171 973 3434.

Liverpool Metropolitan Cathedral (right) to which English Heritage has granted over £1.5 million to aid repairs

9

St Augustine's Abbey

You can celebrate the 1400th anniversary of the arrival in England of St Augustine by visiting the 'cradle of Christianity', the abbey he founded in Canterbury.

This great shrine, which was built the year after he arrived, became the centre of the English Christian movement. It is the burial place of the early Archbishops of Canterbury, as well as of St Augustine himself.

ENGLAND'S

CHRISTIAN

HERITAGE

ENGLISH HERITAGE

Along with the Cathedral, the Abbey is part of the Canterbury World Heritage site. Its foundation represented the most important change in English life since Roman times.

Today you can see the remains of the earliest parts of the Abbey with the help of the new interactive audio tour and follow its long history through displays in the new interpretation centre.

In 596 St Augustine was sent by Pope Gregory from Rome to convert the pagan King Ethelbert of Kent. The party of monks landed the next year at Ebbsfleet in Kent and made their way to Canterbury where the King took up the faith. St Augustine

A stained-glass depiction of St Augustine

was subsequently granted an old church within the city walls – 'built long ago by Roman Christians' – to found his church (now part of Canterbury Cathedral) and the abbey which now bears his name. In so doing St Augustine succeeded in making Christianity the official faith of Kent and thereafter of England.

Although most of the abbey buildings were

The St Pancras Chapel, which forms part of the Abbey complex

destroyed by Henry VIII during the Dissolution of the monasteries there are remarkable remains of the foundations of the original 6th-century church, one of the earliest monastic sites in southern England. Also surviving are fragments of the St Pancras chapel, made from Roman brick and sections of the Norman church and medieval monastery.

To celebrate the 1400th anniversary of the abbey's

Reconstruction of the Abbey from the air

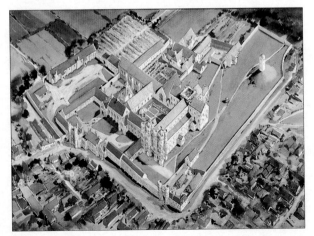

The church from the north west

foundation English Heritage has created many exciting new features to enhance the visitor's day at St Augustine's. See how a medieval abbey worked by letting the new interactive audio tour guide you around the site, bringing to life the remains and explaining the purpose of each section of the large complex.

The new interpretation centre explains the history of the site. A permanent exhibition, created with help from the Heritage Lottery Fund, displays many of the fascinating artefacts that have been excavated during archaeological digs at the site, emphasizing the Abbey's long history. Alongside, a new computer-generated display gives insight into the whole of the Abbey site.

Throughout 1997 special events will be held in conjunction with the Cathedral to mark the anniversary of St Augustine's arrival in England. These will include a special pilgrimage all the way from Rome which will retrace St Augustine's route to England.

The Abbey crypt

● *Visit a Norman Wedding, a delightful and romantic event featuring 11th-century re-enactors, 27–28 June*
● *Enjoy the new visitor facilities, including free interactive audio tour.*
Open *22 March–31 Oct: daily, 10am–6pm (6pm/dusk in Oct).*
1 Nov–31 March: daily, 10am–4pm (closed 24–26 Dec).
Entry *£2.00/£1.50/£1.00.*
✆ *01227 767345*
&. *(some steps)* ⊗ **P** *(nearby)*
🎧* Ⓔ ⑰
➲ *In Longport ¼ m E of Cathedral Close.*
(OS Map 179; ref TR 154578.)
🚌 *From surrounding areas (Tel: 0800 696 996).*
🚉 *Canterbury East & West, both ¾ m.*

11

THE SOUTH WEST

In the South West you'll find many prehistoric marvels, including the greatest wonder of them all – the ancient and mysterious stone circle of Stonehenge in Wiltshire. Nearby is the huge earthwork of Old Sarum, the original site of Salisbury, with the remains of a prehistoric fortress, Norman palace and cathedral. Other highlights include Henry VIII's forts at St Mawes and Pendennis, which have dominated the mouth of the River Fal for over 400 years, and Tintagel Castle with its spectacular cliff-top location and Arthurian connections.

⊙ Abbotsbury Abbey Remains

DORSET (p. 211, 3G)

The remains of a cloister building of this Benedictine abbey, founded in 1044.

Open *Any reasonable time.*
(Site managed by the Ilchester Estates.)
Entry *Free.*
🅿 ⊛
➲ *In Abbotsbury, off B3157, near churchyard.*
(OS Map 194; ref SY 578852.)
🚌 *Upwey 7½m.*

Avebury

WILTSHIRE

See also Silbury Hill, The Sanctuary, West Kennet Avenue, West Kennet Long Barrow and Windmill Hill.

Avebury Stone Circles

Avebury Museum

WILTSHIRE (pp. 211/212, 5J)

The investigation of Avebury Stone Circles was largely the work of Alexander Keiller in the 1930s. He put together one of the most important prehistoric archaeological collections in Britain, and this can be seen in the Avebury Museum.

Avebury Museum

Open *22 March–2 Nov: daily, 10am–6pm. 3 Nov–31 March: daily, 10am–4pm (closed 24–26 Dec, 1 Jan).*
Entry *£1.50 (adult)/80p (child). (Collection on loan to the National Trust.)*
📞 *01672 539250*
🚻 🅿 *(in village)* ⊛ ♿ Ⓔ 🛈
➲ *In Avebury 7m W of Marlborough.*
(OS Map 173; ref SU 100700.)
🚌 *Thamesdown 49A Swindon–Devizes/Marlborough; Wilts & Dorset 5/6 Salisbury–Swindon (Tel: 0345 090 899). All pass close to BR Swindon.*
🚆 *Pewsey 10m, Swindon 11m.*

➊ Avebury Stone Circles

WILTSHIRE (pp. 211/212, 5J)
Complex, gigantic and mysterious, the Circles were constructed 4,000 years ago, originally comprising more than 180 stones. The remains of the Circles still surround the later village of Avebury.

Open *Any reasonable time.
(Site owned and managed by the National Trust.)*
Entry *Free.*
👫 *(in village)* 🅿 ♿ 🐕
➥ *In Avebury 7m W of Marlborough.
(OS Map 173; ref SU 103700.)*
🚌 *Thamesdown 49A Swindon–Devizes/Marlborough; Wilts & Dorset 5/6 Salisbury–Swindon (Tel: 0345 090 899). All pass close to BR Swindon.*
🚂 *Pewsey 10m, Swindon 11m.*

➋ Ballowall Barrow

St Just, CORNWALL
(p. 210, 1A)
In a spectacular position, this is an unusual Bronze Age chambered tomb with a complex layout.

Open *Any reasonable time.
(Site managed by the National Trust.)*
Entry *Free.*
🐕
➥ *1m W of St Just, near Carn Gloose.
(OS Map 203; ref SW 354313.)*

🚌 *Western National 10/A/B, 11/A BR Penzance–St Just, thence 1m (Tel: 01209 719988).*
🚂 *Penzance 8m.*

➋ Bant's Carn Burial Chamber and Halangy Down Ancient Village

St Mary's, ISLES OF SCILLY
(p. 210, 4A)
In a wonderful scenic location, on a hill above the site of the ancient Iron Age village, lies this Bronze Age burial mound with entrance passage and chamber.

Open *Any reasonable time.*
Entry *Free.*
🐕
➥ *1m N of Hugh Town.
(OS Map 203; ref SV 911124.)*

➏ Bayard's Cove Fort

Dartmouth, DEVON
(p. 211, 2E)
A small artillery fort built before 1534 to defend the harbour entrance.

Open *Any reasonable time.
(Site managed by South Hams District Council.)*
Entry *Free.*
❌
➥ *In Dartmouth, on riverfront.
(OS Map 202; ref SX 879510.)*
🚌 *Bayline 200 BR Paignton–Kingswear, 22 Brixham–Kingswear (connections from BR Paignton), thence ferry to*

Dartmouth (Tel: 01803 613226); Western National 89 from Totnes (passes BR Totnes) (Tel: 01392 382800).
🚂 *Paignton 7m via vehicle ferry.*

Bant's Carn burial chamber

➌ Belas Knap Long Barrow

GLOUCESTERSHIRE
(pp. 212/217, 7H)
A good example of a Neolithic long barrow, with the mound still intact and surrounded by a stone wall. The chamber tombs, where the remains of 31 people were found, have been opened up so that visitors can see inside.

Open *Any reasonable time.
(Site managed by Gloucester-shire County Council.)*
Entry *Free.*
🐕
➥ *2m S of Winchcombe, near Charlton Abbots, ½ mile on Cotswold Way.
(OS Map 163; ref SP 021254.)*
🚌 *Castleways from Cheltenham to within 1¼m (Tel: 01242 602949).*
🚂 *Cheltenham 9m.*

Berry Pomeroy Castle (above)
and the castle gatehouse (left)

☯☉ Berry Pomeroy Castle

DEVON (p. 211, 2E)
A romantic late-medieval castle, unusual in combining the remains of a large castle with a flamboyant courtier's mansion. It is reputed to be haunted.

🌣 *Picnic spot of exceptional beauty*.
Open *22 March–31 Oct: daily, 10am–6pm (6pm/dusk in Oct).*
Entry *£2.00/£1.50/£1.00.*
✆ *01803 866618*
🄿 ♿ ♿ *(grounds & ground floor only)* ✖ 🍴 *(not managed by English Heritage)*
➲ *2½m E of Totnes off A385.*
(OS Map 202; ref SX 839623.)
🚌 *Western National 149 BR Torquay–Totnes (passes close to BR Totnes) (Tel: 01392 382800).*
🚃 *Totnes 3½m.*

⬣ Blackbury Camp

DEVON (p. 211, 3F)
An Iron Age hillfort, defended by a bank and ditch.

Open *Any reasonable time.*
Entry *Free.*
✖ 🄿
➲ *1½m SW of Southleigh off B3174/A3052.*
(OS Map 192; ref SY 188924.)
🚃 *Honiton 6½m.*

✠ Blackfriars

Gloucester, GLOUCES-TERSHIRE (pp. 212/217, 7H)
A small Dominican priory church. Most of the original 13th-century church remains, including a rare scissor-braced roof.

Open *Access restricted. Please contact Regional Office for further information (Tel: 0117 975 0700).*
Entry *Free.*
✖
➲ *In Ladybellegate Street off Southgate Street and Blackfriars Walk.*
(OS Map 162; ref SO 830186.)
🚌 *From surrounding areas (Tel: 01452 425543).*
🚃 *Gloucester ½m.*

⬣ Bowhill

Exeter, DEVON (p. 211, 3E)
A mansion of considerable status built c.1500 by a member of the Holland family. The impressive Great Hall has been carefully

14

Blackfriars

restored by English Heritage craftsmen using traditional materials and techniques.

Open *Please contact Regional Office (Tel: 0117 975 0700).*
Entry *Free.*
⊗ P
➲ *1½m SW of Exeter on B3212. (OS Map 192; ref SX 906916.)*
🚌 *Stagecoach Devon C, P from City Centre (Tel: 01392 427711).*
🚃 *Exeter, St Thomas ¾m.*

⊕ Bradford-on-Avon Tithe Barn

WILTSHIRE (pp. 211/212, 5H)
A medieval stone-built barn with slate roof and wooden beamed interior.

Open *Daily, 10.30am–4pm (closed 25 Dec). Keykeeper.*
Entry *Free.*
P ♿ ⊗
➲ *¼m S of town centre, off B3109.*

(OS Map 173; ref ST 824604.)
🚌 *Badgerline X4 Bath–Salisbury, Badgerline 265 Bath–Frome (Tel: 0345 090 899).*
🚃 *Bradford-on-Avon ¼m.*

⊕ Bratton Camp and White Horse

WILTSHIRE (pp. 211/212, 5H)
A large Iron Age hill fort.

Open *Any reasonable time.*
Entry *Free.*
P ⊗

➲ *2m E of Westbury off B3098, 1m SW of Bratton. (OS Map 184; ref ST 900516.)*
🚃 *Westbury 3m.*

⊕ Butter Cross

Dunster, SOMERSET
(p. 211, 4E)
A medieval stone cross.

Open *Any reasonable time. (Site managed by the National Trust.)*
Entry *Free.*
⊗

➲ *Beside minor road to Alcombe, 350m (400 yds) NW of Dunster parish church. (OS Map 181; ref SS 988439.)*
🚌 *Southern National 28 BR Taunton–Minehead, also 38/9 from Minehead to within ½m (Tel: 01823 272033).*
🚃 *Dunster (W Somerset Rly) 1m.*

Bradford-on-Avon Tithe Barn

Carn Euny Ancient Village

CORNWALL (p. 210, 1A)
The remains of an Iron Age
settlement, with foundations
of stone huts and an intriguing curved underground
passage, or *fogou*.

***Open** Any reasonable time.*
***Entry** Free.*
P 🐾

➲ *1¼m SW of Sancreed off A30.*
(OS Map 203; ref SW 402289.)
🚌 *Western National 10/A/B,*
BR Penzance–St Just, to within
2m (Tel: 01209 719988).
🚃 *Penzance 6m.*

✝ Chisbury Chapel

WILTSHIRE
(pp. 211/212, 5J)
A thatched 13th-century
chapel rescued from use
as a farm building.

Carn Euny, the *fogou* entrance

***Open** Any reasonable time.*
***Entry** Free.*
🐾

➲ *On unclassified road*
¼m E of Chisbury off A4
6m E of Marlborough.
(OS Map 174; ref SU 280658.)
🚃 *Bedwyn 1m.*

⊖ Christchurch Castle and Norman House

DORSET (pp. 211/212, 3J)
Early 12th-century Norman
keep, and Constable's house,
built *c.*1160.

***Open** Any reasonable time.*
***Entry** Free.*
🐾

➲ *In Christchurch, near Priory.*
(OS Map 195; ref SZ 160927.)
🚌 *From surrounding areas*
(Tel: 01202 673555).
🚃 *Christchurch ¾m.*

Chysauster Ancient Village

▲⊖ Chysauster Ancient Village

CORNWALL (p. 210, 1A)
A deserted Romano-Cornish
village with a 'street' of eight
well-preserved houses, each
comprising a number of
rooms around an open court.

***Open** 22 March–31 Oct: daily,*
10am–6pm (6pm/dusk in Oct).
Tel: 0831 757934 for details.
***Entry** £1.50/£1.10/80p.*
🚻 P 🐾 ♿

➲ *2½m NW of Gulval*
off B3311.
(OS Map 203; ref SW 473350.)
🚌 *Western National 16*
BR Penzance–St Ives to within
1½m (not Sundays)
(Tel: 01209 719988).
🚃 *Penzance 3½m.*

☉ Cirencester Amphitheatre

GLOUCESTERSHIRE
(pp. 211/212/217, 6H)
A large well-preserved Roman
amphitheatre.

Open *Any reasonable time.*
Entry *Free.*
🐦
● *Next to bypass W of town –*
access from town or along
Chesterton Lane from W end
of bypass onto Cotswold Ave.
Park next to obelisk.
(OS Map 163; ref SP 020014.)
🚌 *Alex Cars/James*
rail-link from BR Kemble
(Tel: 01452 425543).
🚃 *Kemble 4m.*

♙ Cleeve Abbey

SOMERSET (p. 211, 4F)
One of the few 13th-century
monastic sites where you will
see such a complete set of
cloister buildings, including
the refectory with its
magnificent timber roof.

Open *22 March–31 Oct: daily,*
10am–6pm (6pm/dusk in Oct).
1 Nov–31 March: daily,
10am–4pm (closed 24–26
Dec). Closed 1–2pm in winter.
Entry *£2.40/£1.80/£1.20.*
☎ *01984 640377*
🍴👥 Ⓟ ☉ ♿ *(grounds & ground*
floor only) Ⓔ 🛍 ⚒
● *In Washford, ¼m S of A39.*
(OS Map 181; ref ST 047407.)

Cromwell's Castle

🚌 *Southern National 28*
BR Taunton–Minehead, also
38 from Minehead
(Tel: 01823 272033).
🚃 *Washford (W Somerset*
Rly) ½m.

☉ Cromwell's Castle

Tresco, ISLES OF SCILLY
(p. 210, 5A)
Standing on a promontory
guarding the lovely anchorage
between Bryher and Tresco,
this 17th-century round tower
was built to command the
haven of New Grimsby.

Open *Any reasonable time.*
Entry *Free.*
🐦
● *On shoreline, ¾m NW*
of New Grimsby.
(OS Map 203; ref SV 882159.)

Cleeve Abbey

⊕ Dartmouth Castle

DEVON (p. 211, 2E)
This brilliantly positioned defensive castle juts out into the narrow entrance to the Dart estuary, with the sea lapping at its foot. It was one of the first castles constructed with artillery in mind and has seen 450 years of fortification and preparation for war.

Dartmouth Castle

❧ *Picnic spot of exceptional beauty*.
Open *22 March–31 Oct: daily, 10am–6pm (6pm/dusk in Oct). 1 Nov–31 March: Wed–Sun, 10am–4pm (closed 24–26 Dec). Closed 1–2pm in winter.*
Entry *£2.40/£1.80/£1.20.*
℘ **01803 833588**
♗♗ 🅿 *(limited)* 🗋 ⊗ 🕭
➲ *1m SE of Dartmouth off B3205, narrow approach road. (OS Map 202; ref SX 887503.)*

🚌 *Bayline 200 BR Paignton–Kingswear, 22 Brixham–Kingswear (connections from BR Paignton), thence ferry to Dartmouth; Western National 89 from Totnes (passes close to BR Totnes) (Tel: 01932 382800). In all cases 1m walk from Dartmouth or local ferry from Dartmouth to Castle.*
🚂 *Paignton 8m via vehicle ferry.*

⬣ Daws Castle

SOMERSET (p. 211, 5F)
The site where the people of the Saxon town of Watchet sought refuge against the threat of Viking attack.

Open *Any reasonable time.*
Entry *Free.*
🅿 *(layby 200m)* ⊗
➲ *½m W of Watchet off B3191 on cliff top. (OS Map 181; ref ST 062432.)*
🚌 *Southern National 28 BR Taunton–Minehead (Tel: 01823 272033).*
🚂 *Watchet (West Somerset Rly) ¾m.*

⊙⬥ Dupath Well

Callington, CORNWALL (p. 210, 2D)
A charming granite-built well house set over a holy well of *c.*1500 and almost complete.

Open *Any reasonable time. (Site managed by the Cornwall Heritage Trust.)*

Entry *Free.*

⊗

➲ *1m E of Callington off A388.
(OS Map 201; ref SX 374693.)*
🚌 *Western National 76
Plymouth–Callington (passes
BR Plymouth), thence 1m
(Tel: 01752 222666).*
🚄 *Gunnislake 4½m.*

◑ Farleigh Hungerford Castle

SOMERSET (pp.211/212, 5H)
Ruins of a 14th-century castle
with a chapel containing wall
paintings, stained glass and
the fine tomb of Sir Thomas
Hungerford, the builder of the
castle.

Open *22 March–31 Oct: daily,
10am–6pm (6pm/dusk in Oct).
1 Nov–31 March: Wed–Sun,
10am–4pm (closed 24–26 Dec).
Closed 1–2pm in winter.*
Entry *£2.00/£1.50/£1.00.*

Fiddleford Manor

Farleigh Hungerford Castle

✆ *01225 754026*
👬 🅿 ⊗ 🗋 🎧 ♿ *(exterior
only).*
➲ *In Farleigh Hungerford 3½m
W of Trowbridge on A366.
(OS Map 173; ref ST 801577.)*
🚌 *Badgerline X3 Bristol–
Frome (passes BR Bath Spa &
close to BR Frome) to within
1m (Tel: 0117 955 3231).*
🚄 *Avoncliff 2m; Trowbridge
3½m.*

◓ Fiddleford Manor

DORSET (pp. 211/212, 4H)
Part of a medieval manor
house, with a remarkable
interior. The splendid roof
structures in the hall and
upper living room are the
best in Dorset.

Open *22 March–30 Sept: daily,
10am–6pm. 1 Oct–31 March:
daily, 10am–4pm (closed
24–26 Dec, 1 Jan). Keykeeper.*
Entry *Free.*
🅿 ♿ *(ground floor only –
1 step)* ⊗

➲ *1m E of Sturminster
Newton off A357.
(OS Map 194; ref ST 801136.)*
🚌 *Damory 310 from
Blandford (Tel: 01258 453731).*

◔ Gallox Bridge

Dunster, SOMERSET
(p. 211, 4E)
A stone packhorse bridge
with two ribbed arches which
spans the old mill stream.

Open *Any reasonable time.
(Site managed by the
National Trust.)*
Entry *Free.*
♿ ⊗

➲ *Off A396 at S end of Dunster.
(OS Map 181; ref SS 990432.)*
🚌 *Southern National 28 BR
Taunton–Minehead, also 38/9
from Minehead to within ⅛m
(Tel: 01823 272033).*
🚄 *Dunster (W Somerset
Rly) ¾m.*

◕ Garrison Walls

St Mary's, ISLES OF SCILLY
(p. 210, 4A)
You can take a pleasant walk
along the ramparts of these
well-preserved walls and
earthworks, built as part of
the island's defences.

Open *Any reasonable time.*
Entry *Free.*
⊗

➲ *Around the headland
W of Hugh Town.
(OS Map 203; ref SV 898104.)*

⊘ Glastonbury Tribunal

SOMERSET (p. 211, 4G)
A well-preserved medieval town house, reputedly once used as the courthouse of Glastonbury Abbey.

Open *28 March–30 Sept: Sun–Thurs, 10am–5pm (Fri & Sat 5.30pm). 1 Oct–27 March: Sun–Thurs, 10am–4pm.(Fri & Sat 4.30pm). (Site managed by Glastonbury Tribunal Ltd.)*
Entry *Tourist Information Centre free. Display areas £1.50/£1.00/75p.*
℃ 01458 832954
⊗ ⑆ *(ground floor only – 2 steps)* ⑩
➲ *In Glastonbury High St. (OS Map 182; ref ST 499390.)*
🚍 *Badgerline 376, 676, Southern National 29A BR Bristol Temple Meads–Street (Tel: 0117 955 3231).*

⊘ Great Witcombe Roman Villa

GLOUCESTERSHIRE
(pp. 211/212/217, 6H)
The remains of a large villa. Built around three sides of a courtyard, it had a luxurious bath-house complex.

Open *Exterior any reasonable time. Guided tours 26 May, 22 June, 17 Aug, 14 Sept only. Please contact Regional Office for details (Tel 0117 975 0700).*
Entry *Free.*
🅿 ⊗

➲ *5m SE of Gloucester, off A417, ½m S of reservoir in Witcombe Park. (OS Map 163; ref SO 899144.)*
🚍 *Stagecoach City of Gloucester 50 BR Gloucester–Cheltenham to within 1½m (Tel: 01452 527516).*
🚇 *Gloucester 6m.*

✝ Greyfriars

Gloucester,
GLOUCESTERSHIRE
(p. 217, 7H)
Remains of a late 15th-early 16th-century Franciscan friary church.

Open *Any reasonable time.*
Entry *Free.*
⑆ ⊗
➲ *On Greyfriars Walk, behind Eastgate Market off Southgate St. (OS Map 162; ref SO 830186.)*
🚍 *From surrounding areas (Tel: 01452 425543).*
🚇 *Gloucester ½m.*

⚠ Grimspound

Dartmoor, DEVON (p. 210, 3E)
This late Bronze Age settlement displays the remains of 24 huts in an area of four acres enclosed by a stone wall.

Open *Any reasonable time. (Site managed by Dartmoor National Park Authority.)*
Entry *Free.*
⊗

Hailes Abbey (above) with **Christ/Sampson boss (left)** and **a manuscript and seal (above right)**

➲ *6m SW of Moretonhampstead off B3212. (OS Map 191; ref SX 701809.)*
🚍 *Western National 82 Plymouth–Exeter, to within 2m (Tel: 01392 382800).*

✝ Hailes Abbey

GLOUCESTERSHIRE
(pp. 212/217, 7H)
13th-century Cistercian abbey, set in wooded pastureland, with examples of high quality sculpture in the site museum.

Open *22 March–31 Oct: daily, 10am–6pm (6pm/dusk in Oct). 1 Nov–31 March: Wed–Sun, 10am–4pm (closed 24–26 Dec). Closed 1–2pm in winter.*
Entry *£2.40/£1.80/£1.20. Grounds only free. National*

Trust members admitted free. (Site maintained and managed by the National Trust.)
☎ 01242 602398
♿ **P** 🎧 *(also available for the visually impaired, those with learning difficulties and wheelchair users)* ♿ *(general access, 1 step to museum)* ⓦ 🚾 🛍
➲ *2m NE of Winchcombe off B4632.*
(OS Map 150; ref SP 050300.)
🚌 *Castleways from Cheltenham to within 1½m (Tel: 01242 602949).*
🚉 *Cheltenham 10m.*

➲ Halliggye Fogou

CORNWALL (p. 210, 1B)
One of several strange underground tunnels, associated with Iron Age villages, which are unique to Cornwall.

Open *Any reasonable time but completely blocked between*

31 Oct and 31 March. A torch is advisable. (Site managed by the Trelowarren Estate.)
Entry *Free.*
🚾
➲ *5m SE of Helston off B3293 E of Garras on Trelowarren estate. (OS Map 203; ref SW 714239.)*
🚌 *Truronian T2/3 from Helston (Tel: 01872 73453); Western National 2/X links Helston with BR Penzance (Tel: 01209 719988).*
🚉 *Penryn 10m.*

◎ Harry's Walls

St Mary's, ISLES OF SCILLY (p. 210, 4B)
An uncompleted 16th-century fort intended to command the harbour of St Mary's Pool.

Open *Any reasonable time.*
Entry *Free.*
🚾
➲ *¼m NE of Hugh Town. (OS Map 203; ref SV 910110.)*

▲ Hatfield Earthworks

WILTSHIRE (pp. 211/212, 5J)
Part of a Neolithic enclosure complex 3,500 years old, formerly with a Bronze Age barrow in its centre.

Open *Any reasonable time.*
Entry *Free.*
🚾
➲ *5½m SE of Devizes off A342 NE of village of Marden. (OS Map 173; ref SU 091583 or SU 092583).*
🚉 *Pewsey 5m.*

➲ Hound Tor Deserted Medieval Village

Dartmoor, DEVON (p. 210, 3E)
Remains of three or four medieval farmsteads, first occupied in the Bronze Age.

Open *Any reasonable time. (Site managed by Dartmoor National Park Authority.)*
Entry *Free.*
🚾
➲ *1½m S of Manaton off The Ashburton Road. Park in Hound Tor car park, ½m walk. (OS Map 191; ref SX 746788.)*
🚌 *Western National 170/1 Newton Abbot–Tavistock, Summer Suns only (Tel: 01392 382800).*

Harry's Walls

King Doniert's Stone

⊙ Hurlers Stone Circles

CORNWALL (p. 210, 2C)
These three Bronze Age stone circles in a line are some of the best examples of ceremonial standing stones in the South West.

Open Any reasonable time. *(Site managed by the Cornwall Heritage Trust.)*
Entry Free.
🅿 ⊛
➲ ½m NW of Minions off B3254.
(OS Map 201; ref SX 258714.)
🚌 Caradon Riviera BR Liskeard–Higher Tremar, thence 1½m
(Tel: 01579 62226).
🚃 Liskeard 7m.

⊕ Innisidgen Lower And Upper Burial Chambers

St Mary's, ISLES OF SCILLY (p. 210, 4B)
Two Bronze Age cairns, about 30 metres (200 feet) apart,

with stunning views towards St Martins.

Open Any reasonable time.
Entry Free.
⊛
➲ 1¾m NE of Hugh Town.
(OS Map 203; ref SV 921127.)

⊛⊙ Jordan Hill Roman Temple

Weymouth, DORSET (pp. 211/212, 3H)
Foundations of a Romano-Celtic temple enclosing an area of about 22 square metres (240 square feet).

Open Any reasonable time.
Entry Free.
⊛
➲ 2m NE of Weymouth off A353.
(OS Map 194; ref SY 698821.)
🚌 Southern National A from Weymouth
(Tel: 01305 783645).
🚃 Upwey or Weymouth, both 2m.

⊙ King Charles's Castle

Tresco, ISLES OF SCILLY (p. 210, 5A)
At the end of a bracing coastal walk to the northern end of Tresco you will find the remains of this castle built for coastal defence.

Open Any reasonable time.
Entry Free.
⊛
➲ ¾m NW of New Grimsby.
(OS Map 203; ref SV 882161.)

⊙ King Doniert's Stone

St Cleer, CORNWALL (p. 210, 2C)
Two decorated pieces of a 9th-century cross with an inscription believed to commemorate Durngarth, King of Cornwall, who drowned c.875.

Open Any reasonable time. *(Site managed by the Cornwall Heritage Trust.)*
Entry Free.
⊛ 🅿 *(lay-by)*
➲ 1m NW of St Cleer off B3254.
(OS Map 201; ref SX 236688.)
🚌 Caradon Riviera BR Liskeard–St Cleer, thence ½m
(Tel: 01579 62226).
🚃 Liskeard 4m.

Kingswood Abbey Gatehouse

⬟ Kingston Russell Stone Circle

DORSET (p. 211, 3G)
A Bronze Age stone circle of 18 stones.

Open *Any reasonable time.*
Entry *Free.*
☀ 🅿 *(on verge near entrance to Gorwell Farm)*
➲ *2m N of Abbotsbury, 1m along footpath off minor road to Hardy Monument.*
(OS Map 194; ref SY 577878.)
🚌 *Dorchester West or South, both 8m.*

✠ Kingswood Abbey Gatehouse

GLOUCESTERSHIRE
(pp. 211/212/217, 6H)
The 16th-century gatehouse, with a richly carved

mullioned window, is all that remains of the Cistercian abbey.

Open *Exterior any reasonable time. Key for interior obtainable from shop nearby during opening hours.*

Entry *Free.*
🚻 *(adjacent to monument)* ⊗
➲ *In Kingswood off B4060 1m SW of Wotton-under-Edge.*
(OS Map 162; ref ST 748919.)
🚌 *Badgerline 309 Bristol–Dursley (Tel: 0117 955 3231).*
🚆 *Yate 8m.*

⊙ Kirkham House

Paignton, DEVON (p. 211, 2E)
A well preserved, medieval stone house, much restored and repaired, which gives a fascinating insight into life in a town residence in the 15th century.

Open *16 April, 21 May, 18 June, 16 July, 20 Aug, 17 Sept only, 10am–5pm. Please contact Regional Office for details (Tel 0117 975 0700).*
Entry *Free.*
⊗
➲ *In Kirkham St, off Cecil Rd, Paignton.*
(OS Map 202; ref SX 885610.)
🚌 *From surrounding areas (Tel: 01803 613226).*
🚆 *Paignton ½m.*

Kirkham House

✠ Knowlton Church and Earthworks

DORSET (pp. 211/212, 4J)
The ruins of this Norman church stand in the middle of Neolithic earthworks, symbolizing the transition from pagan to Christian worship.

Open *Any reasonable time.*
Entry *Free.*
🗙
➲ *3m SW of Cranborne on B3078.*
(OS Map 195; ref SU 024100.)

❶ Launceston Castle

CORNWALL (p. 210, 3D)
Set on the motte of a Norman castle and commanding the town and surrounding countryside, this medieval castle controlled the main route into Cornwall. The shell keep and tower survive.

Open *22 March–31 Oct: daily 10am–6pm (6pm/dusk in Oct).*

Launceston Castle

Entry *£1.50/£1.10/80p.*
☎ *01566 772365*
⟐ *(outer bailey)* 🗙 🍴
➲ *In Launceston.*
(OS Map 201; ref SX 330846.)
🚌 *Western National 76 Plymouth–Launceston (passes BR Plymouth); Tilleys from Exeter (Tel: 01392 382800).*

❻ Leigh Barton

DEVON (p. 210, 2E)
A small late-medieval domestic complex with a fine gatehouse and three ranges around a galleried courtyard.

Open *Contact Regional Office for details (Tel: 0117 975 0700).*
Entry *Free.*
🗙 🅿 *(limited)* ⟐ *(grounds & ground floor only)*
➲ *2m NW of Kingsbridge at Leigh on unclassified road off B3194.*
(OS Map 202; ref SX 721467.)
🚌 *Western National 93 Plymouth–Dartmouth to within ¾m (passes close to BR Plymouth, with connections from BR Totnes at Kingsbridge) (Tel: 01392 382800).*
🚉 *Ivybridge 10m.*

❻❶ Ludgershall Castle and Cross

WILTSHIRE (pp. 211/212, 5J)
Ruins of an early 12th-century royal hunting palace and a late-medieval cross.

Open *Any reasonable time.*
Entry *Free.*

🅿 *(limited)* ⟐ *(part of site only & village cross)* 🗙
➲ *On N side of Ludgershall off A342.*
(OS Map 184; ref SU 264513.)
🚌 *Stagecoach Hampshire Bus/Wilts & Dorset 7–9 BR Andover–Salisbury (Tel: 0345 090899).*
🚉 *Andover 7m.*

❶ Lulworth Castle

DORSET (pp. 211/212, 3H)
An early 17th-century romantic hunting lodge, Lulworth Castle became a fashionable country house set in beautiful parkland during the 18th century. Gutted by fire in 1929, the exterior is now being restored by English Heritage.

Open *28 March–30 Sept: daily, 10am–6pm. 1 Oct–22 Dec: daily, 10am–4pm.*
Entry *Park: £2.50 (adult)/ £1.50 (child). Castle: £3.00/ £2.00. Joint ticket: £5.00/£3.00. Members may be charged for certain special events held in the park. (Site managed by the Weld Estate.)*
☎ *01929 400510*
🚻 🅿 🗙 ⟐ *(by ramp)* 🏠 🍴
➲ *In east Lulworth off B3070, 3 miles NE of Lulworth Cove.*
(OS Map 194; ref SY 853822.)
🚌 *Garrison Cars 225/7 BR Wool–Lulworth Cove (Tel: 01929 462467); Dorset Queen 220 Dorchester– Lulworth (Tel: 01305 852829).*
🚉 *Wool 4m.*

◉ Lydford Castles And Saxon Town

DEVON (p. 210, 3D)
Standing above the gorge of the River Lyd, this 12th-century tower was notorious as a prison. The earthworks of the original Norman fort are to the south.

Lydford Castle

Open *Any reasonable time. (Site managed by the National Trust.)*
Entry *Free.*
☻ **P**
➲ *In Lydford off A386 8m S of Okehampton. (OS Map 191; Castle ref SX 510848, Fort ref SX 509847.)* 🚌 *Western National 86 Plymouth–Barnstaple (passes BR Plymouth); Devon Bus 187 BR Gunnislake–Exeter (Tel: 01392 382800).*

⓫ ◐ Maiden Castle

DORSET (p. 211, 3G)
This is the finest Iron Age hill fort in Britain. The earthworks are enormous, with a series of ramparts and complicated entrances, but they could not prevent the castle's capture by the Romans *c*.AD 43.

Open *Any reasonable time.*
Entry *Free.*
P ☻
➲ *2m S of Dorchester. Access off A354, N of bypass. (OS Map 194; ref SY 670885.)* 🚉 *Dorchester South or West, both 2m.*

◉ Meare Fish House

SOMERSET (p. 211, 4G)
A simple, well-preserved stone dwelling.

Open *Any reasonable time. Key from Manor House farm.*
Entry *Free.*
☻
➲ *In Meare village on B3151. (OS Map 182; ref ST 458418.)*

Lulworth Castle

Maiden Castle

The abbot's house, Muchelney Abbey

⊘ Merrivale Prehistoric Settlement

Dartmoor, DEVON
(p. 210, 3D)
Two rows of standing stones stretching up to 263 metres (864 feet) across the moors, together with the remains of an early Bronze Age village.

Open *Any reasonable time. (Site managed by Dartmoor National Park Authority.)*
Entry *Free.*
⊗
➲ *1m E of Merrivale. (OS Map 191; ref SX 553746.)*
🚌 *Devon Bus 98/A Tavistock–Princetown; 170/2 Tavistock–Newton Abbot (Tel: 01392 382800).*
🚉 *Gunnislake 10m.*

✠ Muchelney Abbey

SOMERSET
(p. 211, 4G)
The well-preserved remains of the cloisters and abbot's lodging of this Benedictine abbey.

Open *22 March–30 Sept: daily, 10am–6pm.*
Entry *£1.50/£1.10/80p.*
✆ *01458 250664*
🚻 🅿 🛈 ⊗ 🍴 ♿ *(grounds and part of ground floor only).*
➲ *In Muchelney 2m S of Langport. (OS Map 193; ref ST 428248.)*
🚌 *Southern National 54 Taunton–Yeovil (passes close to BR Taunton) to within 2m (Tel: 01823 272033).*

A Tudor wedding at Muchelney Abbey and a stone corbel (above)

⊙ Netheravon Dovecote

WILTSHIRE (pp. 211/212, 5J)
A charming 18th-century brick dovecote, standing in a pleasant orchard, with most of its 700 or more nesting boxes still present.

Open *Exterior viewing only, by written application to English Heritage (South West Regional Office).*
Entry *Free.*
⊛
➲ *In Netheravon, 4½m N of Amesbury on A345.*
(OS Map 184; ref SU 146485.)
🚌 *Wilts & Dorset 5/6 Salisbury–Swindon (passes close to BR Salisbury & Swindon) (Tel: 01722 336855).*
🚂 *Pewsey 9m, Grateley 11m.*

⊛ The Nine Stones

Winterbourne Abbas,
DORSET (p. 211, 3G)
Remains of a prehistoric circle of nine standing stones constructed about 4,000 years ago.

Open *Any reasonable time.*
Entry *Free.*
⊛ **P** *(small layby opposite, next to barn; cross road with care)*
➲ *½m W of Winterbourne Abbas, on A35.*
(OS Map 194; ref SY 611904.)
🚌 *Southern National 31 Weymouth–Taunton (passes BR Dorchester South and Axminster) (Tel: 01305 783645).*
🚂 *Dorchester West or South, both 5m.*

⊙ Notgrove Long Barrow

GLOUCESTERSHIRE
(pp. 212/214/217, 7J)
A Neolithic burial mound with chambers for human remains opening from a stone-built central passage.

Open *Any reasonable time. (Site managed by Gloucestershire County Council.)*
Entry *Free.*
P ⊛
➲ *1½m NW of Notgrove on A436.*
(OS Map 163; ref SP 096211.)
🚌 *Pulham's Moreton-in-Marsh–Cheltenham passes close to BR Moreton-in-Marsh (Tel: 01451 20369).*

⊕⊙ Nunney Castle

SOMERSET (p. 211/212, 5H)
A small 14th-century moated castle which is distinctly French in style.

Open *Any reasonable time.*
Entry *Free.*
♿ *(exterior only)* ⊛
➲ *In Nunney 3½m SW of Frome, off A361 (no coach access).*
(OS Map 183; ref ST 737457.)
🚌 *Badgerline 161/2 Frome–Wells (Tel: 01749 673084)*
🚂 *Frome 3½m.*

Nunney Castle

⚊ Nympsfield Long Barrow
GLOUCESTERSHIRE
(pp. 211/211/217, 6H)
A chambered Neolithic long barrow 30 metres (90 feet) in length.

Open *Any reasonable time.*
(Site managed by Gloucester-shire County Council.)
Entry *Free.*
🅿 ⊛ ♦♦♦ *(public; 50 metres [150 feet])*
➲ *1m NW of Nympsfield on B4066.*
(OS Map 162; ref SO 795014.)
🚌 *Stagecoach Stroud Valleys 15, Stroud–Dursley (passes close to BR Stroud) (Tel: 01452 425543).*
🚃 *Stroud 5m.*

Okehampton Castle motte and keep (right) and viewed from the bluebell wood (above)

⚊ Odda's Chapel
Deerhurst,
GLOUCESTERSHIRE
(pp. 212/217, 7H)
A rare Anglo-Saxon chapel attached, unusually, to a half-timbered farmhouse.

Open *22 March–30 Sept: daily, 10am–6pm. 1 Oct–31 March: daily, 10am–4pm (closed 24–26 Dec, 1 Jan). Keykeeper.*
Entry *Free.*
⊛ 🅿
➲ *In Deerhurst (off B4213) at Abbots Court SW of parish church.*
(OS Map 150; ref SO 869298.)
🚌 *Swanbrook Coaches BR Gloucester–Tewkesbury (Tel: 01452 425543).*
🚃 *Cheltenham 8m.*

⚊⚊ Offa's Dyke
GLOUCESTERSHIRE
(pp. 211/217, 6G)
Three-mile section of the great earthwork built by Offa, King of Mercia 757–96, from the Severn estuary to the Welsh coast as a defensive boundary to his kingdom.

Open *Any reasonable time.*
Entry *Free.*
⊛
➲ *3m NE of Chepstow off B4228. Access via Forestry Commission Tidenham car park. 1m walk (way marked) down to Devil's Pulpit on Offa's Dyke. (Access suitable only for those wearing proper walking shoes; not suitable for very young, old or infirm). (OS Map 162; ref SO 545005–549977.)*
🚌 *Stagecoach Red & White 69 Chepstow–Monmouth to within ½m (Tel: 01633 266366).*
🚃 *Chepstow 7m.*

⚊⚊ Okehampton Castle
DEVON (p. 210, 3D)
The ruins of the largest castle in Devon include the Norman motte and the keep's jagged

Old Wardour Castle from the south (above). Castle stairway to Grand Hall (right)

remains. There is a picnic area and there are also lovely woodland walks.

☻ *Picnic spot of exceptional beauty.*
Open *22 March–31 Oct: daily, 10am–6pm (6pm/dusk in Oct).*
Entry *£2.20/£1.70/£1.10.*
℡ 01837 52844
♿ 🅿 ⊗ 🍴 *(picnic tables available)* 🎧 *(also available for the visually impaired and those with learning difficulties)* ⊛
➲ *1m SW of Okehampton town centre.*
(OS Map 191; ref SX 584942.)
🚌 *Devon General 51, Bow Belle 628, Jennings 629, Western National 187, Tilleys from Exeter (some pass BR Exeter St David's) to within ½m (Tel: 01392 382800).*

☉ Old Blockhouse

Tresco, ISLES OF SCILLY
(p. 210, 5A)
The remains of a small 16th-century gun tower overlooking the white sandy bay at Old Grimsby.

Open *Any reasonable time.*
Entry *Free.*
🐕
➲ *On Blockhouse Point, at S end of Old Grimsby harbour. (OS Map 203; ref SV 898155.)*

✝ Old Sarum

WILTSHIRE (p. 211, 4J)
See pp 30–31 for full details.

☉♡⊜ Old Wardour Castle

WILTSHIRE (p. 211/212, 4H)
The unusual hexagonal ruins of this 14th-century castle are on the edge of a beautiful lake, surrounded by

landscaped grounds, which include an elaborate rockwork grotto.

Open *22 March–31 Oct: daily, 10am–6pm (6pm/dusk in Oct). 1 Nov–31 March: Wed–Sun, 10am–4pm (closed 24–26 Dec). Closed 1–2pm in winter.*
Entry *£1.50/£1.10/80p.*
℡ 01747 870487
♿ 🅿 ♿ *(grounds only)* ⊗ ⊛
➲ *Off A30 2m SW of Tisbury. (OS Map 184; ref ST 939263.)*
🚌 *Wilts & Dorset 26 Salisbury–Shaftesbury (passes BR Tisbury) (Tel: 01722 336855).*
🚉 *Tisbury 2½m.*

OLD SARUM

This great earthwork with its huge banks and ditch lies near Salisbury, on the edge of the Wiltshire chalk plains. It was built by Iron Age peoples around 500BC and was taken over by succeeding settlers and conquerors.

Romans, Saxons and, most importantly, the Normans have all occupied what is now known as Old Sarum. The Normans made it into one of their major strongholds, with a royal castle and a great cathedral. But when the new city we know as Salisbury was founded in the early 13th century, the

ENGLAND'S

CHRISTIAN

HERITAGE

ENGLISH HERITAGE

settlement faded away. Despite its virtual abandonment, a handful of electors still returned a member of Parliament to Westminster until 1832, when a wave of anti-corruption electoral reform swept through the whole of Britain.

Today the remains – of the prehistoric fortress, of the Norman palace, castle and cathedral – evoke powerful memories of the people who have ruled England over the millenia. In addition, the chalk downland, with its many wild flowers, makes it a magical spot.

The great earth banks and ditches, a mile round, of the Iron Age hill fort at Old Sarum were used by successive invaders. It was here, in 1070, that William the Conqueror paid off his army and, in 1085, demanded loyalty from his nobles. A castle, a sumptuous palace and a great cathedral were built within the earthwork. However, disputes between soldiers and priests, and inadequate water supplies, were huge hindrances. In 1226 cathedral and town moved. New Sarum, modern Salisbury with its magnificent cathedral, was built in the valley with plentiful water. The cathedral at Old Sarum was then abandoned, although the castle remained in use until Tudor times.

The Cathedral foundations marked out in the grass

Carved heads from Old Sarum cathedral

Romano-British brooch found at Old Sarum

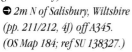 **See displays of Saxon and Norman weaponry and a savage battle re-enacted, complete with mounted Norman knights, 24-25 Aug.**
Open *22 March–31 Oct: daily, 10am–6pm (6pm/dusk in Oct). 1 Nov–31 March: daily, 10am–4pm.*
Entry *£1.90/£1.40/£1.00*
𝄞 01722 335398
P ♦♦ ◔ ੬ *(outer bailey & grounds only)* ⊗ ⊜ ⓘ
⮎ *2m N of Salisbury, Wiltshire (pp. 211/212, 4J) off A345. (OS Map 184; ref SU 138327.)*
🚌 *Wilts & Dorset/Hampshire Bus 3, 5–9 from Salisbury (Tel: 01722 336855).*
🚉 *Salisbury 2m.*

Recreated Saxon warriors

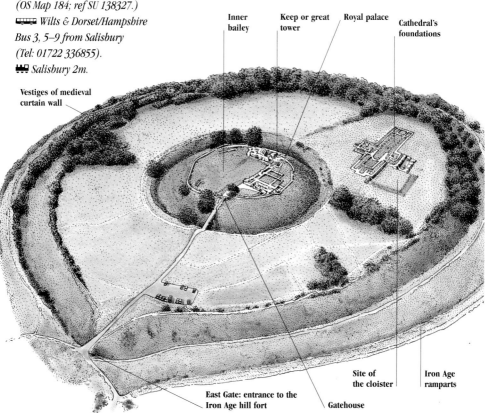

Vestiges of medieval curtain wall

Inner bailey

Keep or great tower

Royal palace

Cathedral's foundations

East Gate: entrance to the Iron Age hill fort

Gatehouse

Site of the cloister

Iron Age ramparts

Portland Castle

● Over Bridge
GLOUCESTERSHIRE
(pp. 212/217, 7H)
A single-arch masonry bridge
spanning the River Severn,
built by Thomas Telford
1825–27.

Open *Any reasonable time.*
Entry *Free.*
⊗ 🅿 *(in layby)*
➲ *1m NW of Gloucester city
centre at junction of A40
(Ross) & A419 (Ledbury).
(OS Map 162; ref SO 817196.)*
🚌 *Frequent services
from BR Gloucester
(Tel: 01452 425543).*
🚆 *Gloucester 2m.*

● Pendennis Castle
CORNWALL (p. 210, 1B)
See pp 34–5 for full details.

● Penhallam
CORNWALL (p. 210, 3C)
Ruins of a medieval manor
house surrounded by a
protective moat.

Open *Any reasonable time.*
Entry *Free.*
⊗ 🅿 *(limited)*
➲ *1m NW of Week St Mary,
off minor road off A39 from
Treskinnick Cross (10 minute
walk from car park).
(OS Map 190; ref SX 224974.)*

● ▲ Porth Hellick Down Burial Chamber
St Mary's, ISLES OF SCILLY
(p. 210, 4B)
Probably the best-preserved
Bronze Age burial mound on
the Islands, with an entrance
passage and chamber.

Open *Any reasonable time.*
Entry *Free.*
⊗
➲ *1½m E of Hugh Town.
(OS Map 203; ref SV 929108.)*

● Portland Castle
DORSET (pp. 211/212, 3H)
One of the best preserved of
Henry VIII's coastal forts,
built of white Portland stone.
It was originally intended to
repel the Spanish and French,
and changed hands several
times during the Civil War.

Open *22 March–31 Oct: daily,
10am–6pm (6pm/dusk in Oct).*
Entry *£2.20/£1.70/£1.10.*
☏ *01305 820539*
🅿 ⊗ ♿ *(ground floor only –
1 deep step)* 🎧 🗂 🐕
➲ *Overlooking Portland
harbour adjacent to RN
helicopter base.
(OS Map 194; ref SY 684743.)*
🚌 *Dorset Transit 1, Smith's
Coaches Weymouth–Portland
(Tel: 01305 783645). Water
bus from Brewers Quay in
Weymouth.*
🚆 *Weymouth 4½m.*

● Ratfyn Barrows
WILTSHIRE (pp. 211/212, 4J)
Part of Bronze Age cemetery
containing burial mounds of
different styles.

Open *Access by consent of
owner only. Contact Regional
Office (Tel: 0117 975 0700).*
Entry *Free.*
➲ *1½m E of Amesbury on both
sides of A303. Barrows can be
seen from A303 (no stopping).
(OS Map 184; ref SU 180417.)*
🚌 *Wilts & Dorset 5–6 Salis-
bury–Swindon, 6–9 Salisbury–
Andover, to within 1m (passes
close to BR Salisbury)
(Tel: 01722 336855)*
🚆 *Salisbury 10m*

✪ Restormel Castle

CORNWALL (p. 210, 2C)
Perched on a high mound,
surrounded by a deep moat,
the huge circular keep of this
splendid Norman castle
survives in remarkably good
condition. It offers splendid
views over the surrounding
countryside.

Open *22 March–31 Oct: daily,
10am–6pm (6pm/dusk in Oct).*
Entry *£1.50/£1.10/80p.*
(*01208 872687*
👫 🅿 🐕 ♿
➲ *1½m N of Lostwithiel
off A390.
(OS Map 200; ref SX 104614).*
🚆 *Lostwithiel 1½m.*

Restormel Castle

✪ Royal Citadel

Plymouth, DEVON (p. 210, 2D)
A dramatic 17th-century
fortress, with walls up to 21
metres (70 feet) high, built to
defend the coastline from the
Dutch, and still in use today.

Open *By guided tour only (1¼
hours) 1 May–30 Sept: 2pm and
3.30pm. Tickets from Plymouth
Dome below Smeaton's Tower
on Hoe. For security reasons
tours may be suspended at
short notice.*
Entry *£2.50/£2.00/£1.50.*
(*01752 775841*
🐕
➲ *At E end of Plymouth Hoe.
(OS Map 201; ref SX 480538.)*
🚌 *From surrounding areas*

(Tel: 01752 222666).
🚆 *Plymouth 1¼m.*

⏏ ✪ St Breock Downs Monolith

CORNWALL (p. 210, 2C)
A prehistoric standing stone,
originally about 5 metres
(16 feet) high, set in
beautiful countryside.

Open *Any reasonable time.
(Site managed by the Cornwall
Heritage Trust.)*
Entry *Free.*
🐕
➲ *On St Breock Downs, 3¾m
SW of Wadebridge off unclassi-
fied road to Rosenannon.
(OS Map 200; ref SW 968683.)*
🚆 *Roche 5½m*

PENDENNIS CASTLE

Pendennis and its neighbour St Mawes Castle face each other across the mouth of the estuary of the River Fal. They are the Cornish end of a chain of castles built by Henry VIII along England's south coast from 1539–1545 as protection against the threat of attack and invasion from France. Many of these castles are in the care of English Heritage. Few of them have ever seen active service, but many,

One of the grotesque water spouts

especially Pendennis, were extended or adapted to meet the changing threats to national security. These came from the French and then the Spanish in the 16th century, and continued right through to World War II. Pendennis today stands as a landmark, with fine seaviews and excellent site facilities, including an introductory exhibition, a museum display and the Guardhouse, which has been returned to its World War I appearance.

Sir Walter Raleigh, who ordered the refortification of Pendennis

The land on which Pendennis stands was originally owned by the Killigrew family, governors of Pendennis for many years. The lodgings fronting the keep were built around 1550 to provide them with more comfortable accommodation.

The Governor's lodging (below), built in the mid-16th century

In the later years of Elizabeth I's reign, a new type of defensive wall with bastions was added around the original fort. Strengthened again prior to the Civil War, Pendennis was host to the future Charles II in 1646, who sailed from there to the Isles of Scilly. It withstood five months of siege before becoming the penultimate Royalist Garrison to surrender on the mainland. Pendennis was heavily rearmed in the late 19th and early 20th centuries, culminating in the installation of huge 6-inch guns during World War II.

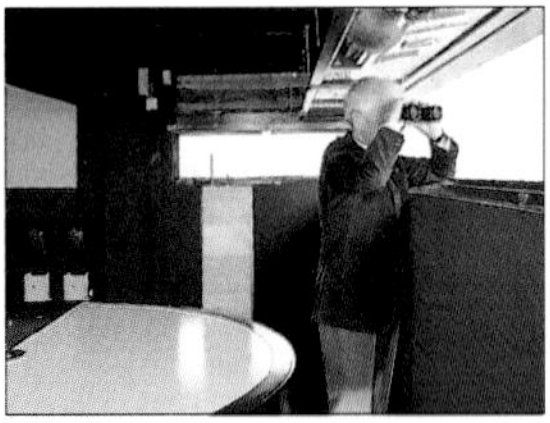

The Battery observation post

Vivid re-creation of the gun defences (nearly 40 historic guns on display).
Free Children's Activity sheet available.
An exciting CD Rom unit with information on English castles' function and purpose.

Open *22 March–31 Oct: daily, 10am–6pm (6pm/dusk in Oct). 1 Nov–31 March: daily, 10am–4pm (closed 24–26 Dec).*
Entry *£2.70/£2.00/£1.40.*
01326 316594

(also available for the visually impaired and those with learning difficulties)
(grounds, parts of keep)
('Pendennis Castle Coffee Shop'; normally open summer season only)
On Pendennis Head, Cornwall (p. 210, 1B), 1m SE of Falmouth. (OS Map 204; ref SW 824318.)
Falmouth Docks ½m.

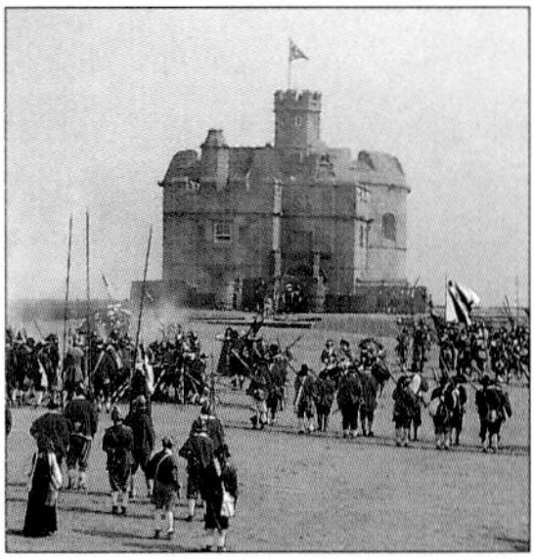

A vivid re-enactment of a 17th-century battle inside the walls of Pendennis

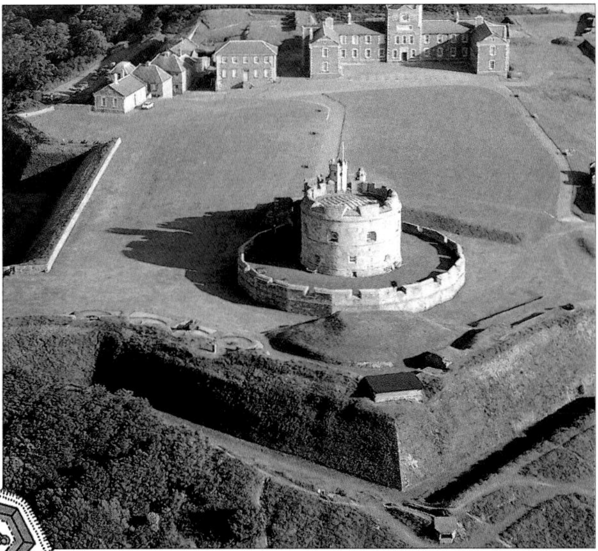

Aerial view of Pendennis from the south east

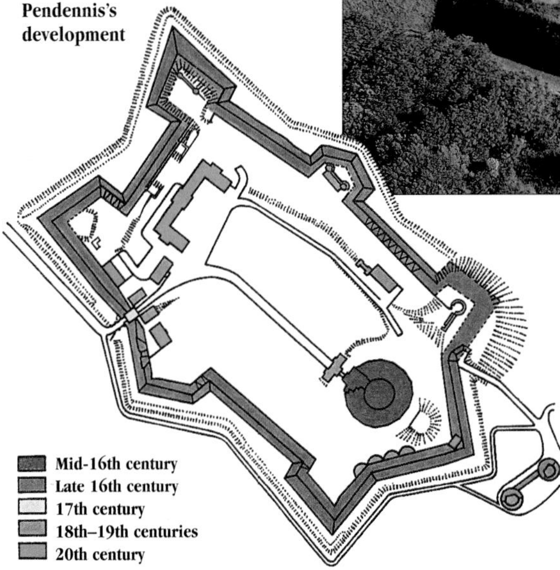
Mid-16th century
Late 16th century
17th century
18th–19th centuries
20th century

Pendennis's development

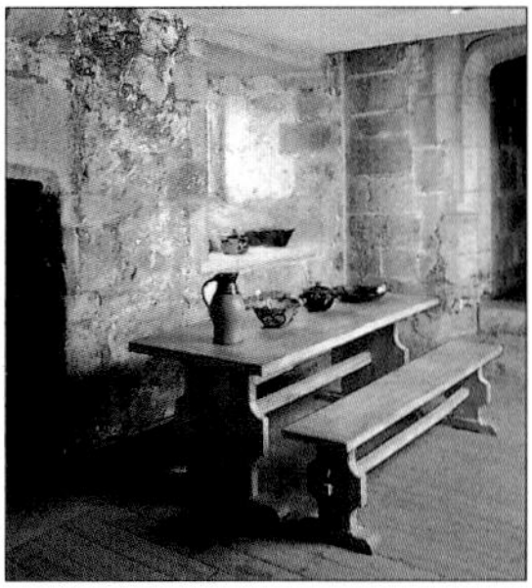

Inside the keep entrance block

St Briavel's Castle

⊖ St Briavel's Castle

GLOUCESTERSHIRE
(pp. 211/217, 6G)
A splendid 12th-century castle now used as a youth hostel, which is appropriate for a building set in such marvellous walking country.

Open *Exterior any reasonable time. Bailey 1 April–30 Sept: daily, 1pm–4pm.*
Entry *Free.*
⊗
➲ *In St Briavel's, 7m NE of Chepstow off B4228. (OS Map 162; ref SO 559046.)*
🚌 *Chepstow 8m.*

⊘ St Catherine's Castle

Fowey, CORNWALL
(p. 210, 2C)
A small fort built by Henry VIII to defend Fowey Harbour.

Open *Any reasonable time.*
Entry *Free.*
⊗ 🅿 *(in Fowey; ½m walk.)*
➲ *¾m SW of Fowey along footpath off A3082. (OS Map 200; ref SX 118508.)*
🚌 *Western National 24*

St Austell–Fowey, thence ¾m (Tel: 01209 719988).
🚌 *Par 4m.*

⛪ St Catherine's Chapel

Abbotsbury, DORSET
(p. 211, 3G)
A small stone chapel, set on a hilltop, with an unusual roof and small turret used as a lighthouse.

Open *Any reasonable time. (Site managed by the Ilchester Estates.)*
Entry *Free.*
⊗
➲ *½m S of Abbotsbury by pedestrian track from village off B3157. (OS Map 194; ref SY 572848.)*
🚌 *Upwey 7½m.*

St Mawes Castle

An aerial view of Sherborne Old Castle

✚ St Mary's Church

Kempley, GLOUCES-TERSHIRE (p. 217, 7G)
A Norman church with superb wall paintings from the 12th–14th centuries.

Open 22 March–30 Sept: daily, 10am–6pm. 1 Oct–31 March: daily, 10am–4pm (closed 24–26 Dec, 1 Jan). Keykeeper.
Entry Free.
⊗
➲ *1m N of Kempley off B4024, 6m NE of Ross-on-Wye.*
(OS Map 149; ref SO 670313.)
🚌 *Ledbury 8m.*

✪ ❀ St Mawes Castle

CORNWALL (p. 210, 1B)
Together with Pendennis, St Mawes Castle was built by Henry VIII to guard the entrance to safe anchorage in the Carrick Roads. Its three huge circular bastions with gun ports were formidable defences indeed. Today the castle stands in delightful sub-tropical gardens featuring plants from around the world. Some of the finest views of the surrounding coastline can be enjoyed from here.

❀ *Free Children's Activity Sheet available.*
Open 22 March–31 Oct: daily, 10am–6pm (6pm/dusk in Oct). 1 Nov–31 March: Wed–Sun, 10am–4pm (closed 24–26 Dec). Closed 1–2pm in winter.
Entry £2.20/£1.70/£1.10.
📞 *01326 270526*
👫 🅿 ⊗ 🕐 🍴 🛏 🎧 ❀
➲ *In St Mawes on A3078.*
(OS Map 204; ref SW 842328.)
🚌 *Western National 51 Truro–St Mawes (Tel: 01209 719988).*
⛴ *Foot Ferry: St Mawes Ferry Co. from Falmouth, Prince of Wales Pier (Tel: 01326 313234). Car via King Harry Ferry at Feoch on B3289 (Tel: 01872 72463).*
🚌 *Falmouth Town, ³⁄₄m walk to Prince of Wales Pier.*

⛰ The Sanctuary

WILTSHIRE (pp. 211/212, 5J)
Possibly 5,000 years old, The Sanctuary consists of two concentric circles of stones and six of timber uprights indicated by concrete posts. The Sanctuary is connected to Avebury by the West Kennet Avenue of standing stones.

Open Any reasonable time. (Site managed by the National Trust.)
Entry Free.
⊗ 🅿 *(in layby)*
➲ *Beside A4, ¹⁄₂m E of West Kennet.*
(OS Map 173; ref SU 118679.)
🚌 *Wilts & Dorset 5/6 Salisbury–Swindon (passes close to BR Swindon) (Tel: 0345 090 899).*
🚌 *Pewsey 9m, Bedwyn 12m.*

➲ ✪ Sherborne Old Castle

DORSET (pp. 211/212, 4G)
The ruins of this early 12th-century castle are a testament to the 16 days Cromwell took to capture it during the Civil War. It was then abandoned.

Open 22 March–31 Oct: daily, 10am–6pm (6pm/dusk in Oct). 1 Nov–31 March: Wed–Sun, 10am–4pm (closed 24–26 Dec). Closed 1–2pm in winter.
Entry £1.50/£1.10/80p.
📞 *01935 812730*
🅿 ⊗ ♿ 🍴
➲ *¹⁄₂m E of Sherborne off B3145.*
(OS Map 183; ref ST 647167.)
🚌 *Sherborne ³⁄₄m.*

Silbury Hill

① Silbury Hill

WILTSHIRE (pp. 211/212, 5J)
An extraordinary artificial
prehistoric mound, the
largest Neolithic construction
of its type in Europe.

Open *Any reasonable time
(no access to hill itself).*
*(Site managed by the
National Trust.)*
Entry *Free.*
&. *(viewing area)* ⊛ 🅿
➲ *1m W of West Kennet on A4.*
(OS Map 173; ref SU 100685.)
🚌 *Thamesdown 49/A*

Totnes Castle

*Swindon–Devizes/Marlborough
Wilts & Dorset 5/6 Salisbury–
Swindon (Tel: 0345 090 899).
All pass within ¾ m and pass
close to BR Swindon.*
🚂 *Pewsey 9m, Swindon 13m.*

⊖ Sir Bevil Grenville's Monument

Lansdown, BATH & N.E.
SOMERSET (p. 211, 5H)
Commemorates the heroism
of a Royalist commander and
his Cornish pikemen at the
Battle of Lansdown.

Open *Any reasonable time.*
Entry *Free.*
⊛ 🅿 *(in layby)*
➲ *4m NW of Bath, on N
edge of Lansdown Hill,
near road to Wick.*
(OS Map 172; ref ST 721703.)
🚌 *Badgerline 2, 702
BR Bath Spa–Ensleigh, thence
2½ m (Tel: 01225 464446).*
🚂 *Bath Spa 4½ m.*

⊜ Stanton Drew Circles and Cove

BATH & N.E. SOMERSET
(p. 211, 5G)
A fascinating assembly of
three stone circles, two
avenues and a burial
chamber makes this one of
the finest Neolithic religious
sites in the country.

Open *Cove – any reasonable
time. Two main stone circles –
access at discretion of owner
who may levy a charge.
Tel: 0117 975 0700 for details.*
Entry *Free but see above.*
⊛
➲ *Circles: E of Stanton Drew
village; Cove: in garden of
Druid's Arms.
(OS Map 172; Circles ref
ST 601634, Cove ref ST 598633.)*
🚌 *Badgerline 376 Bristol–
Yeovil (passes BR Bristol Temple
Meads), alight Pensford, 1½ m
(Tel: 0117 955 3231).*
🚂 *Bristol Temple Meads 7m.*

① Stonehenge

WILTSHIRE (pp. 211/212, 5A)
See pp 40–45 for full details.

● Stoney Littleton Long Barrow

BATH & N.E. SOMERSET
(pp. 211/212, 5H)
This Neolithic burial mound is about 30 metres (100 feet) long and has chambers where human remains once lay.

Open Exterior only – any reasonable time.
Entry Free.
⊛ **P** *(limited)*
➲ *1m S of Wellow off A367.*
(OS Map 172; ref ST 735573.)
🚌 *Bath Spa 6m.*

✝ Temple Church

BRISTOL (p. 211, 5G)
The handsome tower and walls of this 15th-century church defied the bombs of World War II. The graveyard is now a pleasant public garden.

Open Exterior only – any reasonable time.

Trethevy Quoit

Entry Free.
& ⊛
➲ *In Temple St off Victoria St.*
(OS Map 172; ref ST 593727.)
🚌 *From surrounding areas (Tel: 0117 955 3231).*
🚌 *Bristol Temple Meads ¼m.*

ⓩ ♡ Tintagel Castle

CORNWALL (p. 210, 3C)
See pp 48–9 for full details.

ⓩ ♡ Totnes Castle

DEVON (p. 210, 2E)
A superb motte and bailey castle, with splendid views across the roof tops and down to the River Dart – a fine example of Norman fortification.

⊛ *Family Discovery Pack available.*
Open 22 March–31 Oct: daily, 10am–6pm (6pm/dusk in Oct). 1 Nov–31 March: Wed–Sun, 10am–4pm (closed 24–26 Dec). Closed 1–2pm in winter.
Entry £1.50/£1.10/80p.
☎ *01803 864406*
P *(64 metres [210 feet], small charge)* ⊛ 🚃

➲ *In Totnes, on hill overlooking the town.*
(OS Map 202; ref SX 800605.)
🚌 *Totnes ¼m.*

● Tregiffian Burial Chamber

St Buryan, CORNWALL
(p. 210, 1A)
A Neolithic or early Bronze Age chambered tomb by the side of a country road.

Open Any reasonable time. (Site managed by the Cornwall Heritage Trust.)
Entry Free.
⊛
➲ *2m SE of St Buryan on B3315. (OS Map 203; ref SW 430245.)*
🚌 *Penzance 5½m.*

● Trethevy Quoit

St Cleer, CORNWALL
(p. 210, 2D)
An ancient Neolithic burial chamber, standing 2.7 metres (9 feet) high and consisting of five standing stones sur-mounted by a huge capstone.

Open Any reasonable time. (Site managed by the Cornwall Heritage Trust.)
Entry Free.
⊛
➲ *1m NE of St Cleer near Darite off B3254. (OS Map 201; ref SX 259688.)*
🚃 *Caradon Riviera BR Liskeard–Tremar (Tel: 01579 62226)*
🚌 *Liskeard 3½m.*

STONEHENGE

The great and ancient stone circle of Stonehenge is one of the wonders of the world, as old as many of the great temples and pyramids of Egypt, as old as Troy. Stonehenge is not an isolated monument, however. Although visitors over the centuries have tended to focus on the massive stones, these stand at the centre of an extensive prehistoric landscape filled with the

Bronze dagger (left) and gold-plated ornaments from the Stonehenge area

remains of ceremonial and domestic structures. Some are older than the great monument itself. Many of these features – earthworks, burial mounds, and other circular 'henge' monuments – are accessible by road or public footpath. Now a World Heritage Site, Stonehenge and its surroundings remain powerful witnesses to the once great civilization of the Stone and Bronze Ages, between 5000 and 3000 years ago.

What visitors see today are the substantial remnants of the last in a sequence of monuments erected between *c*. 3000 and 1600 BC. Each was a circular structure, aligned along the rising of the sun at the midsummer solstice. The first 'Stonehenge' consisted of a circular bank and ditch with

a ring of 56 wooden posts, now known as Aubrey Holes. Later monuments all used, and re-used, the great stones we see today, which were brought from some distance away. The final phase comprised an outer circle of huge standing stones – super-hard sarsens, from the Marlborough Downs –

The best-surviving section of the outer circle of sarsen stones

The final phase of Stonehenge's construction

South Barrow (site of station stone)

Station stone

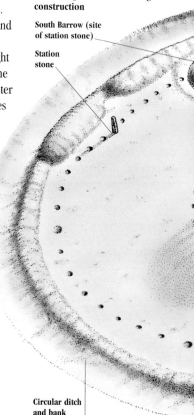

Circular ditch and bank

and topped by lintels making a continuous ring. Inside this stood a horseshoe of still larger stones, five pairs of uprights with a lintel across each pair, known as trilithons. Stones were connected using mortice and tenon and tongue and groove joints, possibly copying previous wood construction techniques. Smaller bluestones, from the Preseli Mountains in south Wales, were arranged in a circle and a horseshoe within the great sarsen stone circle and horseshoe. In an earlier phase these bluestones had been erected in a different arrangement.

Fallen stones showing the mortice and tenon fixing

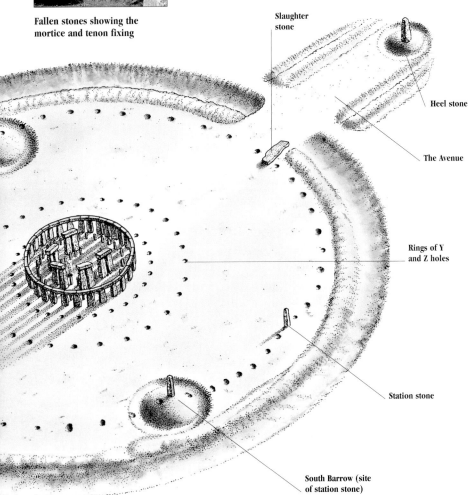

Slaughter stone

Heel stone

The Avenue

Rings of Y and Z holes

Station stone

South Barrow (site of station stone)

A possible method of raising the sarsen stones into an upright setting

There has always been intense debate over quite what purpose Stonehenge served. Certainly it was the focal point for thousands of years within a ceremonial landscape. It also represented a huge investment of labour and time. The stones were carried tens, sometimes hundreds, of kilometres by land and water. Huge efforts were needed to transport the stones, and then to shape and raise them. It must have been a sophisticated society to command the amount of labour, to design and construct this and the many other surrounding monuments.

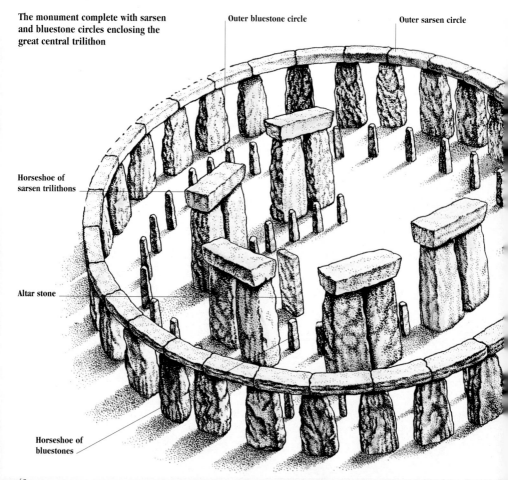

The monument complete with sarsen and bluestone circles enclosing the great central trilithon

Outer bluestone circle

Outer sarsen circle

Horseshoe of sarsen trilithons

Altar stone

Horseshoe of bluestones

A likely method of raising a lintel to the top of two sarsens

Stonehenge's orientation on the rising and setting sun has always been one of its most remarkable features. Whether this was simply because the builders came from a sun-worshipping culture, or because – as some scholars have believed – the circle and its banks were part of a huge astronomical calendar, remains a mystery.

What cannot be denied is the ingenuity of the builders of Stonehenge. With just very basic tools at their disposal, they shaped the stones and formed the mortices and tenons that linked uprights to lintels. Using antlers and bones, they dug the pits to hold the stones and made the banks and ditches that enclosed them.

Digging tools of the type used at Stonehenge

Stonehenge from the air in winter

A dressed sarsen from the outer circle

There are direct links with the people who built Stonehenge in their artefacts: tools, pottery and even the contents of their graves. Some of these are displayed in the museums at Salisbury and Devizes.

Burial mounds, which possibly contained the graves of ruling families, are also integral to the landscape. The long barrows of the New Stone

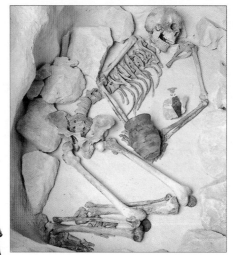

A man buried *c*.2000 BC, holding a pottery drinking vessel

Pottery funerary vessels of the early Bronze Age

Age, and the various types of circular barrows that came after, are still visible, as are other earthworks and monuments. Some, such as the long oval earthwork to the north,

the Cursus, once thought to be a chariot race course, remain enigmatic. The Cursus and other parts of the Stonehenge landscape may be visited. Woodhenge, two miles to the

Map with the barrows and monuments in the Stonehenge area

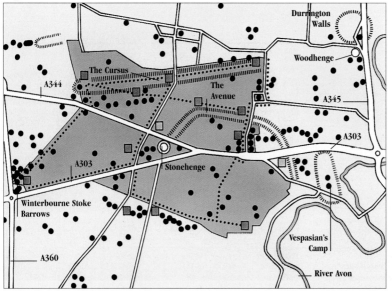

The chalk and grass landscape, with the Cursus, the Stonehenge circle, and clusters of barrow burials

An artist's impression (below) of a possible reconstruction of Woodhenge

surrounded by 1,500 acres of land owned by the National Trust with excellent walks.)

☎ 01980 624715

🅿 ⛏ 🚻 ♿ 🎫 *(also available in French, German and Japanese; large print and braille guides in English only)* 🎧* *(available in six languages & hearing loop) .*

➲ *2m W of Amesbury, Wiltshire (pp. 211/212, 5J) on junction*

north east, was a wooden oval post structure aligned with the summer solstice sun and contemporary with the first phase of Stonehenge.

Stonehenge and its surrounding monuments have been an object of fascination and appeal since well before the dawn of recorded history.

William Cunnington (below), one in a great line of antiquarians, who studied Stonehenge around 1800

❂ *Interactive audio tour of the facts and legends of Stonehenge, available in six languages.*
❂ *Superb gift shop.*
Open *16 March–31 May: daily, 9.30am–6pm. 1 June–31 Aug: daily, 9am–7pm. 1 Sept–15 Oct: daily, 9.30am–6pm. 16 Oct–15 March (1998): daily, 9.30am–4pm (closed 24–26 Dec).*
Entry *£3.70/£2.80/£1.90. Family ticket (2 adults & 3 children) £9.00. National Trust members admitted free. (Under the guardianship and managed by English Heritage. The site is*

A303 and A344/A360. (OS Map 184; ref SU 123422.) 🚌 *Wilts & Dorset 3 BR Salisbury–Stonehenge (Tel: 01722 336855).* 🚉 *Salisbury 9½m.*

Midsummer sunrise

⚠ Uley Long Barrow (Hetty Pegler's Tump)

GLOUCESTERSHIRE
(pp. 211/212/217, 6H)
Dating from around 3000 BC, this 55 metre- (180 foot-) long Neolithic chambered burial mound is unusual in that its mound is still intact.

Open *Any reasonable time. (Site managed by Gloucester-shire County Council.)*
Entry *Free.*
🐕
➲ *3½m NE of Dursley on B4066. (OS Map 162; ref SO 790000.)*
🚌 *Stagecoach Stroud Valleys 15 Stroud–Dursley (passes close to BR Stroud) (Tel: 01452 425543).*
🚃 *Stroud 6m.*

⚠ Upper Plym Valley

Dartmoor, DEVON (p. 210, 2D)
Scores of prehistoric and medieval sites covering six square miles of ancient landscape.

Open *Any reasonable time. (Sites managed by the National Trust.)*
Entry *Free.*
🐕
➲ *4m E of Yelverton. (OS Map 202.)*
🚌 *Western National 82, 98A Plymouth–Exeter (passes BR Plymouth) (Tel: 01392 382800).*

⚠ West Kennet Avenue

Avebury, WILTSHIRE
(pp. 211/212, 5J)
An avenue of standing stones, which ran in a curve from Avebury Stone Circles to The Sanctuary, probably dating from the late Neolithic Age.

Open *Any reasonable time. (Site owned and managed by the National Trust.)*
Entry *Free.*
♿ *(on roadway)* 🐕
➲ *Runs alongside B4003. (OS Map 173; ref SU 105695.)*
🚌 *Thamesdown 49A Swindon–Marlborough; Wilts & Dorset 5/6 Salisbury–Swindon (Tel: 0345 090 899). All pass close to BR Swindon.*
🚃 *Pewsey 9m, Swindon 12m.*

⚠ West Kennet Long Barrow

WILTSHIRE (pp. 211/212, 5J)
A Neolithic chambered tomb, consisting of a long earthen mound containing a passage with side chambers, and with the entrance guarded by a large stone.

Open *Any reasonable time. (Site managed by the National Trust.)*
Entry *Free.*
🅿 *(in layby)* 🐕
➲ *¾m SW of West Kennet along footpath off A4. (OS Map 173; ref SU 104677.)*
🚌 *Thamesdown 49A Swindon–Devizes/Marlborough; Wilts & Dorset 5/6 Salisbury–*

West Kennet Long Barrow

Swindon (Tel: 0345 090 899).
All to within 1m. All pass close
to BR Swindon.
🚃 Pewsey 9m, Swindon 13m.

⬤ Windmill Hill

WILTSHIRE (pp. 211/212, 5J)
Neolithic remains of three
concentric rings of ditches,
enclosing an area of 21
acres.

Open *Any reasonable time.
(Site owned and managed by
the National Trust.)*
Entry *Free.*
🚻

➲ *1½m NW of Avebury.*
(OS Map 173; ref SU 086714.)
🚌 *Thamesdown 49A
Swindon–Devizes/Marlborough;
Wilts & Dorset 5/6 Salisbury–
Swindon. All to within 1m.*

All pass close to BR Swindon
(Tel: 0345 090 899).
🚃 Swindon 11m.

⬤ Winterbourne Poor Lot Barrows

DORSET (p. 211, 3G)
Part of an extensive 4,000-
year-old Bronze Age cemetery.

Open *Any reasonable time.*
Entry *Free.*
🚫

➲ *2m W of Winterbourne
Abbas, S of junction of A35 with
minor road to Compton
Valence. Access via Wellbottom
Lodge – 180 metres (200 yards)
E along A35 from junction.
(OS Map 194; ref SY 590906.)*
🚌 *Southern National 31
Weymouth–Taunton (Passes BR
Dorchester South and Axmin-
ster) (Tel: 01305 783645).*
🚃 *Dorchester West or South,
both 7m.*

⬤ Woodhenge

WILTSHIRE (pp. 211/212, 5J)
Neolithic ceremonial
monument of *c.*2300 BC,
consisting of a bank and
ditch and six concentric rings
of timber posts, now shown
by concrete markers. The
entrance and long axis of the
oval rings points to the rising
sun on Midsummer Day.
See p. 45 for more details.

Open *Any reasonable time.*
Entry *Free.*
🅿 ♿ 🚻

➲ *1½m N of Amesbury, off
A345 just S of Durrington.
(OS Map 184; ref SU 151434.)*
🚌 *Wilts & Dorset 5/6
Salisbury–Swindon (passes
close to BR Salisbury &
Swindon), 16 from Amesbury
(Tel: 01722 336855).*
🚃 *Salisbury 9m.*

Yarn Market

⊙ Yarn Market

Dunster, SOMERSET
(p. 211, 4E)
A 17th-century octagonal
market hall.

Open *Any reasonable time.
(Site managed by the
National Trust.)*
Entry *Free.*
♿ 🚻

➲ *In Dunster High St.
(OS Map 181; ref SS 992437.)*
🚌 *Southern National 28 BR
Taunton–Minehead to within
¼m, also 39 from Minehead
(Tel: 01823 272033).*
🚃 *Dunster (W Somerset
Rly) ½m.*

TINTAGEL CASTLE

With its specacular location on one of England's most dramatic coastlines, Tintagel Castle is a place of legends. Joined to the mainland by a narrow neck of land, Tintagel Island faces the full force of the Atlantic. On the mainland itself, the gaunt remains of the medieval castle, thought to date from the second quarter of the 13th century, represent only one phase in a long history of occupation. Even before Richard, Earl of Cornwall, built his castle there, Tintagel

Merlin and baby Arthur

had come to be associated with King Arthur, as the great warrior leader's birthplace. The legend, depicted in Geoffrey of Monmouth's fabulous History (written c. 1139), has lived on. Today, fact and fiction lie inextricably intertwined. We know for sure, however, that with the surf thundering against the cliffs and the waves breaking over the threshold of Merlin's cave, Tintagel remains one of the most awe-inspiring and romantic spots in Britain.

After a period as a Roman settlement and military outpost, Tintagel is thought to have been the stronghold of a Celtic king during the fifth and sixth centuries. An early Christian church stands on the site of what may have been a cemetery for important men. Here legend and archaeology come together. Whether one of those men was King Mark, whose nephew Tristan fell in love with Isolt (or Isolde), history cannot tell. Their doomed romance is part of Tintagel's story, as are

Geoffrey of Monmouth's tales, in which Uther Pendragon, aided by Merlin, seduced Queen Igerna at Tintagel. Tintagel's Arthurian connection was later renewed by Alfred, Lord Tennyson in his *Idylls of the King*. The remains of the 13th-century castle are breathtaking. Steep stone steps, stout walls and rugged windswept cliff edges encircle the Great Hall, where Richard, Earl of Cornwall, may once have feasted. The emphasis at Tintagel is always on the word 'may' as it has so many legends and unanswered questions.

Tintagel Castle ruins

The so-called
Merlin's cave

Thomas Hardy's fanciful
reconstruction of Tintagel

King Arthur receives Excalibur
from the Lady in the Lake

❂ *Family Discovery Pack
and free Children's Activity
Sheet available.*
Open *22 March–31 Oct: daily,
10am–6pm (6pm/dusk in Oct).
1 Nov–31 March: daily, 10am–4pm
(closed 24–26 Dec).*
Entry *£2.70/£2.00/£1.40*
✆ **01840 770328**
⌂ ♦♦ ❂ 🅿 *(in Tintagel village)* ⊗
Ⓓ *(Please note steep climb up
steps to reach castle.)*
➲ *On Tintagel Head, Cornwall
(p. 210, 3C), ½m along uneven
track from Tintagel, no vehicles.
(OS Map 200; ref SX 048891.)*
🚌 *Western National 122, 125
from Wadebridge (with
connections from BR Bodmin
Parkway) (Tel: 01209 719988);
Fry's service from Plymouth
(Tel: 01840 770256).*

The Island of Tintagel

THE SOUTH EAST

The sites across the South East span the centuries, ranging from the Roman villa at Lullingstone to the huge tunnel complex underneath Dover Castle, used throughout World War II. Celebrate the 1400th anniversary of the arrival of St Augustine in Kent with a visit to the Abbey he founded in 598. New visitor facilities include a facinating museum and interactive audio tours. Explore the battlefield where King Harold fell in 1066 and relive the invasion of William the Conqueror. Royal heritage dominates the Isle of Wight where Carisbrooke Castle, once prison to King Charles I, and Osborne House, Queen Victoria's 'place of one's own', give glimpses of past royal life. At Walmer Castle the tradition continues, with the Queen Mother's new garden opening in early summer.

Appuldurcombe House

♡ ➲ Appuldurcombe House

ISLE OF WIGHT (p. 212, 3K)
Although now mainly a shell, Appuldurcombe was once the grandest house on the Isle of Wight. The fine 18th-century baroque-style house retains its elegant east front and stands in its own ornamental grounds, designed by 'Capability' Brown. The rolling green landscape beyond makes this an idyllic setting. An exhibition of prints and photographs depicts the house and its history.

Open *1 April–31 Oct: daily, 10am–6pm (6pm/dusk in Oct). (Site managed by Mr & Mrs Owen.)*

Bayham Old Abbey

Entry £2.00/£1.50/£1.00.
(01983 852484
♦♦ P & ⌂ ☞
➲ *½m W of Wroxall off B3327. (OS Map 196; ref SZ 543800.)*
🚌 *Southern Vectis 92 W. Cowes–Ventnor, 7/A Ryde–Yarmouth (Tel: 01983 827005).*
🚉 *Shanklin 3½m.*
⛴ *Ryde 11m (Wightlink. Tel: 01705 827744); West Cowes 12m; East Cowes 12m (Red Funnel. Tel: 01703 334010).*

⛪ Battle Abbey and Battlefield

SUSSEX (p. 213, 4N)
See pp 52–5 for full details.

⛪ Bayham Old Abbey

SUSSEX (p. 213, 4N)
Ruins of a house of 'white' canons, founded in *c*.1208,

in an 18th-century landscaped setting. The Georgian House (Dower House) is also open to the public.

Open *22 March–31 Oct: daily, 10am–6pm (6pm/dusk in Oct).*
Entry *£2.00/£1.50/£1.00.*
☎ *01892 890381*
♛♟📷🚻👜🛍
➲ *1¾m W of Lamberhurst off B2169.*
(OS Map 188; ref TQ 651366.)
🚌 *Autopoint/Wealden 256 BR Tunbridge Wells–Wadhurst (Tel: 0800 696 996).*
🚉 *Frant 4m.*

⛪ Bishop's Waltham Palace

HAMPSHIRE (p. 212, 4K)
This medieval seat of the Bishops of Winchester once stood in an enormous park. Wooded grounds still surround the mainly 12th- and 14th-century remains, including the Great Hall and three-storey tower, as well as the moat which once enclosed the palace. Much

Bishop's Waltham Palace shield

was destroyed in a fire by Parliamentarians in the Civil War after the Battle of Cheriton in 1644, but the ground floor of the Dower House is intact and furnished as a 19th-century farmhouse, with an exhibition on the powerful Winchester Bishops on the first floor.

Open *22 March–31 Oct: daily, 10am–6pm (6pm/dusk in Oct). Keykeeper in winter, please telephone 01732 778030.*
Entry *£2.00/£1.50/£1.00.*
☎ *01489 892460*
♛ *(nearby in Bishop's Waltham)*
📷 ♿ *(grounds only)* 🚻 🛍
➲ *In Bishop's Waltham 5m from junction 8 of M27.*
(OS Map 185; ref SU 552173.)

🚌 *Stagecoach Hampshire Bus 69 Winchester–Southsea (passes close to BR Winchester) (Tel: 01256 464501); Solent Blue Line/Provincial 48A/C Eastleigh–Fareham (passes close to BR Eastleigh) (Tel: 01703 226235). All pass close to BR Fareham.*
🚉 *Botley 3½m.*

⛪ Boxgrove Priory

SUSSEX (p. 212, 4L)
Remains of the Guest House, Chapter House and church of a 12th century priory.

Open *Any reasonable time.*
Entry *Free.*
📷 📷
➲ *N of Boxgrove, 4m E of Chichester on minor road off A27.*
(OS Map 197; ref SU 909076.)
🚌 *Stagecoach Coastline 58 BR Chichester–Littlehampton (passes BR Barnham) (Tel: 01243 783251).*
🚉 *Chichester 4m.*

Bishop's Waltham Palace

1066 BATTLE OF HASTINGS
ABBEY & BATTLEFIELD

The one date in English history that everyone can remember is 1066: the Battle of Hastings, when the conquering Normans vanquished the Anglo-Saxons on 14 October. There is just as much myth surrounding the conflict as known fact. The two armies did not even fight at Hastings, but at the place which became the town of Battle, 6 miles inland. There, on the valley slopes, it is possible to

retrace the lines of conflict. In the ruins of the abbey that King William built to atone for the blood spilt, you may stand on the very spot where the defeated King Harold fell.

A visit to the battlefield itself provides an unparalleled chance to absorb the reality of the conquest and its aftermath. Battle Abbey stands at one of the turning points of English history.

It was never a foregone conclusion that William would win at Battle. Only days before, Harold had won a famous victory in the north at Stamford Bridge against the King of Norway. William *did* win, but only after a great struggle. Today an audio tape tour re-creates the sounds of the battle, as you stand exactly where the English were, watching the Normans advance towards them. With the English occupying the high ground, the Normans were forced to fight uphill. They overcame this disadvantage by fighting both on foot and horseback, while the English dismounted, using swords or their huge two-handed axes. The course of the battle was reversed when the Normans pretended to flee, but then turned back to cut down the English who had broken ranks in pursuit. The final assault by William was preceded by a devastating volley of arrows. The Bayeux Tapestry depicts an arrow hitting Harold in the eye. He did not die directly from that wound, but was later cut down by a Norman sword. On Harold's death his army fled, the Normans in pursuit.

William the Conqueror

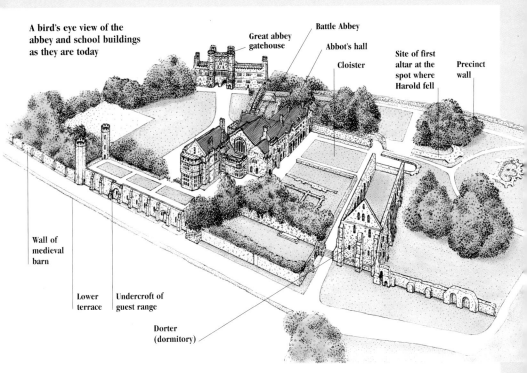

A bird's eye view of the abbey and school buildings as they are today

Great abbey gatehouse

Battle Abbey

Abbot's hall

Cloister

Site of first altar at the spot where Harold fell

Precinct wall

Wall of medieval barn

Lower terrace

Undercroft of guest range

Dorter (dormitory)

Once William had quelled the nation in 1070, ruthlessly crushing any opposition to his rule, he founded Battle Abbey to atone for the terrible loss of life at the Battle of Hastings. A few portions of the abbey remain today, but little of the church or features dating back to the early Normans. The best-preserved and most impressive part is the Great Gatehouse, finest of all surviving medieval abbey entrances, which was built around 1338.

The site of the battle, with the abbey remains in the background

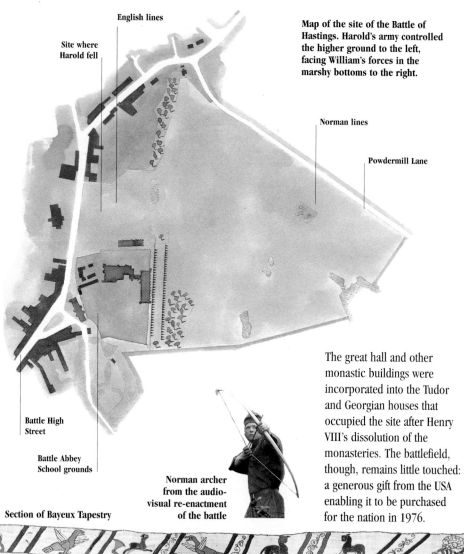

English lines

Site where
Harold fell

Map of the site of the Battle of
Hastings. Harold's army controlled
the higher ground to the left,
facing William's forces in the
marshy bottoms to the right.

Norman lines

Powdermill Lane

Battle High
Street

Battle Abbey
School grounds

Norman archer
from the audio-
visual re-enactment
of the battle

Section of Bayeux Tapestry

The great hall and other
monastic buildings were
incorporated into the Tudor
and Georgian houses that
occupied the site after Henry
VIII's dissolution of the
monasteries. The battlefield,
though, remains little touched:
a generous gift from the USA
enabling it to be purchased
for the nation in 1976.

A re-enactment of the Battle of Hastings (left)

Battle of Hastings'; Abbot's Hall open to the public during school summer holidays only.
Entry £3.50/£2.60/£1.80. Family ticket (2 adults & 3 children) £8.80.
☎ 01424 773792
🄿 (charge payable) 🎧* (also available for the visually impaired, those in wheelchairs or with learning difficulties, and in French, German and Japanese) ⅃ (some steps)
🚻 (nearby) ⓘ ⊕ ⊡ ⓦ ⓔ
➲ In Battle, East Sussex (p. 213, 4N), at S end of High St. (OS Map 199; ref TQ 749157.) Battle is reached by road by turning off A21 onto the A2100.
🚌 Stagecoach South Coast/ Maidstone & District 4/5 Maidstone–Hastings; Eastbourne Buses 30 BR Eastbourne–Battle; Hastings & District RE Group BR Rye– BR Battle, summer, Suns only (Tel: 01273 474747).
🚆 Battle ½m.

☻ See a fascinating display of World War II encampments, displays of Allied and German troops, military vehicles, 25-pounder guns and a battle set in 1944, 25–26 May.
☻ Exciting range of interactive displays and exhibitions, an audio-visual interpretation of the battle, and a new interactive audio tour of the history of the battlefield and abbey that guides you around the grounds.
☻ Family Discovery Pack and free Children's Activity Sheet available.
☻ Children's activity area with outdoor playground.

Open 22 March–31 Oct: daily, 10am–6pm (6pm/dusk in Oct). 1 Nov–31 March: daily, 10am–4pm (closed 24–26 Dec). Film/audio-visual – '1066, The

⊙ Bramber Castle

SUSSEX (p. 212, 4M)
The remains of a Norman
castle gatehouse, walls and
earthworks.

Open *Any reasonable time.*
Entry *Free.*
P *(limited)* ⊛
➲ *On W side of Bramber
village off A283
(OS Map 198; ref TQ 187107.)*
🚌 *Brighton & Hove 20
BR Shoreham-by-Sea–Steyning
(Tel: 01273 886200).*
🚉 *Shoreham-by-Sea 4½m*

⊙ Calshot Castle

HAMPSHIRE (p. 212, 3K)
This century, the fort has
been part of both an RN
and an RAF base. Spectacular
views of the Solent can be
seen from the roof. Henry
VIII built this coastal fort to
command the sea passage to
Southampton. The barrack
room has been restored to

its pre-World War I artillery
garrison appearance,
complete with bunks
and uniform.

Open *22 March–31 Oct: daily,
10am–6pm (6pm/dusk in Oct).*
Entry *£1.80/£1.40/90p.*
☎ 01703 892023
P ♦♦ ♿ *(Keep: ground floor
only; toilets)* ⊗ 🗂 ⊛
➲ *On spit 2m SE of
Fawley off B3053.
(OS Map 196; ref SU 488025.)*
🚌 *Solent Blue Line X9, 39
Southampton-Calshot (passes
BR Southampton) to within 1m
(Tel: 01703 226235).*

⊙ Camber Castle

SUSSEX (p. 213, 4O)
A rare example of an
Henrician fort surviving
in its original plan.

Open *1 July–30 Sept: Sat,
2–5pm. Monthly guided walks
of Rye Harbour Nature Reserve
including Camber Castle.
Please telephone the Reserve*

Camber Castle

*Manager (01797 223862) for
further information. (Site
managed by Rye Harbour
Nature Reserve.)*
Entry *£2.00/£1.50/£1.00.
Friends of Rye Harbour Nature
Reserve free.*
☎ 01797 223862
⊛
➲ *Access by a delightful 1m
walk across fields, off the A259,
1m S of Rye off harbour road.
(OS Map 189; ref TQ 922185.)*

**Calshot Castle (middle) and
the restored barrack room
(below and far left)**

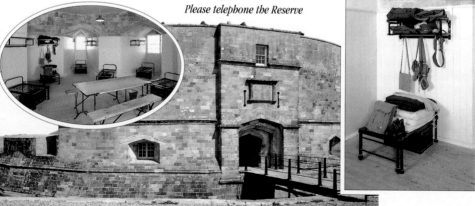

🚌 *From surrounding areas to Rye, thence 1¼m (Tel: 01273 474747).*
🚃 *Rye 1¼m*

⊘ Carisbrooke Castle

ISLE OF WIGHT (p. 212, 3K)
See pp 58–61 for full details.

⊖ Conduit House

Canterbury, KENT (p. 213, 5P)
The Conduit House is the monastic waterworks which supplied nearby St Augustine's Abbey.

Open *Any reasonable time. Exterior viewing only.*
Entry *Free.*
➲ *Approximately 5–10 minutes' walk from St Augustine's Abbey. Situated within the new St Martin's Heights housing estate, St Martin's Avenue, Canterbury. (OS Map 179; ref TR 159585.)*
🚌 *Stagecoach East Kent C1/C2 from railway stations to bus station, thence C5 (Tel: 01227 472082).*
🚃 *Canterbury East or West, both 1½m.*

⊘ Deal Castle

KENT (p. 213, 5P)
Crouching low and menacing, the huge, rounded bastions of this austere fort, built by Henry VIII, once carried 119 guns. It is a fascinating castle to explore, with long, dark passages, battlements, and a huge basement with an exhibition on England's coastal defences.

⊛ **Free Children's Activity Sheet available.**
Open *22 March–31 Oct: daily, 10am–6pm (6pm/dusk in Oct). 1 Nov–31 Mar: Wed–Sun, 10am–4pm (closed 24–26 Dec).*
Entry *£2.80/£2.10/£1.40.*
☎ *01304 372762*
🚻 ☐ 🎧 *(also available for the visually impaired, those with learning difficulties, and in French and German)* ♿ *(courtyards & ground floor only, parking available)* ⊛
➲ *SW of Deal town centre. (OS Map 179; ref TR 378521.)*

🚌 *From surrounding areas (Tel: 0800 696 996).*
🚃 *Deal ½m.*

⊘ Donnington Castle

BERKSHIRE (p. 212, 5K)
Built in the late 14th century, the twin towered gatehouse of this castle survives amidst some impressive earthworks.

Open *Any reasonable time (exterior viewing only).*
Entry *Free.*
🅿 ♿ *(steep slopes within grounds)* ⊛
➲ *1m N of Newbury off B4494. (OS Map 174; ref SU 461694.)*
🚌 *Bennett's 130/4 from Newbury (passes close to BR Newbury) (Tel: 01635 248423).*
🚃 *Newbury 1¾m.*

⊘ Dover Castle

KENT (p. 213, 4P)
See pp 64–71 for full details.

Deal Castle: from the air (below) and a passageway (left)

CARISBROOKE CASTLE

The Redvers Shield of Arms

From time immemorial, whosoever controlled Carisbrooke controlled the Isle of Wight. The castle sits at the very heart of the island, and has been a fixture since its foundation as a Saxon camp during the 8th century. Carisbrooke's royal connections date from the end of the 13th century when it was purchased from the Redvers family by Edward I. For a brief period the castle occupied the centre of the national and political stage when Charles I was imprisoned there from 1647 to 1648, before being taken for trial and execution in London. His story is commemorated in the Charles I rooms and in the many exhibits relating to his imprisonment.

The compact set of castle buildings demonstrates every phase of construction from the Saxon era to the present. Remnants of the Saxon wall run below the shell of the stone Norman keep, high on its artificial mound. The discomfort of the keep was diminished with the building of a great hall and private apartments for the Redvers family, who ruled the island and Carisbrooke from 1100 to 1293. The last of them, the young Countess Isabella, was a most ambitious builder. She was among the first in the country to put glass into domestic windows. Remains of her beautiful chapel show an individual taste. The castle fell into royal hands when Edward I bought it on Isabella's death.

The Norman keep

Motte

A re-enaction of King Charles I when imprisoned at Carisbrooke (left), and a replica of the seal of Sir George Carey, Governor of the castle from 1583 to 1603 (below)

The castle was refortified in the 16th century against the threat of invasion by Catholic Spain in 1588. When Spain threatened to invade England again in the late 1590s, Sir George Carey, the Governor, persuaded Elizabeth I to improve the defences still further.

The 12th-century keep, on its artificial mound, towers above the later great hall and private apartments (right)

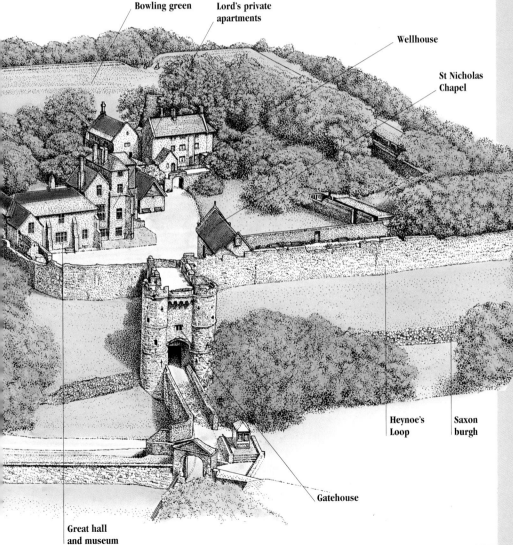

Bowling green

Lord's private apartments

Wellhouse

St Nicholas Chapel

Great hall and museum

Gatehouse

Heynoe's Loop

Saxon burgh

Queen Elizabeth I's Governor, Sir George Carey, (above) and the windows that replaced the one through which Charles I tried to escape (left)

Although Carisbrooke saw no action in the English Civil War, it housed the defeated King Charles I in 1647–8. The castle was prepared for its new inhabitant while the government decided his future. Charles tried escaping twice, before he was taken to London to be tried.

Less distinguished prisoners had been used to tread the waterwheel, drawing water up the well's 49-metre (161-feet) depth. In the 17th century donkeys were introduced and they are still there today, providing a very popular attraction for visitors. The castle's museum was founded by Princess Beatrice, Victoria's daughter, governor 1896–1944, and symbol of a continuing royal presence felt throughout the Isle of Wight. An interactive museum in the Old Coach House, displaying the history of the castle, rounds off a pleasant visit.

Charles I's daughter Elizabeth, who died at Carisbrooke of pneumonia in 1650

St Nicholas Chapel
(left)

Edwardian decoration from the
St Nicholas Chapel (above)

❹ *Free Children's Activity*
Sheet available.
❹ *An exciting CD Rom unit*
provides information on the
castles of England, their
functions and purpose.
❹ *New for 1997 – the donkey*
centre with exhibition, inter-
pretation boards and stables.

Open 22 March–31 Oct: daily,
10am–6pm (6pm/dusk in Oct).

1 Nov–31 March: daily,
10am–4pm (closed 24–26 Dec).
Entry *£4.00/£3.00/£2.00.*
Family ticket £10.
✆ 01983 522107
🚹 🅿 🍴 *(The Coach House Café;*
open Easter–October) 🎧 *(also*
available for the visually
impaired and those with learn-
ing difficulties) ♿ *(grounds &*
lower levels only) 🎟 ✴ 🚾 Ⓔ 🗊
➲ *1¼m SW of Newport, Isle of*
Wight (p. 212, 3K).
(OS Map 196; ref SZ 486877.)
🚌 *Southern Vectis 7/A/B,*
11/12 from Newport, Yarmouth
& Ventnor to within ¼m
(Tel: 01983 827005).
🚂 *Ryde Esplanade 9m; Wootton*
(IoW Steam Rly) 5m.
⛴ *West Cowes 5m; East Cowes*
6m (Red Funnel, tel: 01703
334010); Fishbourne 6m; Ryde
8m; Yarmouth 9m (Wightlink,
tel: 01705 827744).

A donkey drawing water using
the treadmill (below)

The Norman keep, built
before 1136

⊕ Down House

KENT (p. 213, 5N)
See pp 74–7 for full details.

⊖ Dymchurch Martello Tower

KENT (p. 213, 4O)
One of many artillery towers which formed part of a chain of strongholds intended to resist invasion by Napoleon. It is fully restored, with a 24-pounder gun on the roof.

***Open** 28–31 March: 12–4pm. 1 May–31 July: weekends, 12–4pm. 1–31 Aug: daily, 12–4pm. For further details please telephone Area Manager, Dover Castle, 01304 211067. (Open with the assistance of Shepway District Council.)*
***Entry** £1.00/80p/50p.*
⊛

➲ *Access from High Street, not from seafront.*
(OS Map 189; ref TR 102294.)
🚌 *Stagecoach East Kent 11, 12/A, Stagecoach South Coast 711 Folkestone–Hastings (passes close to BR Folkestone Central) (Tel: 0800 696 996).*
🚉 *Sandling 7m; Dymchurch (R H & D Rly), adjacent.*

⊖ Eynsford Castle

KENT (p. 213, 5N)
One of the first stone castles built by the Normans. The moat and remains of the curtain wall and hall can still be seen.

***Open** 1 March–30 Sept: daily, 10am–6pm. 1 Oct–28 Feb: 10am–4pm.*
***Entry** Free.*

Eynsford Castle

🅿 ♿ ⊛
➲ *In Eynsford off A225.*
(OS Map 177; ref TQ 542658.)
🚌 *Kentish Bus 13, 415 BR Eynsford–Dartford (Tel: 0800 696 996).*
🚉 *Eynsford 1m.*

⊖ Farnham Castle Keep

SURREY (p. 212, 5L)
A motte and bailey castle, once one of the seats of the Bishop of Winchester, which has been in continuous occupation since the 12th century.

***Open** 22 March–30 Sept: daily, 10am–6pm.*
***Entry** £2.00/£1.50/£1.00.*
✆ **01252 713393**
🅿 🎧 ⊛
➲ *½m N of Farnham town centre on A287.*
(OS Map 186; ref SU 839474.)
🚌 *From surrounding areas (Tel: 01737 223000).*
🚉 *Farnham ¾m.*

✠ Faversham: Stone Chapel

KENT (p. 213, 5O)
The remains of a small medieval church incorporating part of a 4th-century Romano-British pagan mausoleum.

***Open** Any reasonable time. (Site managed by the Faversham Society.)*
***Entry** Free.*
⊛

➲ *1¼m W of Faversham on A2.*
(OS Map 178; ref TQ 992614.)
🚌 *Stagecoach East*
Kent/Chalkwell Coaches 333
Maidstone–Faversham
(passes BR Faversham)
(Tel: 0800 696996).
🚃 *Faversham 1½m.*

ⓐ Flowerdown Barrows

HAMPSHIRE (p. 212, 4K)
Round barrows of a Bronze Age burial site which were once part of a larger group.

Open Any reasonable time.
Entry Free.
🐾

➲ *In Littleton, 2½m NW of*
Winchester off A272.
(OS Map 185; ref SU 459320.)
🚌 *Stagecoach Hampshire*
Bus 68/A/C from Winchester
(passes BR Winchester)
(Tel: 01256 464501).
🚃 *Winchester 2m.*

ⓞ Fort Brockhurst

HAMPSHIRE (p. 212, 3K)
This was a new type of fort, built in the 19th century to protect Portsmouth with formidable fire-power. Largely unaltered, the parade ground, gun ramps and moated keep can all be viewed. An exhibition illustrates the history of Portsmouth's defences.

⦿ *See nesting birds, and look out for ghostly activity*

Farnham Castle Keep

in Prisoner Cell No 3!
⦿ *View the RAF Gosport Aviation Heritage Exhibition.*
Open 22 March–30 Sept: daily, 10am–6pm.
Entry £2.00/£1.50/£1.00.
☎ *01705 581059*
Ⓔ 👫 🅿 ♿ ♿ *(grounds & ground floor only; toilets)*
➲ *Off A32, in Gunner's Way, Elson, on N side of Gosport.*
(OS Map 196; ref SU 596020.)
🚌 *Provincial 1–7*
Fareham–Gosport Ferry (passes BR Fareham, also Gosport Ferry links with BR Portsmouth & Southsea) (Tel: 0345 023067).
🚃 *Fareham 3m.*

ⓞ Fort Cumberland

HAMPSHIRE (p. 212, 3K)
Constructed in the shape of a wide pentagon by the Duke of Cumberland in 1746. The fort was occupied by the Royal Marines until 1973 and is perhaps the most impressive piece of 18th-century defensive architecture remaining in England.

Open 27 July, 27 Sept: by guided tour only. Advance booking is required for tours, please telephone 01732 778030.
Entry £2.00/£1.00.
➲ *In the Eastney district of Portsmouth on the estuary approach via Henderson Road, a turning off Eastney Road, or from the Esplanade.*
(OS Map 196; ref SZ 682992.)
🚌 *Provincial 16/A, BR Portsmouth and Southsea–Hayling Ferry (Tel: 01705 650967).*
🚃 *Fratton 2m.*

THE SECRET WARTIME TUNNELS AT DOVER CASTLE

The white cliffs of Dover are among England's most celebrated sights, yet hidden underground is a fascinating and secret world. On top of the cliffs stands the ancient and mighty fortress of Dover Castle but below, running deep into the ground, are miles of tunnels. First used during the Napoleonic wars, their greatest moment came nearly 150 years later when they became a nerve centre in World War II and were the headquarters from which the Dunkirk evacuation was masterminded.

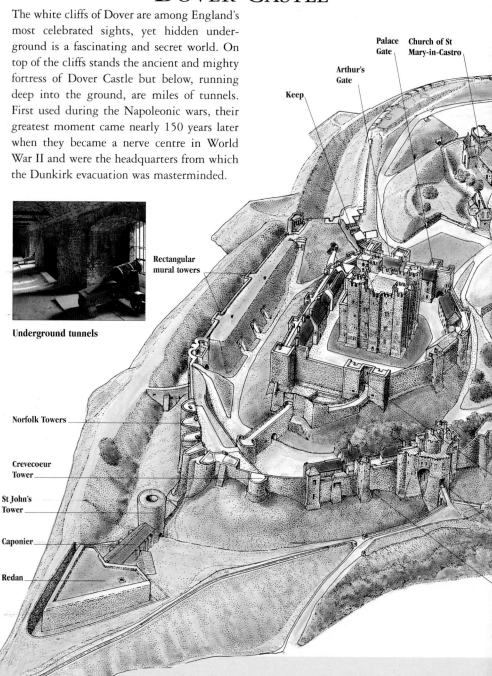

Underground tunnels

Palace Gate

Church of St Mary-in-Castro

Arthur's Gate

Keep

Rectangular mural towers

Norfolk Towers

Crevecoeur Tower

St John's Tower

Caponier

Redan

The labyrinth of tunnels under Dover Castle reached the height of their importance during World War II when they were a vital headquarters during the darkest hours of Britain's struggle. Today you can experience life as it was for the 700 personnel in the worst days of the war.

World War II gun embrasures on the eastern ramparts

Roman *Pharos*

Admiralty Lookout

Entrance to secret wartime tunnels

Canon's Gate

Reconstructed repeater station

Relive the drama as a wounded Battle of Britain pilot is taken into the underground hospital to fight for his life in the operating theatre and move on to see the Command Centre in which Churchill hatched the most desperate plans – the ones that eventually led to victory.

Fulbert of Dover's Tower

Hurst's Tower

Say's Tower

Gatton Tower

Peveril's Tower and Gate

Queen Mary's Tower

King's Gate

Constable's Tower and Gate

Treasurer's Tower

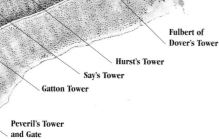

Winston Churchill and Admiral Ramsay plotting in the tunnels

Secret wartime tunnels

Whoever first had the idea of tunnelling under Dover Castle can hardly have anticipated the dramas that would unfold underground. The rabbit warren of tunnels has been the centre of military operations from the Napoleonic Wars almost to the present. The Dunkirk evacuation in 1940 was its finest hour. Visitors may experience for themselves what military life was like underground.

Tunnelling operations began in earnest in 1797 when Dover was fortified in readiness for a French invasion. Seven tunnels (running with damp and prone to collapse) were dug for the soldiers and officers who were filling both castle and town to overflowing.

When French threats ended, the tunnels fell into disuse until they came back into their own in World War II. Vice-Admiral Ramsay, who was commanding the Straits of Dover, occupied the underground tunnels from the outbreak of war.

Some of the first tunnels at Dover may have been made by attackers digging under the castle walls during medieval sieges (below).

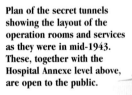

Plan of the secret tunnels showing the layout of the operation rooms and services as they were in mid-1943. These, together with the Hospital Annexe level above, are open to the public.

Visitors' entrance

Ventilation shaft

Entrance to secret wartime tunnels (left)

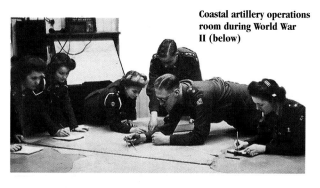

Coastal artillery operations room during World War II (below)

Spy artefacts from World War II

The reconstructed telephone exchange

Ventilation shafts

Ventilation shafts

Admiralty casemate incorporating the central communications office, naval cipher office and Dynamo ops room

300 FT

250 FT

HOSPITAL ANNEXE

200 FT

CASEMATE LEVEL

Stores
Latrines

150 FT

Canteen and kitchen

Coding and cypher room

Post Office Tunnel for equipment and batteries

Admiral's operation room

Admiral's cabin

Coding office

Dormitories and offices

DUMPY LEVEL

Telephone exchange and anti-aircraft and coastal artillery operation room

Cypher office

SEA LEVEL

In May 1940, as France fell before the German advance, these tunnels became the nerve centre for Operation Dynamo – the evacuation of the British Expeditionary Force (BEF) and French troops from Dunkirk's beaches.

Ramsay and his staff worked round the clock for nine days. On 26 May some 400,000 troops were awaiting rescue. The best estimate was that 45,000 could be brought back. Dunkirk was ablaze. Pleasure craft, fishing boats, sailing barges streamed across the Channel as tenders from the beaches. The Allied forces and rescue ships were sitting targets. Yet, by 4 June, all were evacuated. In total, 338,000 men came back: the BEF and 139,000 French soldiers.

Under sustained German air attack through the war,

Anti-aircraft operations room

Dover's tunnels acquired a new importance as shelter for the Combined Headquarters.

Additional tunnels were dug, telecommunications systems were installed, and even a hospital was established. Hundreds of men and women worked and lived under ground in the most unpleasant conditions of damp and piercing cold.

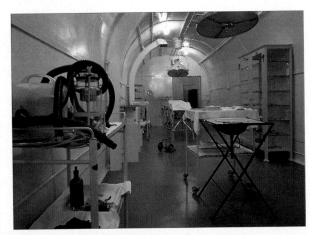

The underground hospital on the Annexe level

A WWII re-enactment at Dover

A tour of Dover Castle

Dover Castle is a sturdy reminder of some of the toughest fighting days in England's past.

Henry II

William the Conqueror strengthened the defences that Harold built, the monumental keep was built for Henry II, as were the walls of the Inner Bailey, and the eastern part of the outer curtain wall. Their designs were innovative, with regularly spaced towers for the Inner Bailey, and the curtain wall's gatehouses and flanking towers. The works were completed under Henry III.

Spiral stairs leading to all floors of the keep

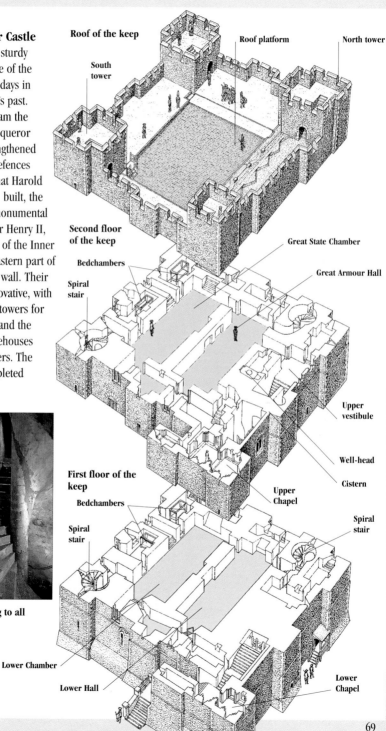

Roof of the keep

South tower

Roof platform

North tower

Second floor of the keep

Bedchambers

Spiral stair

Great State Chamber

Great Armour Hall

Upper vestibule

Well-head

Cistern

First floor of the keep

Bedchambers

Spiral stair

Upper Chapel

Spiral stair

Lower Chamber

Lower Hall

Lower Chapel

The keep, the central strong tower built in the 1180s, is the obvious starting point for visitors. Its three-towered forebuilding, carrying the entry staircase and two chapels, is one of the most elaborate of all. The upper chapel, reserved for the royal family's use, is especially fine, with its rich decoration and its style of Norman, crossing over into Gothic. The former royal apartments, with their central halls and intimate chambers,

are still most impressive in their monumental scale, despite having lost most of their original decoration. Although most of the medieval buildings have gone, Henry III's great hall survives. It is incorporated into the Georgian barracks which are one of the features of Dover's continued military importance long after many other castles had fallen into picturesque decay. Queen Elizabeth's 'Pocket Pistol' is a survival of the Tudor

age of defence. A great gun, 7.3 metres (24 feet) long, it was actually made in 1544 for Henry VIII. The castle's outer defences, which were innovative in military design, provide a fascinating, and lengthy, walk through history.

The Avranches Tower, purpose-built in the 1180s for archers, is approached via the

The Pocket Pistol

The Prince of Wales, later George V, a notable Constable

A view of the castle featuring the curtain wall, Peverell's Tower and the keep

magazines and the artillery works of the Napoleonic Wars. The Bell Battery, originally for six guns, was built as part of the programme of refortification that began in the 1750s.

On the cliff edge, with panoramic views over the town and out to sea, there are the remains of the Admiralty Lookout and Signal Station used in both World Wars. Soldiers and sailors have guarded the English approaches from this spot for well over 800 years.

Dover Castle has something for everyone interested in the nation's past. With the end of World War II, the tunnels were adapted to become a Regional Seat of Government in the event of nuclear catastrophe, before being finally abandoned by the Home Office in 1984. In the 1990s, the tunnels' wartime secrets are open for all to see.

St Mary-in-Castro and *Pharos*

☻ *For easy access around the site take a free ride on the new land train.*
☻ *Come and meet Henry VIII and his court at a lively re-enactment, 4–5 May.*
☻ *The Princess of Wales' Royal Regiment, a lively exhibition of regimental history from the 1600s to the present day.*
☻ *Live and Let Spy exhibition in the Keep.*
☻ *Children's play area in the keep.*
☻ *Exciting CD-Rom unit with information on English castles' functions and purpose.*

Interior of St Mary-in-Castro

Open *22 March–31 Oct: daily, 9.30am–6pm (6pm/dusk in Oct). 1 Nov–31 March: daily, 10am–4pm (closed 24–26 Dec).* **Entry** *£6.00/£4.50/£3.00. (includes admission to secret wartime tunnels, by guided tour only – last tour begins at 5pm (summer) and 3pm (winter). Family ticket (2 adults & 3 children) £15.* ✆ *01304 201628* Ⓔ ⛺ ♿ ♿ Ⓟ ♨ *(The Keep Restaurant; for private functions tel: 01304 205830)* 🎧 *(Two separate tours – for grounds only and for medieval underground works only – available in French, German and Japanese.)* 🎧* *(underground hospital.)* ♿ *(courtyard & grounds – some very steep slopes)* ♿ 🏧 ➲ *On E side of Dover. (OS Map 179; ref TR 326416.)* 🚌 *Stagecoach East Kent 90 from BR Dover Priory (Tel: 0800 696 996).* 🚆 *Dover Priory 1½m.*

Constable's Gate

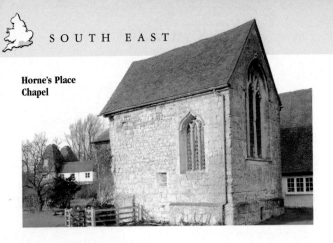

Horne's Place Chapel

✞ Horne's Place Chapel

Appledore, KENT (p. 213, 4O)
This 14th-century domestic chapel was once attached to the manor house. The house and chapel are privately owned.

Open By arrangement. Please telephone 01304 211067.
Entry Free.
P *(nearby)* ⊗
➲ 1½m N of Appledore.
(OS Map 189; ref TQ 957307.)
🚌 Appledore 2½m.

◑ Hurst Castle

HAMPSHIRE (pp. 211/212, 3J)
This was one of the most sophisticated fortresses built by Henry VIII, and later strengthened in the 19th and 20th centuries, to command the narrow entrance to the Solent. There are two exhibitions in the castle, and two huge 38-ton guns from the fort's armaments.

Open 22 March–30 June: daily, 10am–5.30pm. 1 July–31 Aug: daily, 10am–6pm. 1 Sept–31 Oct: daily, 10am–5.30pm. (Site managed by Hurst Castle Services.)
Entry £2.00/£1.50/£1.00.
✆ 01590 642344
👫 ☕ ('Castle Cafe'; weekends only April and May, daily June–Sept) ⊗
➲ On Pebble Spit S of Keyhaven. Best approached by ferry from Keyhaven, telephone 01590 642500 (June–Sept, 9am–2pm) or answerphone 01425 610784, for ferry details.
(OS Map 196; ref SZ 319898.)
🚌 Wilts & Dorset 123/4 Bournemouth–Lymington (passes BR New Milton) to within 2½m, or 1m to ferry (Tel: 01202 673555).
🚌 Lymington Town 4½m to Keyhaven, 6½m to Fort.

◐ King James's and Landport Gates

Portsmouth, HAMPSHIRE (p. 212, 3K)
These gates were once part of the 17th-century defences of Portsmouth.

Open Exterior any reasonable time.
Entry Free.
⊗
➲ King James's Gate: forms entrance to United Services Recreation Ground (officers) on Park Rd; Landport Gate: as above, men's entrance on St George's Rd. (OS Map 196; King James's Gate ref SU 638000, Landport Gate ref SU 634998.)

▲ Kit's Coty House and Little Kit's Coty House

KENT (p. 213, 5N)
Ruins of two prehistoric burial chambers, taking their name from the Celtic phrase for 'tomb in the woods'.

Hurst Castle

Kit's Coty House

Open *Any reasonable time.*
Entry *Free.*

⊛

➲ *W of A229 2m N of Maidstone.
(OS Map 188; ref TQ 745608
& TQ 745604.)*
🚌 *Maidstone & District 101,
126, BR Maidstone East–
Gillingham (Tel: 0800
696 996).*
🚂 *Aylesford 2½ m.*

✠ Knights Templar Church

Dover, KENT (p. 213, 4P)
Standing across the valley
from Dover Castle are the
foundations of a small
circular 12th-century church.

Open *Any reasonable time.*
Entry *Free.*

⊛

➲ *On the Western Heights
above Dover.
(OS Map 179; ref TR 313408.)*
🚂 *Dover Priory ¾ m.*

**Lullingstone
gaming counters**

❂ Lullingstone Roman Villa

KENT (p. 213, 5N)
The villa, discovered in 1939,
was one of the most exciting
finds of the century. Dating
from *c*.100 AD, but extended
during 300 years of Roman
occupation, much is visible
today. The original villa was
fronted by a verandah, with
projecting wings. At later
remodellings, the bath houses
were extended and a large
apsed dining room was
added with two mosaic
panels, depicting scenes
from classical legend. An
early shrine in the cellar has
frescoes of water nymphs.
Grave goods and other relics
are evidence of the
paganism prac-
tised here before
Christianity
arrived when
some rooms were converted
into a chapel. The villa had
been abandoned by 420, most
of the remains lying hidden
for 1500 years.

**❂ Free Children's Activity
Sheet available.**
Open *22 March–31 Oct: daily,
10am–6pm (6pm/dusk in Oct).
1 Nov–31 March: daily,
10am–4pm (closed 24–26 Dec).*
Entry *£2.00/£1.50/£1.00*
✆ *01322 863467*
🚻 🅿 🎧 *(also available for the
visually impaired and those
with learning difficulties and
in French and German)* ⊛ Ⓓ
➲ *½ m SW of Eynsford off A225
off junction 3 of M25. Follow
A20 towards Brands Hatch.
(OS Map 177; ref TQ 529651.)*
🚂 *Eynsford ¾ m.*

**The mosaic floor (below), and a
bronze flagon from Lullingstone
Roman Villa (left)**

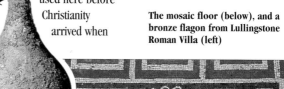

DOWN HOUSE

Charles Darwin was perhaps the most influential scientist of the 19th century. It was from his study at Down House that he worked on the scientific theories that first scandalized and then revolutionized the Victorian world, culminating in the publication of the most significant book of the century, *On the Origin of Species by means of Natural Selection*, in 1859. His home for forty years, Down House was the centre of his intellectual world and even now his study remains full of his notebooks and journals, and mementoes from his epic voyage of discovery that took him most famously to the Galapagos Islands.

Charles Darwin

The house is currently being restored so that by the summer of 1997 you can visit Darwin's much-loved family home in the tranquil Kent countryside. Visitors can wander in the gardens along the 'Sandwalk', as Darwin did every morning to compose his thoughts before beginning his scientific studies.

From the outside, Down House looks like an everyday mid-Victorian family home, lying on the edge of a Kent village. Its significance lies in the influence of its remarkable former owner who made this house his home for forty years.

Charles Darwin returned to Britain from his epic voyage on HMS *Beagle* around South America in 1836 and at first lived in London. He had already achieved a certain fame through the reports he had sent back throughout his five-year journey and his writings continued to be well received. Following the marriage to his cousin, Emma Wedgwood, and the first signs of his own poor health, he decided, in 1842, to move away from the capital into the peace and open space of the

The house from the gardens

countryside. Although not his ideal choice, he at first thought Down House 'oldish and ugly', it did allow him and his large family the freedom and space that had not been possible in London. Originally a farmhouse, the main structure of the house was built in the late 18th century. The move to Kent allowed him to live the quiet and happy life of a family man while at the same time correlating the discoveries from which he formed the revolutionary theory of evolution through natural selection.

A watercolour of Down House painted in 1880 by Goodwin

The principal asset of the house is that it remains much as it was when Darwin lived there. Most special of all is the ground-floor study which was the centre of his life, in which are collected some of the 3,500 objects connected with his work that still remain at Down House. This quiet room contains the chair he used and the desk at which he sat to write his famous works. Scattered around the study are some of his prized possessions, the most important of which is the huge original bound manuscript of the journal from his five year voyage on HMS *Beagle*.

The Cary microscope Darwin used on *HMS Beagle*

The study in which Darwin worked for forty years as it is today (above) and his notebooks from the *Beagle*

Charles Darwin at Down House with his eldest son, William

The study also houses the ingenious instruments which he used to collect his data, including the portable microscope, made by Cary of London, his pocket pistols and 'life preserver'. And there are reminders of the vilification Darwin underwent when his theories were published. Going against the conceptions of the age, both scientific and religious, Darwin bore the brunt of the outrage with equanimity. He himself kept *Punch* cartoons that derided his theories and the cruellest of caricatures from *Vanity Fair*. Scattered elsewhere around the house are objects as diverse as a stuffed giant tortoise and the underwear Darwin wore as a baby.

In later life the study became a sanctuary into which Darwin could retreat for hours at a time. A carefully placed mirror allowed him to see who was coming up the drive. He even had a lavatory built into one corner of the room so that he need never leave the room if he did not wish to.

Darwin's happiest years were spent at Down House. After *On the Origin of Species* had been published in 1859, he was able to concentrate more on his family. His family came first above all else, including his work. Early photographs show him affectionately holding his eldest son, William, and the great

A page from Charles Darwin's *Journal*

delight he took in becoming a father is readily apparent.

He also found time to make several additions to the simple three-storey house. At various times he extended both the drawing room and his wife's bedroom, and he also built the kitchen wing.

Little remains of the original garden except for the 'Sandwalk', Darwin's 'thinking path', around which he strolled every morning.

Down House is currently undergoing restoration to return the ground floor rooms to how they would have been in the 1870s. An exhibition area on the first floor will

***HMS Beagle* in the Straits of Magellan**

Darwin's desk in the Old Study (above)

Open *Down House will be opening to the public in July. For further information on opening times and admission prices please contact the Regional Office (0171 973 3479) or Customer Services (0171 973 3434).*

♿ 🅿 ♿ (throughout)

🕮 💻 ⊗ 🗋 🎞

⮕ In Luxted Road, Downe, Kent (p. 213, 5N) off A21 near Biggin Hill.

🚂 Orpington 5m or Bromley South 8m.

Memorabilia from Darwin's journey on the *Beagle* (left)

capture the essence of Darwin's life and work and convey the importance of his ideas.

When the Darwin Museum at Down House opens in the Summer of 1997 it will do justice to the memory and influence of this country's best known scientist: a man who once modestly said, 'I have dabbled in several branches of natural history...'

Maison Dieu

☉ Maison Dieu

Ospringe, KENT (p. 213, 5O)
Part of a medieval complex of
Royal lodge, almshouses and
hospital, it is much as it was
400 years ago, with a crown-
post roof and a decorative
16th-century ceiling. It
contains an exhibition about
Ospringe in Roman times.

*Open 28 March–31 Oct:
weekends and Bank Holidays,
2–5pm. For further details
contact The Faversham Society
on 01795 534542. Keykeeper in
winter. (Site managed by
The Faversham Society.)*
Entry £1/80p/50p.
🚹🚻 ⊗

➲ *In Ospringe on A2, ½m
W of Faversham.
(OS Map 178; ref TR 002608.)*
🚌 *Stagecoach East Kent/
Chalkwell Coaches 333,
Maidstone–Faversham
(passes BR Faversham)
(Tel: 0800 696 996).*
🚊 *Faversham ¾m.*

⊕ Medieval Merchant's House

Southampton, HAMPSHIRE
(p. 212, 4K)
Life in the Middle Ages is
vividly evoked by the brightly
painted cabinets and colourful wall hangings authentically
re-created for this 13th-
century town house, originally
built as shop and home for a
prosperous wine merchant.

⊛ *Free Children's Activity
Sheet available.*
*Open 22 March–31 Oct: daily,
10am–6pm (6pm/dusk in Oct).*
Entry £2.00/£1.50/£1.00.
✆ *01703 221503*

🚹🚻 ∩ *(also available for the
visually impaired and those
with learning difficulties)*
⌖ *(one step)* ⌂ ⊗
➲ *58 French Street, ¼m S of
city centre just off Castle Way
(between High St and Bugle St)
(OS Map 196; ref SU 419112.)*
🚌 *Southampton Citybus
17A/B, 27 from BR Southampton
(Tel: 01703 553011).*
🚊 *Southampton ¾m.*

♰ Milton Chantry

Gravesend, KENT
(p. 213, 5N)
A small 14th-century building
which housed the chapel of
a leper hospital and a family
chantry. It later became a
tavern and, in 1780, part
of a fort.

*Open 1 April–30 Sept:
Tues–Fri and bank holidays,
1–5pm (closed Tues after bank
holiday); Sat–Sun, 10am–5pm.
1 Nov–31 March: Fri–Sun,
10am–4pm. For school parties
and exhibition tel: 01474
321520. (Closed 25–26 Dec,
1 Jan). (Site managed by
Gravesend Borough Council.)*
Entry £1.50/75p.
⊗
➲ *In New Tavern Fort Gardens
E of central Gravesend off A226.
(OS Map 177; ref TQ 652743).*
🚌 *From surrounding areas
(Tel: 0800 696 996.)*
🚊 *Gravesend ¾m.*

Medieval Merchant's House

Netley Abbey

HAMPSHIRE (p. 212, 4K)

A 13th century Cistercian abbey converted in Tudor times for use as a house. Watch out for ghostly figures drifting amongst the ruins.

Netley Abbey East window

Open *Any reasonable time.*
Entry *Free.*
☎ 01705 378291
P ♿ 🐕 🚻 *(nearby, across road near estuary)*
➔ *In Netley, 4m SE of Southampton, facing Southampton Water.*
(OS Map 196; ref SU 453089.)
🚌 *Southampton Citybus 16/C. BR Southampton–Hamble (Tel: 01703 553011).*
🚂 *Netley 1m.*

Northington Grange

Northington Grange

HAMPSHIRE (p. 212, 4K)

Magnificent neoclassical country house, built at the beginning of the 18th century.

Open *Any reasonable time (exterior viewing only).*
Entry *Free.*
P ♿ *(with assistance)* 🐕
➔ *4m N of New Alresford off B3046.*
(OS Map 185; ref SU 562362.)
🚌 *Oakley Buses 309 Basingstoke–Alresford to within ½m (passes close to BR Basingstoke) (Tel: 01256 780731).*
🚂 *Winchester 8m.*

Netley Abbey

Pevensey Castle (above and right)

⊙ Old Soar Manor

Plaxtol, KENT (p. 213, 5N)
The remains of a late 13th-
century knight's manor
house, comprising the two-
storey solar and chapel.
There is an exhibition to visit.

Open *28 March–30 Sept: daily,
10am–6pm. Keykeeper. (Site
maintained, managed and
owned by the National Trust.)*
Entry *Free.*
✆ *01732 810378*

Old Soar Manor

⊗ 🅿 *(limited) (National Trust
Kent & East Sussex office)*
➲ *1m E of Plaxtol.
(OS Map 188; ref TQ 619541.)*
🚌 *Wealden Beeline 222 BR
Borough Green–BR Tunbridge
Wells; East Surrey 404
Sevenoaks–Plaxtol; on both
alight E end of Plaxtol,
thence ¾m by footpath
(Tel: 0800 696 996).*
🚉 *Borough Green &
Wrotham 2½m.*

☺⊛ Osborne House

ISLE OF WIGHT (p. 212, 3K)
See pp 82–5 for full details.

⊙ Pevensey Castle

EAST SUSSEX (p. 213, 3N)
William the Conqueror landed
at Pevensey on September 28
1066. He may have used the
Roman Shore Fort as a
shelter for his troops. Today
you can see the ruins of the

medieval castle including
remains of an unusual keep
enclosed within its walls, originally dating back to the 4th-
century Roman fort Anderida.

⊛*See a special performance
of George Bernard Shaw's
classic comedy,* **Androcles &
the Lion,** *15 June.*
Open *22 March–31 Oct: daily,
10am–6pm (6pm/dusk in Oct).
1 Nov–31 March: Wed–Sun,
10am–4pm (closed 24–26
Dec). Closed 1–2pm in winter.*
Entry *£2.00/£1.50/£1.00.*
✆ *01323 762604*
🅿 *(charge payable)* ♿ ♟
(nearby) ⊛ 🔊 *(also available
for the visually impaired and
those with learning difficulties)*
🍴 *('Castle Cottage Tearoom
and Restaurant')*
➲ *In Pevensey off A259.
(OS Map 199; ref TQ 645048.)*
🚌 *Eastbourne Buses 30,
Stagecoach South Coast 711,
from Eastbourne
(Tel: 01273 474747).*
🚉 *Pevensey & Westham ½m.*

⊙ Portchester Castle

HAMPSHIRE (p. 212, 3K)
A residence for kings and a
rallying point for troops, this
grand castle has a history
stretching back nearly 2,000
years. There are Roman walls,
the most complete in Europe,
substantial remains of the
castle and an exhibition
telling the story of Portchester.

Portchester Castle (above and right)

🕮 *See how Saxons & Vikings lived and watch a re-enactment of a savage battle between them, 30–31 March.*
🕮 *Free Children's Activity Sheet and CD-Rom showing details on English castles.*
Open *22 March–31 Oct: daily, 10am–6pm (6pm/dusk in Oct). 1 Nov–31 March: daily, 10am–4pm (closed 24–26 Dec).*
Entry *£2.50/£1.90/£1.30.*
☎ *01705 378291*
🅿 ⅶ *(grounds & lower levels only)* ⅶⅶ *(in car park)* 🛈 🗂 🏛 Ⓔ
➲ *On S side of Portchester off A27, Junction 11 on M27. (OS Map 196; ref SU 625046.)*
🚌 *Provincial 1A/C, 5 Fareham–Southsea to within ¼ m (Tel: 01705 650967).*
🚇 *Portchester 1m.*

Richborough Castle

🕮 Reculver Towers and Roman Fort
KENT (p. 213, 5P)
Standing in a country park, a 12th-century landmark of twin towers and the walls of a Roman fort.

Open *Any reasonable time (external viewing only).*
Entry *Free.*
☎ *01227 366444*
ⅶⅶ 🅿 ⅶ *(ground floor only – long slope up from car park)* 🐕
➲ *At Reculver 3m E of Herne Bay. (OS Map 179; ref TR 228694.)*
🚌 *Stagecoach East Kent/ Regent 635 from Herne Bay (Tel: 0800 696 996).*
🚇 *Herne Bay 4m.*

🕮🕮 Richborough Castle, Roman Fort
KENT (p. 213, 5P)
This fort and township date back to the Roman landing in AD43. The fortified walls and the massive foundations of a triumphal arch which stood 25 m (80 ft) high still survive.

🕮 *Beautiful picnic spot.*
Open *22 March–31 Oct: daily, 10am–6pm (6pm/dusk in Oct).*
Entry *£2.00/£1.50/£1.00.*
☎ *01304 612013*
🅿 ⅶ 🎧 🐕 🏛
➲ *1½ m N of Sandwich off A257. (OS Map 179; ref TR 324602.)*
🚇 *Sandwich 2m.*

OSBORNE HOUSE

Osborne House was 'a place of one's own, quiet and retired', for Queen Victoria and Prince Albert. They found tranquillity on the Isle of Wight, far from the formality of court life at Buckingham Palace and Windsor Castle. The house they built was set among terraced gardens and filled with treasured mementoes. Victoria died at Osborne in 1901, still mourning her beloved Albert, who had died in middle age. Edward VII gave the house to the nation shortly afterwards. With recent restoration, it has become one of the most evocative memorials to Britain's longest-reigning monarch.

Prince Albert and Queen Victoria

With royalty, most things are relative. When visitors see Osborne for the first time, knowing that the young Victoria and Albert had wanted a modest country home, they are surprised by its scale and magnificence. The house is set on rising ground overlooking the Solent, where the ships that helped Britannia rule the waves sailed to and fro. Two tall towers in an Italian style dominate, above fountains set on terraces and rolling wooded parkland. Inside, magnificence abounds – the Indian room, marbled pillars, gilding, statuary, grand paintings. The full, even overfull, interiors seem

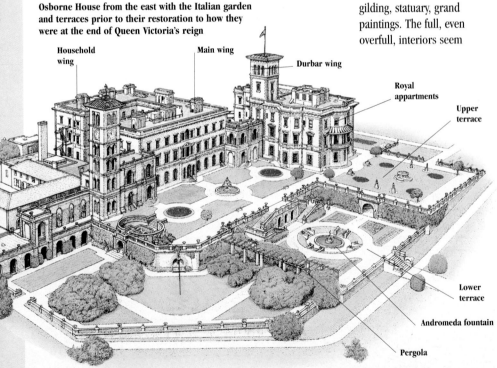

Osborne House from the east with the Italian garden and terraces prior to their restoration to how they were at the end of Queen Victoria's reign

Household wing

Main wing

Durbar wing

Royal appartments

Upper terrace

Lower terrace

Andromeda fountain

Pergola

Queen Victoria's bedroom

typically Victorian, but the contents remind us that this family had links with all the crowned heads of Europe. Despite the idea of cosy domesticity at Osborne, the formality of monarchy and its role as head of the British empire, are never far away.

Victoria married Albert in 1840, three years after she had come to the throne. They were dismayed by the places in which they were expected to live. Windsor was a rambling old castle, with smelly drains – their typhoid germs killed Prince Albert in 1861.

The Billiard Room

Victoria and Albert bought Osborne in 1845, and began dismantling the existing relatively small house. Its ambitious replacement was the work of Thomas Cubitt, best known for his buildings in London.

The new house was Italianate, rather than in the Gothic idiom one often associates with the Victorians. The first part was ready for occupation by 1846 and the main structure was completed by 1851.

Queen Victoria photographed with many of her family in 1898

This speed was the result of both Cubitt's skill and Albert's unflagging Teutonic zeal. Osborne's completion was also the year of the Great Exhibition – Albert's greatest achievement – held in the Crystal Palace in Hyde Park. Victoria and Albert with their many children embodied the family ideal and helped restore respect for the monarchy following its low esteem under George IV and William IV. Queen Victoria enthused to her uncle Leopold, King of the Belgians, that Albert had 'raised monarchy to the highest

pinnacle of respect, and rendered it popular beyond what it ever was in this country'. Although of necessity state affairs took place at Osborne, it was essentially a family holiday home. The queen had her first experience of sea bathing there – she liked it until she put her head under the water.

Victoria and Albert's nine children were given more freedom at Osborne. They could play in their own little home, Swiss Cottage, which was given to them on Victoria's birthday in 1854. As a memento of their youth

Victoria commissioned marble sculptures of their infant arms, which still lie in ghostly display.

A new routine helped ease painful memories after Albert died and Victoria went into the mourning from which she never fully emerged. Growing numbers of grand- and great-grand-children filled the house at Christmas, while Princess Beatrice, Victoria's youngest daughter, became her mother's companion. The princess lived

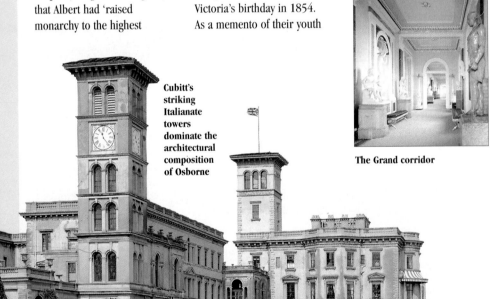

Cubitt's striking Italianate towers dominate the architectural composition of Osborne

The Grand corridor

in the Durbar wing, Osborne's last addition, built by craftsmen from India in 1890–91 to provide more formal state rooms.

Queen Victoria died on 22 January 1901 on a couch bed in the Queen's Bedroom. The private royal suite was closed to all except members of the royal family until the Queen gave permission in 1954 for full public access.

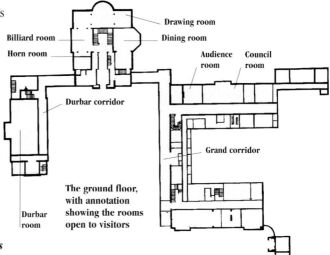

Drawing room
Billiard room
Dining room
Horn room
Audience room
Council room
Durbar corridor
Grand corridor
Durbar room
The ground floor, with annotation showing the rooms open to visitors

❋ *Come and watch 'Soldiers of the Queen', Redcoats, Gunners and Lancers of 1897 parading at Osborne, 25–26 May.*
❋ *Enjoy a Victorian carriage ride to the Swiss Cottage area.*
❋ *Free Children's Activity Sheet available.*

The Durbar room, the last addition to Osborne

Open *22 March–30 Sept: daily, House, 10am–5pm (last admission 4.30pm), Grounds, 10am–6pm (last admission 5pm). 1 Oct–31 Oct: daily, House and Grounds, 10am–5pm/dusk (last admission 4pm).*
Entry *House and Grounds £6.00/£4.50/£3.00. Grounds only £3.50/£2.60/£1.80 (separate ticket available April–May,* *Sept–Oct only). Family ticket (2 adults & 3 children) £15.*
✆ 01983 200022
🚪 Ⓔ ⚥ 🅿 🍴 *('Keepers Kitchen')*
&. *(exterior and ground floor only; vehicles with disabled passengers may set them down at the house entrance before returning to car park)*
① ✖ ♻ ✿

➤ *1m SE of East Cowes, Isle of Wight (p. 212, 3K).*
(OS Map 196; ref SZ 516948.)
🚌 *Southern Vectis 4 Ryde– E Cowes, 5 Newport–E Cowes (Tel: 01983 827005).*
🚉 *Ryde Esplanade 7m; Wootton (IoW Steam Rly) 3m.*
⛴ *East Cowes (Red Funnel) 1½m (Tel: 01703 334010); Fishbourne (Wightlink) 4m; Ryde (Wightlink) 7m (Tel: 01705 827744).*

⊘⊙ Richborough Roman Amphitheatre

KENT (p. 213, 5P)
Ditch associated with the
nearby 3rd-century castle.

Open *Difficult access through
farmed field. Please telephone
Richborough Castle (01304
612013) for details.*
Entry *Free.*
➲ *1¼m N of Sandwich off A257,
Junction 7 of M2, onto A2.
(OS Map 179; ref TR 321598.)*
🚉 *Sandwich 1¾m.*

⊘ Rochester Castle

KENT (p. 213, 5N)
Built on the Roman city wall,
this Norman bishop's castle
was a vital royal stronghold.

Open *1 April–30 Sept: daily,
10am–6pm. 1 Oct–31 March:
daily, 10am–4pm (closed
25–27 Dec).(Site managed
by Rochester upon Medway
City Council.)*
Entry *£2.60/£2.00/£1.30.*

Rochester Castle with the tide out

(01634 402276
🚻 *(public, in castle grounds)*
🎧 ⊗ ◎ 🖺
➲ *By Rochester Bridge (A2),
Junction 1 of M2 and
Junction 2 of M25.
(OS Map 178; ref TQ 742686.)*
🚌 *From surrounding areas
(Tel: 0800 696 996).*
🚉 *Rochester ½m.*

✝ Royal Garrison Church

Portsmouth, HAMPSHIRE
(p. 213, 3K)
Originally a hospice for
pilgrims, this 16th-century
chapel became the Garrison
Church after the Dissolution.
Expertly restored in the
1860s but fire-bombed in
1941, the chancel survived
and there is still plenty to see.

Open *22 March–30 Sept:
Mon–Fri, 11am–4pm. Keykeeper
in winter (tel: 01705 378291).*
Entry *Free.*
(01705 378291
🅿 *(nearby)* ♿ ⊗
➲ *On Grand Parade S of
Portsmouth High St.
(OS Map 196; ref SU 633992.)*
🚌 *From surrounding areas
(Tel: 01962 868944).*
🚉 *Portsmouth Harbour ¾m.*

✝ St Augustine's Abbey

Canterbury, KENT
(p. 212, 3K)
See pp 8–11 for full details.

St Augustine's Cross

✝ St Augustine's Cross

Ebbsfleet, KENT (p. 213, 5P)
19th-century cross, in
Celtic design, marking
the traditional site of St
Augustine's landing in 597.

Open *Any reasonable time.*
Entry *Free.*
♿ ⊗
➲ *2m E of Minster off B29048.
(OS Map 179; ref TR 340641.)*
🚌 *Thanet Bus 01 Ramsgate–
Sandwich (Tel: 0800 696 996).*
🚉 *Minster 2m.*

⊖⊙ St Catherine's Oratory

ISLE OF WIGHT (p. 212, 3K)
Affectionately known as the
Pepperpot, this 14th-century

lighthouse, erected following the wreck of the wine ship *St Marie*, stands on the highest point of the island.

Open *Any reasonable time (external viewing only). (Site maintained and managed by the National Trust.)*
Entry *Free.*
🅿 ⊛
➲ *¾m NW of Niton.*
(OS Map 196; ref SZ 494773.)
🚌 *Southern Vectis 6/A Ventnor–Newport, 7/A Yarmouth–Ryde, to within ½m or 1m depending on route (Tel: 01983 562264).*
🚉 *Shanklin 9m.*
⛴ *West Cowes 14m; East Cowes 14m (Red Funnel. Tel: 01703 334010); Yarmouth 15m (Wightlink. Tel: 01705 827744).*

✚ St John's Commandery

Swingfield, KENT
(p. 213, 4P)
A medieval chapel, converted into a farmhouse in the 16th century. It has a fine moulded plaster ceiling and a remarkable timber roof.

Open *Any reasonable time for exterior viewing. Internal viewing by appointment only, tel. 01304 211067 for details.*
Entry *Free.*
⊛
➲ *2m NE of Densole off A260. (OS Map 179; ref TR 232440.)*

🚌 *Stagecoach East Kent 16 BR Folkestone Central– Canterbury to within 1m (Tel: 0800 696 996).*
🚉 *Kearsney 4m.*

✚ St Leonard's Tower

West Malling, KENT
(p. 213, 5N)
An early and particularly fine example of a Norman tower keep, built *c.*1080 by Gundulf, Bishop of Rochester.

Open *Any reasonable time for exterior viewing. To view interior, please contact West Malling Parish Council Mon–Fri, 9am–12pm, tel: 01732 870872.*
Entry *Free.*
♿ *(grounds only)* ⊛
➲ *On unclassified road W of A228. (OS Map 188; ref TQ 675570.)*
🚌 *Maidstone & District 70 from Maidstone, Mercury 151 from Chatham (Tel: 0800 696 996).*
🚉 *West Malling 1m.*

♿⛵ Silchester Roman City Walls and Amphitheatre

HAMPSHIRE (p. 212, 5K)
The best preserved Roman town walls in Britain, almost one-and-a-half miles around, with an impressive, recently restored amphitheatre.

Open *Any reasonable time.*
Entry *Free.*
🅿 ⊛
➲ *On minor road 1m E of Silchester. (OS Map 175; ref SU 643624.)*
🚌 *Stagecoach Hampshire Bus 44A from Basingstoke (passes BR Bramley) to within 1m (Tel: 01256 464501).*
🚉 *Bramley or Mortimer, both 2¾m.*

✚ Stone Chapel

See Faversham: Stone Chapel, p.60

St Leonard's Tower

♡ ⊕ Sutton Valence Castle

KENT (p. 213, 5O)

The ruins of a 12th-century stone keep built to monitor the important medieval route across the Weald from Rye to Maidstone.

Open *Any reasonable time.*
Entry *Free.*
⊛
➲ *5m SE of Maidstone in Sutton Valence village on A274. (OS Map 188; ref TR 815491.)*
🚌 *Maidstone & District/ Fuggles/Chalkwell 12 Maidstone– Tenterden (passes BR Headcorn) (Tel: 0800 696 996).*
🚉 *Headcorn 4m, Hollingbourne 5m.*

⊙ Temple Manor

Rochester, KENT (p. 213, 5N)

The 13th-century manor house of the Knights Templar.

Open *2 days notice is required, please telephone 01634 827980 for details.*

(Site managed by Rochester upon Medway City Council.)
Entry *Free.*
🅿 ♿ *(grounds only)* ⊛
➲ *In Strood (Rochester) off A228.*
(OS Map 178; ref TQ 733686.)
🚌 *From surrounding areas (Tel: 0800 696 996).*
🚉 *Strood ¾m.*

⛪ Titchfield Abbey

HAMPSHIRE (p.212, 4K)

Remains of a 13th-century abbey overshadowed by a grand Tudor gatehouse.

Open *22 March–31 Oct: daily, 10am–6pm (6pm/dusk in Oct). 1 Nov–31 March: daily, 10am– 4pm. (Site managed by The Titchfield Abbey Association.)*
Entry *Free.*
🅿 ♿ ⊛
➲ *½m N of Titchfield off A27. (OS Map 196; ref SU 541067.)*
🚌 *Solent Blue Line 26 Fareham–Southampton (Tel: 01703 226235).*
🚉 *Fareham 2m.*

Upnor Castle

⊗ ⊖ Upnor Castle

KENT (p. 213, 5N)

Well preserved 16th-century gun fort, built to protect Queen Elizabeth I's warships. However in 1667 it failed to resist the Dutch navy, which stormed up the Medway destroying half the English fleet.

Open *1 April–30 Sept: daily, 10am–6pm. Please telephone 01634 827980 for further details. (Site managed by Rochester upon Medway City Council.)*
Entry *£2.60/£1.90/£1.30.*
☎ *01634 718742*
🚻 🅿 *(at a slight distance from castle – park before village)*
♿ *(grounds only)* ⊕ 🎧
➲ *At Upnor, on unclassified road off A228.*
(OS Map 178; ref TQ 758706.)
🚌 *Mercury 197 from BR Chatham; otherwise 120, 191/4/6 Chatham–Hoo, alight Wainscott, thence 1m (Tel: 0800 696 996).*
🚉 *Strood 2m.*

Titchfield Abbey

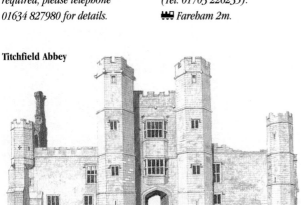

✪ ✿ Walmer Castle and Gardens

KENT (p. 213, 5P)
See pp 90–1 for full details.

♰ Waverley Abbey

SURREY (p. 212, 4L)
First Cistercian house in England, founded in 1128. The remaining ruins date from the 13th century.

Open *Any reasonable time.*
Entry *Free.*
🅿 *(limited)* ✆
➲ *2m SE of Farnham off B3001 and off junction 10 of M25.*
(OS Map 186; ref SU 868453.)
🚌 *Farnham 2m.*

⊖ Western Heights

Dover, KENT (p. 213, 4P)
Parts of moat of 19th-century fort built to fend off a French attack. Now part of the White Cliffs Countryside Project.

Open *Any reasonable time.*
Entry *Free.*
✆ *01304 241806*

✆ 🅿
➲ *Above Dover town on W side of Harbour.*
(OS Map 179; ref TR 312408.)
🚌 *Dover Priory ¾m.*

♰ Wolvesey Castle (Old Bishop's Palace)

Wolvesey, HAMPSHIRE
(p. 212, 4K)
One of the greatest medieval buildings in England, the Palace was the chief residence of the Bishops of Winchester. Its extensive ruins still reflect their importance and wealth. The last great occasion was on 25th July, 1554 when Queen Mary and Philip of Spain held their wedding breakfast in the East Hall.

Open *22 March–31 Oct: daily, 10am–6pm (6pm/dusk in Oct). Keykeeper in winter (Tel: 01732 778030).*
Entry *£1.50/£1.10/80p.*
✆ *01962 854766*

Wolvesey Castle

Yarmouth Castle

♿ ✆
➲ *¾m SE of Winchester Cathedral, next to the Bishop's Palace; access from College St.*
(OS Map 185; ref SU 484291.)
🚌 *From surrounding areas (Tel: 0345 023067).*
🚌 *Winchester ¾m.*

✪ Yarmouth Castle

ISLE OF WIGHT (p. 212, 3J)
This last addition to Henry VIII's coastal defences was completed in 1547. It houses exhibitions of paintings of the Isle of Wight and photographs of old Yarmouth.

🌳 *Picnic spot with views over the Solent.*
🌳 *New shop now open.*
Open *22 March–31 Oct: daily, 10am–6pm (6pm/dusk in Oct).*
Entry *£2.00/£1.50/£1.00.*
✆ *01983 760678*
♿ *(ground floor only)*
🏪 ✆ 🅿 *(coach & car park 200yds, limited roadside of 1hr)*
➲ *In Yarmouth adjacent to car ferry terminal.*
(OS Map 196; ref SZ 354898.)
⛴ *Yarmouth (Wightlink) adjacent (Tel: 01705 827744).*

89

WALMER CASTLE AND GARDENS

Walmer Castle was among the first of a new breed of castle. It was one of the many forts built along the south coast by Henry VIII in the early 16th century, that were specially designed to defend against the new threat of attack by gunpowder. Unlike a medieval castle it is low and squat, with hugely thick walls able to withstand the mightiest bombardment. Its spherical bastions held heavy armament which could be deployed against an attacking fleet. The castle was

Wellington's famous boots

later transformed into an elegant stately home that serves as a residence of the Lords Warden of the Cinque Ports. Past Wardens include William Pitt the Younger, the Duke of Wellington, and Sir Winston Churchill. Today, Walmer is still visited by the present Lord Warden, HM the Queen Mother, and some rooms used by her are open to visitors.

Another treat is the magnificent Queen Mother's Garden, open to the public for the first time this summer.

Built to withstand the wrath of the French and Spanish following Henry VIII's break with the Roman Catholic Church, the defences of Walmer Castle have in fact never been put to the test. Early 1539 saw England under the threat of invasion and Henry built a series of castles from Cornwall to Kent, which ended with the linked fortresses of Deal, Walmer and Sandown. The expected attack

The Duke of Wellington's Room

never materialized and, although the castles of the Downs were brought to readiness again in 1588 to repel the Spanish Armada, no fighting took place.

Walmer was transformed when it became the official residence of the Lords Warden of the Cinque Ports, an ancient title that originally involved control of the five most important medieval ports on the south coast.

The castle and its extensive gardens, looking inshore from the beach

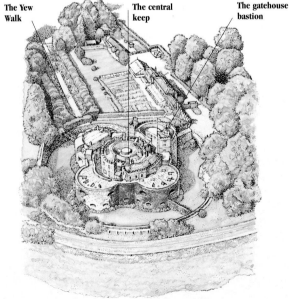

The Yew Walk

The central keep

The gatehouse bastion

The castle from the Yew Walk

including two rooms that are now a museum dedicated to the Duke of Wellington.

Open *22 March–31 Oct: daily, 10am–6pm (6pm/dusk in Oct). 1 Nov–31 Mar: Wed–Sun, 10am–4pm (closed Jan–Feb and when Lord Warden in residence).* ***Entry*** *£4.00/£3.00/£2.00.*
℆ 01304 364288
♿ 🅿 (nearby approach to castle) 🎧 (also available for the visually impaired, those with learning difficulties, and in French and German)
♿ (courtyard & garden only, parking available) ✖ 🚻
➲ On coast S of Walmer, Kent (p. 213, 5P), on A258. Junction 13 off M20 or from M2 to Deal. (OS Map 179; ref TR 378501.)
🚌 From surrounding areas (Tel: 0800 696 996).
🚉 Walmer 1m.

By the eighteenth century the position of Warden was largely ceremonial, although it retained immense prestige and a substantial salary. The Duke of Dorset was the first Lord Warden to use Walmer. He undertook the original transformation of the fort into a stately home, increasing the number of first-floor rooms by extending the living quarters out over the bastions. Further additions were made by Earl Granville, Lord Warden from 1865, who commissioned the extension of the gatehouse bastion.

The magnificent gardens surrounding the castle owe much to the enthusiasm of another Lord Warden, William Pitt the Younger, and much of his early landscaping remains.

The castle is full of memories of former Lords Warden,

William Pitt's gaming chair (above) and the gardens in summer (right)

GREATER LONDON

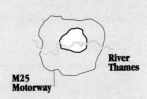

M25 Motorway

River Thames

Escape the stresses and strains of the capital by visiting the fascinating English Heritage sites in London. Kenwood, on the edge of Hampstead Heath, is set in a beautiful landscaped park with a lake which forms the perfect backdrop for summer concerts. It houses the Iveagh Bequest, one of the most important collections of paintings ever given to the nation. Also magnificent are Chiswick House and Marble Hill House, both original Palladian masterpieces by the River Thames.

Albert Memorial: a gilded angel

⊙ Albert Memorial

Kensington, GREATER LONDON (p. 212, 6M)
An elaborate national memorial by George Gilbert Scott to commemorate the Prince Consort. Finally completed in 1876, the figure of the Consort sits on a pyramid of 868 brick arches and has above it a lofty Gothic canopy supported by granite columns. The memorial is undergoing extensive conservation by English Heritage, explained in an exhibition and video in the Visitor Centre.

· **Open** *22 March–30 Sept: daily, 10am–6pm. 1 Oct–31 March: daily, 9am–3.30pm.*
Entry *Free.*
✆ *0171 225 1059*
🚌 *Frequent from surrounding areas (Tel: 0171 222 1234).*
🚆 *Victoria 1½m.*
Tube *South Kensington ½m.*

🏠 Chapter House, Pyx Chamber and Abbey Museum

Westminster Abbey, GREATER LONDON (p. 213, 6M)
The Chapter House, built by the royal masons in 1250, contains some of the finest medieval English sculpture to be seen. The building is octagonal, with a central

Mural of the Apocalypse of St John in the Chapter House, Westminster Abbey

column, and still has its original floor of glazed tiles. The 11th-century Pyx Chamber now houses the Abbey treasures. The Abbey museum contains medieval royal effigies.

Open *22 March–30 Sept: daily, 10am–5.30pm. 1 Oct–31 March: daily, 10am–4pm (closed 24–26 Dec). Liable to be closed at short notice on State occasions. Pyx Chamber 10.30am–4pm all year.*
Entry *£2.50/£1.90/£1.30.*
℘ 0171 222 5897
🅰 ❌ ⓦ ⃞
➲ *Approach either through the Abbey or through Dean's Yard and the cloister.*
🚌 *Frequent from surrounding areas (Tel: 0171 222 1234).*
🚉 *Victoria and Charing Cross both ¾m, Waterloo 1m.*
Tube *Westminster ¼m.*

🅰 ❀ Chiswick House

Chiswick, GREATER LONDON (p. 212, 5M)
See pp 94–5 for full details.

❂ Coombe Conduit

Kingston-Upon-Thames, GREATER LONDON (p. 212, 5M)
Built by Henry VIII to supply water to Hampton Court Palace, three miles away, Coombe Conduit consists

of two small buildings (one now a ruin) connected by an underground passage.

Open *By appointment only. Please contact House Manager at Marble Hill House on 0181 892 5115.*
Entry *Free.*
🚌 *Frequent from surrounding areas (Tel: 0171 222 1234).*
🚉 *Kingston-upon-Thames ¼m.*

🅰 ❀ Eltham Palace

Eltham, GREATER LONDON (p. 213, 5M)
A fascinating blend of a medieval royal palace and a 1930's Art Deco country house. Step from the 15th-century Great Hall, straight into the lost pre-War world with a suite of striking Modernist interiors.

Open *22 March–5 Oct: Thurs, Fri and Sun, 10am–6pm. These dates are provisional since conservation work may cause*

closure in 1997. Please contact Eltham Palace or Customer Services on 0171 973 3434 for details .
Entry *House & gardens £4.00/£3.00/£2.00. Gardens only £2.00/£1.50/£1.00. House & Great Hall only £2.50/£1.90/£1.25.*
℘ 0181 294 2548
❌
➲ *¾m N of A20 off Court Yard, SE9.*
🚌 *Frequent from surrounding areas (Tel: 0171 222 1234).*
🚉 *Eltham or Mottingham, both ½m.*

The Chapter House, Westminster Abbey

CHISWICK HOUSE

Close to the centre of London lies one of the first and finest English Palladian villas, surrounded by beautiful gardens. It was designed by the third Earl of Burlington who sought to create the kind of house and garden found in the suburbs of ancient Rome. He was one of the foremost architects of his generation and a

Inigo Jones

great promoter of the Palladian style first pioneered in England by Inigo Jones. He designed the villa to serve as a fitting showcase for his large collection of art and books. Today you can enjoy the house and its lavish interiors before stepping outside into the classical gardens – a perfect complement to the house itself.

The sumptuous decoration of Chiswick's interior is by William Kent. He created rooms whose vibrancy contrasts strongly with the purity of Burlington's exterior. You can enjoy the lavish Blue Velvet Room, Lord

Burlington's private study, with its gilded decoration and fabulous ceiling paintings, and look through the magnificent Gallery towards the octagonal Saloon.

Following new research into the House's original decoration, the domed Saloon will be redecorated and displayed to match its appearance in Burlington's day. The Gallery has been enhanced by a magnificent pair of gilt carved and marble-topped

The Palladian facade (below) and the ornate Blue Velvet Room (left)

The Red Velvet Room (above) looking through to the Round Room

tables originally made for Lord Burlington at Chiswick House in 1730. They return to their original position as the focal point of the Gallery.

Kent also produced the designs for the beautiful 18th-century gardens which are still in their original layout. The symmetrical lawns are dotted with classical statues, obelisks and urns, while neoclassical temples are hidden away among the trees.

The lake which Kent created snakes its way through the

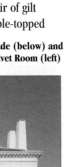

The Cascade (above) at the southern end of the lake being excavated by archaeologists before its recent restoration

The extensive grounds include a magnificent Camellia House

house and its extensive grounds, as well as Lord Burlington himself, letting you enjoy one of the jewels of London to the full.

Open *22 March–31 Oct: daily, 10am–6pm (6pm/dusk in Oct). 1 Nov–31 March: Wed–Sun, 10am–4pm (closed 24–26 Dec).* *Entry £2.50/£1.90/£1.30.* *℘ 0181 995 0508* *⚲ (in grounds)* **P** *(off westbound A4)* *☊ (also available for the visually impaired, those with learning difficulties, and in French and German)* *ᵶ (exterior & ground floor only)* ⬛ ⊛ ⬜ ⊪ *('Burlington Café'; open daily in summer, weekends only in winter.)* *Pre-booked tours available.* *➲ Burlington Lane, London, W4 (p. 212, 5M).* *🚌 190 Hammersmith– Richmond; E3 Greenford– Chiswick (Tel: 0171 222 1234).* *🚃 Chiswick ½m.* *Tube Turnham Green ¾m.*

grounds. At the southern end is the Cascade, recently the subject of extensive restoration managed by English Heritage in partnership with the London Borough of Hounslow, and with help from the Chiswick House Friends and the Heritage Lottery Fund. Built in 1738 to Kent's designs, it mimics an underground river flowing from a rocky hillside before pouring into the lake. It never worked properly in its day and precisely how it worked is still uncertain. Its setting has now been complemented by new planting, while new water features have been introduced into the central arches of the main structure and of the rustic bridge, with burbling pools resembling springs pouring into the lake.

An exhibition, along with an introductory video, tells the complete story of the

❿ Jewel Tower

Westminster, GREATER
LONDON (p. 213, 5M)
One of two surviving buildings
of the original Palace of
Westminster, the Jewel Tower
was built c.1365 to house the
personal treasure of Edward
III. It was subsequently used
as a storehouse and government office. The exhibition,
'Parliament Past and Present',
shows how Parliament works
and a new touch-screen
computer gives a virtual
reality tour of both Houses
of Parliament.

Open *22 March–31 Oct: daily,*
10am–6pm (6pm/dusk in Oct).
1 Nov–31 March: daily, 10am–
4pm (closed 24–26 Dec).

Closed 1–2pm.
Entry £1.50/£1.10/80p.
☎ 0171 222 2219
⊗ ☐
➲ *Opposite S end of Houses of*
Parliament (Victoria Tower).
🚌 *Frequent from surround-*
ing areas (Tel: 0171 222 1234).
🚄 *Charing Cross ¾m, Victoria*
and Waterloo, both 1m.
Tube *Westminster ¼m.*

❼ ✿ Kenwood

Hampstead, GREATER
LONDON (p. 212, 6M)
See pp 98–9 for full details.

❽ London Wall

Tower Hill, GREATER
LONDON (p. 213, 6M)
The best preserved piece of
the Roman Wall, heightened

Jewel Tower

in the Middle Ages, which
formed part of the eastern
defences of the City of London.

Open *Any reasonable time.*
Entry *Free.*
🍴 ♿ ⊗
➲ *Near Tower Hill underground*
station, EC3.
🚌 *Frequent from surround-*
ing areas (Tel: 0171 222 1234).
🚄 *Fenchurch Street ¼m.*
Tube *Tower Hill, adjacent.*

❾ ✿ Marble Hill House

Twickenham, GREATER
LONDON (p. 212, 5M)
A magnificent Thames-side
Palladian villa built 1724–29
for Henrietta Howard,
Countess of Suffolk, set in
66 acres of parkland. The
Great Room has lavish gilded
decoration and architectural
paintings by Panini. The
house also contains an
important collection of early
Georgian furniture, the
Lazenby Bequest Chinoiserie

Marble Hill House: the
Great Room

collection and an 18th-century lacquer screen. There is a display on the ground floor with an introductory film about the house, grounds, and the life and times of Henrietta Howard.

● *Enjoy 'Regency Life', a special event revealing history through fascinating presentations, 4–5 May.*
● *Free Children's Activity Sheet available.*
Open *22 March–31 Oct: daily, 10am–6pm (6pm/dusk in Oct). 1 Nov–31 March: Wed–Sun, 10am–4pm (closed 24–26 Dec).* **Entry** *£2.50/£1.90/£1.30.*
𝄞 *0181 892 5115*
⛟ ⑪ *('Coach House Cafe', open March–Oct)* ⌕ 🅿 *(at Richmond end of Marble Hill Park)* ♿ *(exterior & ground floor only; toilets)* 🚲 ⊛ 🛍 *Pre-booked group tours available.*
➲ *Richmond Road, Twickenham.*
🚃 *Frequent from surrounding areas (Tel: 0171 222 1234).*

Marble Hill House

🚉 *St Margarets ½m, Richmond or Twickenham 1m.* **Tube** *Richmond 1m.*

⊕ Ranger's House

Blackheath, GREATER LONDON (p. 213, 5M)
A handsome red brick villa built *c.*1700, on the edge of Greenwich Park, with a splendid bow-windowed gallery. The Architectural Study Collection is displayed in the Coach House, showing interesting domestic architectural features from London dwellings of the 18th–19th centuries.

Open *22 March–31 Oct: daily, 10am–6pm (6pm/dusk in Oct). 1 Nov–31 March: Wed–Sun, 10am–4pm (closed 24–26 Dec).* **Entry** *£2.50/£1.90/£1.30.*
𝄞 *0181 853 0035*
⛟ 🅿 *(in Chesterfield Walk)* ⊗ ⌕ Ⓔ *Pre-booked group tours available.*

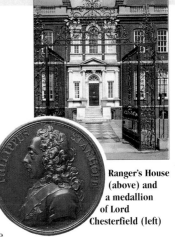

Ranger's House (above) and a medallion of Lord Chesterfield (left)

➲ *Chesterfield Walk, Blackheath, SE10.*
🚌 *LT 53 Oxford Circus–Plumstead (Tel: 0171 222 1234).*
🚉 *Maze Hill ½m, Greenwich or Blackheath ¾m.*

✝ Winchester Palace

Southwark, GREATER LONDON (p. 213, 6M)
The west gable end, with its unusual round window, is the prominent feature of the remains of the Great Hall of this 13th-century town house of the Bishops of Winchester, damaged by fire in 1814.

Open *Any reasonable time.* **Entry** *Free.*
⛟ ♿ ⊗
➲ *Near Southwark Cathedral, at corner of Clink St & Storey St, SE1.*
🚌 *Frequent from surrounding areas (Tel: 0171 222 1234).*
🚉 *and* **Tube** *London Bridge ¼m.*

KENWOOD

Standing in splendid, landscaped grounds on the edge of Hampstead Heath, Kenwood contains the most important private collection of paintings ever given to the nation. There is a selection of Old Masters, among the finest the 'Self-Portrait' by Rembrandt and 'The Guitar Player' by Vermeer, and paintings by such eminent British artists as Gainsborough, Turner and Reynolds. The outstanding neoclassical house was remodelled by Robert Adam, 1764–79, and includes his magnificent library. Outside, the historic landscaped park, with sloping lawns and a lake, forms the perfect setting for the waterside concerts that are held here in the summer.

Lord Mansfield's lion

In the 18th century Kenwood was occupied by a succession of Scottish lords. For the great judge, Lord Mansfield, Robert Adam transformed the brick house into a majestic villa. Later Earls of Mansfield remodelled the parkland and Kenwood remained in the family until 1922. When developers attempted to buy the estate, the grounds were saved by public purchase; the brewing magnate Edward Cecil Guinness, first Earl of Iveagh, bought the house and bequeathed it and his collection of pictures to the nation in 1927.

⊕ *Free Children's Activity Sheet available*.

***Open** 22 March–31 Oct: daily, 10am–6pm (6pm/dusk in Oct). 1 Nov–31 March: daily, 10am–4pm (closed 24–25 Dec). The Upper Hall (first floor) is open at weekends.*

***Entry** Free.*

✆ *0181 348 1286*

⌂ ⚲ 🅿 ⑪ ('The Brewhouse', open all year. Ring 0181 341 5384 for functions) ⊚ (also available for the visually impaired and those

Sculptures by
Hepworth and Moore

Mount Tyndal
Slopes

The
Elms

Beech
Mount

The concert bowl by the lake, venue for perfect summer concerts

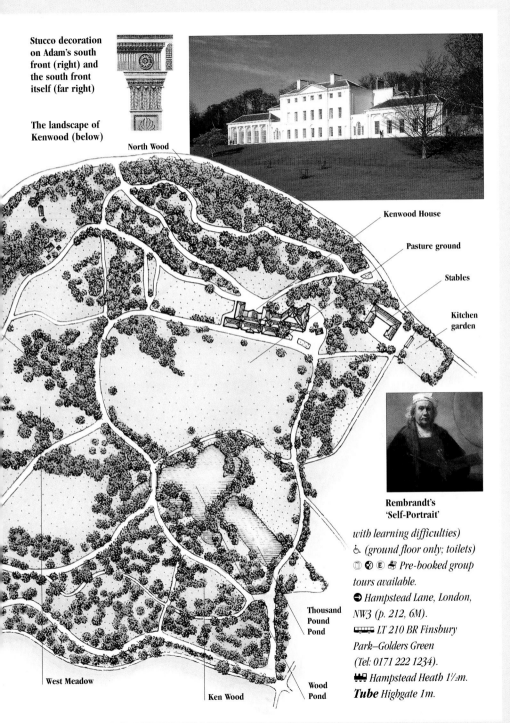

Stucco decoration on Adam's south front (right) and the south front itself (far right)

The landscape of Kenwood (below)

North Wood

Kenwood House

Pasture ground

Stables

Kitchen garden

Rembrandt's 'Self-Portrait'

with learning difficulties)
& *(ground floor only; toilets)*
Ⓘ Ⓕ Ⓔ 🚌 *Pre-booked group tours available.*
➡ *Hampstead Lane, London, NW3 (p. 212, 6M).*
🚌 *LT 210 BR Finsbury Park–Golders Green (Tel: 0171 222 1234).*
🚇 *Hampstead Heath 1½m.*
Tube *Highgate 1m.*

Thousand Pound Pond

West Meadow

Ken Wood

Wood Pond

99

THE EASTERN COUNTIES

Cambridgeshire

Norfolk

Suffolk

Essex

The Eastern Counties are scattered with Roman sites, castles spanning the centuries, chapels, priories and windmills. You'll even find a prehistoric flint mine. On the grandest scale is Audley End, a Jacobean house in Essex with a magnificent landscaped garden. Tilbury Fort, at the mouth of the Thames has defended London since Elizabethan times, while medieval castles are epitomised by the impressive solidity of Framlingham in Suffolk and the grandeur of the coastal keep at Orford with its views over the Suffolk marshes.

⊞❀ Audley End House and Park

ESSEX (p. 213/214, 7N)
See pp 102–5 for full details.

⊙➲ Baconsthorpe Castle

NORFOLK (p. 215, 10O)
Remains of the gate-houses of a large 15th-century fortified manor house, partly surrounded by a moat.

***Open** All year: daily, 10am–4pm.*
***Entry** Free.*
🅿 ⊛
➲ *¾m N of village of Baconsthorpe off unclassified road 3m E of Holt.*
(OS Map 133; ref TG 122382.)
🚃 *Sheringham 4½m.*

➲ Berney Arms Windmill

NORFOLK (p. 215, 9P)
A wonderfully situated marsh mill, one of the best and largest remaining in Norfolk, with seven floors, making it a landmark for miles around. Built to grind a constituent of cement, it was in use until

Binham Priory

Berney Arms Windmill

1951, ending its days pumping water to drain surrounding marshes.

***Open** 22 March–30 Sept: daily, 9am–5pm. Closed 1–2pm.*
***Entry** £1.10/80p/60p.*
☎ *01493 700605*
⊛
➲ *3½m NE of Reedham on N bank of River Yare. Accessible by boat, or by footpath from Halvergate (3½m).*
(OS Map 134; ref TG 465051.)
🚃 *Berney Arms ¼m.*

✚ Binham Priory

NORFOLK (p. 215, 10O)
Extensive remains of a Benedictine priory, of which the original nave of the church still continues in use as the parish church.

***Open** Any reasonable time.*
***Entry** Free.*
⊛

➥ ¼m NW of village of Binham-on-Wells on road off B1388.
(OS Map 132; ref TF 982399.)
🚌 Sanders, Wells Community Bus from Wells-next-the-Sea; Eastern Counties Coastliner Great Yarmouth–Sheringham–Hunstanton (Tel: 0500 626116).

⊘ Binham Wayside Cross

NORFOLK (p. 215, 10O)
Medieval cross marking the site of an annual fair held from the reign of Henry I until the 1950s.

Open Any reasonable time.
Entry Free.
🚻

➥ On village green adjacent to Priory.
(OS Map 132; ref TF 982399.)
🚌 Sanders, Wells Community Bus from Wells-next-the-Sea; Eastern Counties Coastliner Great Yarmouth–Sheringham–Hunstanton (Tel: 0500 626116).

⊘ Blakeney Guildhall

NORFOLK (p. 215, 10O)
The surviving basement, most likely used for storage, of a large 14th-century building, probably a merchant's house.

Open Any reasonable time.
Entry Free.
🚻

➥ In Blakeney off A149.
(OS Map 133; ref TG 030441.)
🚌 Sanders, Wells Community Bus from Wells-next-the-Sea;

Bury St Edmunds Abbey

Eastern Counties Coastliner Great Yarmouth–Sheringham–Hunstanton
(Tel: 0500 626116).
🚆 Sheringham 9m.

⊘ Burgh Castle

NORFOLK (p. 215, 9P)
Impressive walls, with projecting bastions, of a Roman fort built in the late 3rd century as one of a chain to defend the coast against Saxon raiders.

Open Any reasonable time.
Entry Free.
🚻

➥ At far W end of Breydon Water, on unclassified road 3m W of Great Yarmouth.
(OS Map 134; ref TG 475046.)
🚌 Eastern Counties 219, Great Yarmouth Transport 23 from Great Yarmouth (Tel: 0500 626116).
🚆 Great Yarmouth 5m.

Blakeney Guildhall

⚓ Bury St Edmunds Abbey

SUFFOLK (p. 215, 8O)
A Norman tower and 14th-century gatehouse of a ruined Benedictine abbey, church and precinct. The visitor centre has interactive diplays.

Open Abbey all year: weekdays, 7.30am–dusk, weekends and Bank Holidays, 9am–dusk. For opening hours of visitor centre please telephone 01284 763110. (Site managed by St Edmundsbury Borough Council.)
Entry Free.
🚻

➥ E end of town centre.
(OS Map 155; ref TL 858642.)
🚌 From surrounding areas (Tel: 01473 583358).
🚆 Bury St Edmunds 1m.

AUDLEY END

Audley End was one of the great wonders of the nation when it was built by the first Earl of Suffolk, Lord Treasurer to James I. It was on the scale of a great royal palace, and soon became one when Charles II bought it in 1668 for £50,000: using it as a base when he attended the nearby Newmarket races. Returned to the Suffolks after his death, substantial parts of the house were demolished.

Even so, what remains is one of the most significant Jacobean houses in England. Successive owners have since placed their stylistic imprint both within the graceful exterior and in the surrounding parkland.

As we see it now, Audley End's interior with its historic picture collecton and furniture is largely the product of its owner in the mid-19th century, the third Lord Braybrooke. The challenge for the visitor today is to piece together the many changes over time that have created such a harmonious whole.

The first Lord Braybrooke (left) remodelled Audley End in the late 18th century

The rooms at Audley End are a blend of many generations of taste – the differences sometimes subtly combined, sometimes dramatically exploited. The main structure has remained remarkably little-altered since the main front court was demolished in 1708, and the east wing came down in 1735.

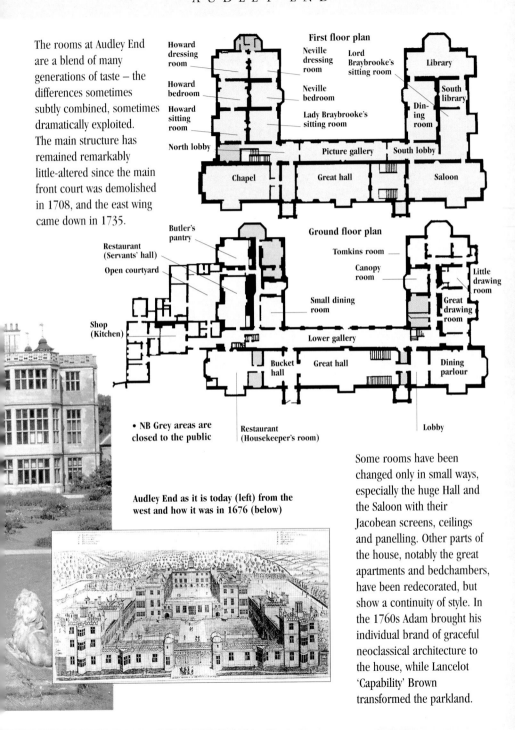

First floor plan

Howard dressing room
Neville dressing room
Lord Braybrooke's sitting room
Library
Howard bedroom
Neville bedroom
South library
Howard sitting room
Lady Braybrooke's sitting room
Dining room
North lobby
Picture gallery
South lobby
Chapel
Great hall
Saloon

Ground floor plan

Butler's pantry
Restaurant (Servants' hall)
Tomkins room
Open courtyard
Canopy room
Little drawing room
Small dining room
Great drawing room
Shop (Kitchen)
Lower gallery
Bucket hall
Great hall
Dining parlour
Restaurant (Housekeeper's room)
Lobby

• NB Grey areas are closed to the public

Audley End as it is today (left) from the west and how it was in 1676 (below)

Some rooms have been changed only in small ways, especially the huge Hall and the Saloon with their Jacobean screens, ceilings and panelling. Other parts of the house, notably the great apartments and bedchambers, have been redecorated, but show a continuity of style. In the 1760s Adam brought his individual brand of graceful neoclassical architecture to the house, while Lancelot 'Capability' Brown transformed the parkland.

Audley End and the Ring Hill Temple **painted by William Tomkins *c.* 1785**

The Georgian 'Gothick' chapel survives, but many of the other 18th-century decorative schemes were replaced. The fourth Lord Braybrooke was more interested in archaeology and ornithology than redecorating. His collection of stuffed birds and animals are a real feature of the house. After Audley End was requisitioned in World War II the ninth Lord Braybrooke resumed possession and in 1948 the house was sold to English Heritage's predecessor, the Ministry of Works. Much has been done recently to restore the park and the Victorian

The Little Drawing Room (above)

Sir John Griffin Griffin, later fourth Baron Howard de Walden and first Baron Braybrooke, introduced sweeping changes before he died in 1797. The third Baron Braybrooke, who inherited house and title in 1825, stamped his taste equally firmly and with longer-lasting results. He installed his huge picture collection, filled the rooms with furnishings, and reinstated some of the original Jacobean feel to the state rooms.

gardens, including the magnificent parterre. A free exhibition and special guidebook focus on the extensive grounds, with their lake, river and ornamental gardens. On a summer afternoon, Audley End's beauty and historical continuity are readily apparent.

Heraldic crests (left) adorn the plaster ceiling in the great hall

⏺ *Come and enjoy the beautiful blooms and displays at an Autumn flower festival, designed and arranged by the Cambridge Group of Flower Clubs, 6–7 Sept.*

Open *22 March–30 Sept: Wed–Sun and Bank Holidays, 11am–6pm. Last admissions 5pm. 1 Oct–31 Oct: Wed–Sun, 10am–3pm, house by guided tour only.*

Entry *to house and grounds £5.50/£4.10/£2.80, family ticket (2 adults & 3 children) £13.80. Grounds only £3.30/£2.50/ £1.30, family ticket £8.30.*

☎ **01799 522399** *(information line)*

🕴🕴 ⑂ *(Audley End Restaurant)*

🅿 ⅔ *(substantial groundfloor area and gardens only)* 🚽 ☕ 🌱

🎫 📱 🎧 *(a new audio tour will be introduced in 1997). French and German guide books available. No photography allowed within house.*

➤ *1m W of Saffron Walden, Essex (p. 213/214, 7N) on B1383 (M11 exits 8, 9 Northbound only, & 10). (OS Map 154; ref TL 525382.)*

🚌 *Hedingham/Viceroy 59 from BR Audley End, Eastern National 301, Townlink 504 Bishops Stortford–Saffron Walden (Tel: 0345 000333).*

🚆 *Audley End 1¼m.*

The Doll's House (right) is a miniature version of early 19th-century high life at Audley End

A tour around the Great Hall at Audley End (above)

⊘ Caister Roman Site

NORFOLK (p. 215, 9P)

The remains of a Roman site, possibly a fort, including part of a defensive wall, a gateway and buildings along a main street.

Open *Any reasonable time. (Site managed by Great Yarmouth Borough Council.)*
Entry *Free.*
(P)

◗ *Near Caister-on-Sea, 3m N of Great Yarmouth. (OS Map 134; ref TG 518125.)*
⬚⬚⬚ *Great Yarmouth Transport 8, Eastern Counties 223, 622–6, 701/5/7, 723/6 (Tel: 0500 626116).*
⬛⬛ *Great Yarmouth 3m.*

✪ Castle Acre: Bailey Gate

NORFOLK (p. 215, 9N)

The north gateway to the medieval planned town of Acre with flint towers.

Castle Acre Priory (below and right)

Castle Acre Castle

Open *Any reasonable time.*
Entry *Free.*
(P)

◗ *In Castle Acre, at E end of Stocks Green, 5m N of Swaffham. (OS Map 132; ref TF 817152.)*

⊖ ✪ Castle Acre Castle

NORFOLK (p. 215, 9O)

The remains of a Norman manor house, which became a castle with earthworks, set by the side of the village.

Open *Any reasonable time.*
Entry *Free.*
(P)

◗ *At E end of Castle Acre, 5m N of Swaffham. (OS Map 132; ref TF 819152.)*

✟ Castle Acre Priory

NORFOLK (p. 215, 9N)

The great west front of the 12th-century church of this Cluniac priory still rises to its full height and is elaborately

106

decorated, whilst the prior's lodgings and porch retain their roofs. The delightful herb garden, re-created to show herbs used in medieval times for both culinary and medicinal purposes, should not be missed.

Open *22 March–31 Oct: daily, 10am–6pm (6pm/dusk in Oct). 1 Nov–31 March: Wed–Sun, 10am–4pm (closed 24–26 Dec).*
Entry *£2.75/£2.10/£1.40.*
(01760 755394
♦♦♦ ⌒ (also available for the visually impaired, those with learning difficulties and in French) **P** *& (ground floor & grounds only)* ☻ 🍴 🄼 🗋
➲ ¼m W of village of Castle Acre, 5m N of Swaffham. (OS Map 132; ref TF 814148.)

❶ Castle Rising Castle

NORFOLK (p. 215, 10N)
A fine mid 12th-century domestic keep, set in the centre of massive defensive earthworks, once palace and prison to Isabella, "She-Wolf" dowager Queen of England. The keep walls stand to their original height and many of the fortifications are intact.

Open *22 March–31 Oct: daily, 10am–6pm (6pm/dusk in Oct). 1 Nov–31 March: Wed–Sun, 10am–4pm (closed 24–26 Dec). Closed 1–2pm in winter.*
Entry *£2.10/£1.60/£1.10.*

(01553 631330
🗋 ♦♦♦ **P** *& (exterior only; toilets)* ⌒ ☻
➲ 4m NE of King's Lynn off A149. (OS Map 132; ref TF 666246.)
🚌 *Eastern Counties 410/1 King's Lynn–Hunstanton (Tel: 01553 772343).*
🚉 *King's Lynn 4½m.*

❶ Church of the Holy Sepulchre

Thetford, NORFOLK
(p. 215, 8O)
The ruined nave of a priory church of the Canons of the Holy Sepulchre, the only surviving remains in England of a house of this order.

Open *Any reasonable time.*
Entry *Free.*
☻
➲ On W side of Thetford off B1107. (OS Map 144; ref TL 865831.)
🚌 *From surrounding areas (Tel: 0500 626116).*
🚉 *Thetford ¾m.*

Castle Rising Castle

❶ ❺ Cow Tower

Norwich, NORFOLK
(p. 215, 9P)
A circular brick tower, which once formed part of the 14th-century city defences.

Open *Any reasonable time.*
Entry *Free.*
☻
➲ In Norwich, near cathedral. (OS Map 134; ref TG 240091.)
🚌 *From surrounding areas (Tel: 0500 626116).*
🚉 *Norwich ½m.*

❶ Creake Abbey

NORFOLK (p. 215, 10O)
The ruins of the church of an Augustinian abbey.

Open *Any reasonable time.*
Entry *Free.*
☻
➲ 1m N of North Creake off B1355. (OS Map 132; ref TF 856395.)
🚌 *Bus: Wells Community Bus, Sanders Wells-next-the-Sea–Fakenham, Mon, Thu, Sat (Tel: 0500 626116).*

Framlingham Castle (above) and a Victorian gunnery re-enactment (right)

✝ Denny Abbey
CAMBRIDGESHIRE
(p. 214, 10N)

What at first appears to be an attractive stone-built farm-house is actually the remains of a 12th-century Benedictine abbey founded by the Countess of Pembroke which, at different times, also housed the Knights Templar and Franciscan nuns.

⊛ 'The Farmland Museum', opens Spring 1997.
Open *22 March–31 Oct: daily, 12–5pm.*
Entry *£3.20/£2.40/£1.20. Joint admission ticket with museum. Abbey free for English Heritage members.*

Denny Abbey

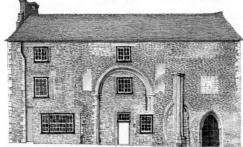

℡ 01223 860489
🅿 ⊛ ♿ *(grounds & ground floor only)* 🚻
➲ *6m N of Cambridge on A10. (OS Map 154; ref TL 495684.)*
🚌 *Stagecoach Cambus 109 Cambridge–Ely (passes close to BR Waterbeach) (Tel: 01223 423554).*
🚉 *Waterbeach 3m.*

✝ Duxford Chapel
CAMBRIDGESHIRE
(p. 214, 8N)

A medieval chapel once part of the Hospital of St John.

Open *Telephone 01799 522842 for opening arrangements.*
Entry *Free.*
⊗
➲ *Adjacent to Whittlesford station off A505. (OS Map 154; ref TL 486472.)*
🚉 *Whittlesford, adjacent.*

◐ Framlingham Castle
SUFFOLK (p. 215, 8P)

A superb 12th-century castle which, from the outside, looks almost the same as when it was built. From the continuous curtain wall, linking 13 towers, there are excellent views over Framlingham and the charming reed-fringed mere. At different times, the castle has been a fortress, an Elizabethan prison, a poor house and a school. The many alterations over the years have led to a pleasing mixture of historical styles. The Lanman Museum, containing a local history collection, can be seen for a small extra charge.

❹ **Walk along the full length of the towering castle walls. Activity book for children available.**
Open *22 March–31 Oct: daily, 10am–6pm (6pm/dusk in Oct). 1 Nov–31 March: daily, 10am–4pm (closed 24–26 Dec).*
Entry *£2.60/ £2.00/£1.30.*
☎ **01728 724189**
✖ Ⓔ 📷 🅿 ♿ *(grounds & ground floor only)* ⓘ ⓜ 🎧*
➲ *In Framlingham on B1116. (OS Map 156; ref TM 287637.)*
🚌 *Eastern Counties 82 from Ipswich (passes close to BR Woodbridge) (Tel: 01473 583358).*
🚉 *Wickham Market 6½m; Saxmundham 7m.*

⊕⊖ⓘ Grime's Graves

NORFOLK (p. 215, 9O)
These remarkable Neolithic flint mines, unique in England, comprise over 300 pits and shafts. The visitor can descend some 10m (30ft) by ladder into one excavated shaft, and look

Grime's Graves, aerial view

Grime's Graves

along the radiating galleries, where the flint for making axes and knives was extracted.

❹ **Climb down into a prehistoric flint mine.**
Open *22 March–31 Oct: daily, 10am–6pm (6pm/dusk in Oct). 1 Nov–31 March: Wed–Sun, 10am–4pm (closed 24–26 Dec). Last visit to pit 20 minutes before closing. Closed 1–2pm.*
Entry *£1.60/£1.20/80p.*
☎ **01842 810656**
🅿 ♿ *(exhibition area only; access track rough)* ⊛ 📷 ⓘ
➲ *7m NW of Thetford off A134. (OS Map 144; ref TL 818898.)*
🚌 *Eastern Counties/Whippet 200 Thetford–Newmarket, alight Santon Downham thence 2m (Tel: 01473 583358).*
🚉 *Brandon 3½m.*

❂ Hadleigh Castle

ESSEX (p. 213, 6N)
The curtain wall and two towers of this 13th-century castle survive almost to their full height and overlook the Essex marshes and Thames estuary.

Open *Any reasonable time.*
Entry *Free.*
☎ **01760 755161**
✖ ♿ *(hilly)*
➲ *¾m S of A13 at Hadleigh. (OS Map 178; ref TQ 810860.)*
🚌 *Thamesway and Southend Transport services from surrounding areas to within ½m (Tel: 0345 000 333).*
🚉 *Leigh-on-Sea 1½m by footpath.*

⊙⊕⊛ Hill Hall

ESSEX (p. 213, 6N)
This fine Elizabethan mansion has some of the earliest Renaissance decoration in the country. Rare wall paintings of mythological and biblical subjects date from the same period. The house is surrounded by parkland landscaped by Repton.

Open *The Hall is undergoing major building works and is not normally open to the public. Any open day will be announced in the members'* magazine, Heritage Today, *and the local press.*
Entry *Free.*
☎ **01992 561657**
ⓘ 🅿 ⊛ 🍴 ♿ *(ground floor and grounds).*
➲ *3m E of Epping on unclassified road to Theydon Mount. From M11 – Junction 7, S on B1393 to Epping, then as above. (OS Map 167; ref TQ 489994.)*
Tube *Epping 2½m.*

⛪ Isleham Priory Church

CAMBRIDGESHIRE
(p. 215, 8N)
Rare example of an early
Norman church. It has
survived little altered
despite being later
converted to a barn.

Open *Any reasonable time.*
Keykeeper (please follow
instructions shown at site
or telephone regional office
01604 730320 for details).
Entry *Free.*
⊗

➲ *In Isleham, 16m NE of*
Cambridge on B1104.
(OS Map 143; ref TL 642744.)
🚌 *Stagecoach Cambus 122*
Cambridge–Soham
(Tel: 01223 423554).
🚉 *Newmarket 8½m; Ely 9m.*

⊙ Landguard Fort

Felixstowe, SUFFOLK
(pp. 213/215, 7P)
An 18th-century fort, with
later additions. There is a
museum featuring displays
of local history.

Leiston Abbey

Open *Landguard Fort is*
undergoing major building
works and is not normally
open to the public. Open days
will be announced in the
members' magazine, Heritage
Today, *and the local press.*
Entry *Museum adults*
£1/children 50p. (no
unaccompanied children).
☎ *01394 286403 (evenings)*
🅿 ⊗ ⓜ 🍽

➲ *1m S of Felixstowe*
near docks.
(OS Map 169; ref TM 284318.)

🚌 *Eastern Counties 75–9*
Ipswich–Felixstowe Dock to
within ¾m (but with F4
from Felixstowe to Fort
Summer Suns only)
(Tel: 01473 253734).
🚉 *Felixstowe 2½m.*

⛪ Leiston Abbey

SUFFOLK (p. 215, 8P)
The remains of this abbey for
Premonstratensian canons
include a restored chapel.

Isleham Priory

Open *Any reasonable time.*
Entry *Free.*

🅿 ♿ ☻

➲ *1m N of Leiston off B1069.*
(OS Map 156; ref TM 445642.)

🚌 *Eastern Counties/ Eastern National 80/1, 166/7, Country Travel 80 Ipswich–Aldeburgh (passes close to BR Saxmundham) (Tel: 01473 583358).*

🚃 *Saxmundham 5m.*

⛰ Lexden Earthworks and Bluebottle Grove
Colchester, ESSEX
(pp. 213/215, 7O)
Parts of a series of earthworks, once encompassing 12 square miles, which protected Iron Age Colchester and were subsequently added to by the conquering Romans.

Open *Any reasonable time.*
(Sites managed by Colchester Borough Council.)
Entry *Free.*

☻

➲ *2m W of Colchester off A604. (OS Map 168; ref TL 965246 [Lexden Earthworks] and TL 975245 [Bluebottle Grove].)*

🚌 *Colchester Transport 5 from BR Colchester (Tel: 01206 44449).*

🚃 *Colchester or Colchester Town, both 2½m.*

Longthorpe Tower (right) and one of the wall paintings (above)

☻ Longthorpe Tower
CAMBRIDGESHIRE
(p. 214, 9M)
The finest example of 14th-century domestic wall paintings in northern Europe. They show many secular and sacred objects, including the Wheel of Life, the Labors of the Months, the Nativity and King David. The tower, with the Great Chamber that contains the paintings, is part of a fortified manor house.

Open *22 March–31 Oct: weekends and Bank Holidays only, 10am–6pm (6pm/ dusk in Oct). Closed 1–2pm.*
Entry *£1.10/80p/60p.*

☻

✆ *01733 268482*

➲ *2m W of Peterborough on A47.*
(OS Map 142; ref TL 163983.)

🚌 *Viscount 14 from Peterborough, 367 Peterborough–Oundle (Tel: 01733 54571); Midland Fox/Woods 747 Peterborough–Leicester (Tel: 0116 251 1411).*

🚃 *Peterborough 1½m.*

EASTERN COUNTIES

Mistley Towers
ESSEX (pp.213/215, 7O)
The remains of a church designed by Robert Adam and built in 1776. It was unusual in having towers at both the east and west ends.

Open *Key available from Mistley Quay Workshops (Tel: 01206 393884). (Site managed by Mistley Thorn Residents Association.)*
Entry *Free.*
(exterior only)
On B1352, 1½m E of A137 at Lawford, 9m E of Colchester. (OS Map 169; ref TM 116320.) Eastern National 102-4 Colchester–Harwich (Tel: 0345 000 333). Mistley ¼m.

Moulton Packhorse Bridge
SUFFOLK (p. 215, 8N)
Medieval four-arched bridge spanning the River Kennett.

Open *Any reasonable time.*
Entry *Free.*
In Moulton off B1085, 4m E of Newmarket. (OS Map 154; ref TL 698645.) Kennett 2m.

North Elmham Chapel
NORFOLK (p. 215, 10O)
Remains of a Norman chapel converted into a fortified dwelling and enclosed by

earthworks in the late 14th century by the notorious Bishop of Norwich, Hugh le Despencer.

Open *Any reasonable time. (Site managed by North Elmham Parish Council.)*
Entry *Free.*
6m N of East Dereham on B1110. (OS Map 132; ref TF 988217.)

Old Merchant's House: glass door panel (above) and interior (top)

Old Merchant's House, Row 111 House and Greyfriars' Cloisters
Great Yarmouth, NORFOLK (p. 215, 9P)
Two 17th-century Row Houses, a type of building unique to Great Yarmouth, containing original fixtures and displays of local architectural fittings salvaged from bombing in 1942–43. Nearby are the remains of a Franciscan friary, with rare early wall paintings, accidentally discovered during bomb damage repairs.

Open *22 March–31 Oct: daily, 10am–5pm. Guided tours hourly: depart Row 111 house at 10am, 11am, 12pm, 2pm, 3pm, 4pm & 5pm.*
Entry *£1.60/£1.20/80p.*
01493 857900
Great Yarmouth, make for

South Quay along riverside and
dock, ½m inland from beach.
Follow signs to dock and south
quay. (OS Map 134; ref TG
525072 [Houses] and TG
525073 [Cloisters].)
🚌 From surrounding areas
(Tel: 0500 626116).
🚃 Great Yarmouth ½m.

⊙ Orford Castle

SUFFOLK (p. 215, 8P)
A royal castle built for coastal
defence in the 12th century.
A magnificent keep survives
almost intact with three
immense towers reaching to
30m (90 feet). Inside a spiral
stair leads to a maze of
rooms and passageways.

⊛ *Free Children's Activity
Sheet available*
⊛ *CD Rom unit with information on English castles.*
Open *22 March–31 Oct: daily,
10am–6pm (6pm/dusk in Oct).
1 Nov–31 March: Wed–Sun,*

10am–4pm (closed 24–26
Dec). Closed 1–2pm in winter.
Entry £2.10/£1.60/£1.10.
☎ *01394 450472*
🅿 ⊗ ⓘ
➥ *In Orford on B1084
20m NE of Ipswich.
(OS Map 169; ref TM 419499.)*
🚌 *Belle 160, Eastern
Counties 122, Suffolk County
Villager Woodbridge–Orford
(passes close to BR Woodbridge)
(Tel: 01473 583358).*
🚃 *Wickham Market 8m.*

⊖ Prior's Hall Barn

Widdington, ESSEX
(pp. 213/214, 7N)
One of the finest surviving
medieval barns in south-east
England and representative
of the aisled barns of north-
west Essex.

Open *22 March–30 Sept:
Sat & Sun, 10am–6pm.*

Prior's Hall Barn, Widdington

*Telephone 01799 522842
for further details.*
Entry *Free.*
⊗ ♿
➥ *In Widdington, on
unclassified road 2m SE
of Newport, off B1383.
(OS Map 167; ref TL 538319.)*
🚌 *Eastern National 301
Bishops Stortford–Saffron
Walden (Tel: 0345 000 333).*
🚃 *Newport 2m.*

⛪ St Botolph's Priory

Colchester, ESSEX
(p. 215, 7O)
The nave, with an impressive
arcaded west end, of the first
Augustinian priory in England.

Open *Any reasonable time.
(Site managed by Colchester
Borough Council.)*
Entry *Free.*
⊗
➥ *Colchester, near Colchester
Town station.
(OS Map 168; ref TL 999249.)*
🚌 *From surrounding areas
(Tel: 0345 000 333).*
🚃 *Colchester Town, adjacent.*

Orford Castle

St John's Abbey Gate

✝ St James's Chapel
Lindsey, SUFFOLK
(pp. 213/215, 7O)
A little 13th-century
chapel with thatched
roof and lancet windows.

Open All year: daily,
10am–4pm.
Entry Free.
✼ & (single step)
➲ On unclassified road
½m E of Rose Green,
8m E of Sudbury.
(OS Map 155; ref TL 978443.)
🚌 Suffolk Bus 156 from
Ipswich–Ely, Sun only
(Tel: 01473 583358).
🚉 Sudbury 8m.

✝ St John's Abbey Gate
Colchester, ESSEX
(pp. 213/215, 7O)
This fine abbey gatehouse,
in East Anglian flintwork,
survives from the Benedictine
abbey of St John.

Open Any reasonable time.
(Site managed by Colchester
Borough Council.)
Entry Free.
✼ &
➲ On S side of central
Colchester.
(OS Map 168; ref TL 998248.)
🚌 From surrounding areas
(Tel: 0345 000 333).
🚉 Colchester Town ¼m.

✝ St Olave's Priory
NORFOLK (p. 215, 9P)
Remains of an Augustinian
priory founded nearly 200
years after the death in 1030
of the patron saint of Norway,
after whom it is named.

Open Any reasonable time.
Entry Free.
✼
➲ 5½m SW of Great Yarmouth
on A143.
(OS Map 134; ref TM 459996.)
🚉 Haddiscoe 1¼m.

Saxtead Green Post Mill

◉ Saxtead Green Post Mill
SUFFOLK (p. 215, 8P)
A fine example of a post mill,
where the superstructure
turns on a great post to face
the wind. The mill, which
ceased production in 1947,
is still in working order and
you can climb the wooden
stairs to the various floors,
which are full of fascinating
mill machinery.

Open 22 March–31 Oct: Mon–
Sat, 10am–6pm (6pm/dusk in
Oct). Closed 1–2pm.
Entry £1.60/£1.20/80p.
☎ 01728 685789
✼ 🎧
➲ 2½m NW of Framlingham
on A1120.
(OS Map 156; ref TM 253645.)
🚌 Eastern Counties 82, 99,
120 from Ipswich (passes
close to BR Woodbridge)
(Tel: 01473 583358).
🚉 Wickham Market 9m.

✝ Thetford Priory
NORFOLK (p. 215, 8N)
The 14th-century gatehouse is
the best preserved part of this
Cluniac priory built in 1103.
The extensive remains include
the plan of the cloisters.

Open Any reasonable time.
Entry Free.
✼
➲ On W side of Thetford
near station.
(OS Map 144; ref TL 865836.)

🚌 *From surrounding areas (Tel: 0500 626116).*
🚉 *Thetford ¼m.*

⊙ Thetford Warren Lodge

NORFOLK (p. 215, 9O)

The ruins of a small, two-storeyed medieval house, set in pleasant woods, which was probably the home of the priory's gamekeeper.

Open *Any reasonable time.*
Entry *Free.*
🅿️

➲ *2m W of Thetford off B1107. (OS Map 144; ref TL 839841.)*
🚌 *Eastern Counties 131/2 Bury St Edmunds–Brandon (passes close to BR Thetford) (Tel: 0500 626116).*
🚉 *Thetford 2½ m.*

⊙⊜ Tilbury Fort

ESSEX (p. 213, 5N)

The largest and best preserved example of 17th-century military engineering in England, commanding the Thames and showing the development of fortifications over the following 200 years. Exhibitions, the powder magazine and the bunker-like 'casemates' demonstrate how the fort protected London from seaborne attack – there's even a chance to fire an anti-aircraft gun!

Open *22 March–31 Oct: daily, 10am–6pm (6pm/dusk in Oct).*

1 Nov–31 March: Wed–Sun, 10am–4pm (closed 24–26 Dec).
Entry *£2.20/£1.70/£1.10. £1 to fire anti-aircraft gun.*
📞 *01375 858489*
🅿️ Ⓔ 👫 🎧 ♿ *(exterior, fort square & magazines)* 🏪
➲ *½m E of Tilbury off A126. (OS Map 177; ref TQ 651754.)*
🚌 *Harris Bus 380 BR Standford-le-Hope–Tilbury Riverside; Thameside 382 BR Grays–Tilbury Riverside (Tel: 0345 000 333).*
🚉 *Tilbury Town 1½m.*

✠ Waltham Abbey Gatehouse and Bridge

ESSEX (p. 213, 6M)

A late 14th-century abbey gatehouse, part of the cloister and 'Harold's Bridge'.

Open *Any reasonable time. (Sites managed by Lee Valley Park.)*

Tilbury Fort (below) and gun emplacement (right)

Entry *Free.*
🅿️
➲ *In Waltham Abbey off A112. (OS Map 166; ref TL 381008.)*
🚌 *Frequent services from BR Waltham Cross (Tel: 0345 000 333).*
🚉 *Waltham Cross 1¼m.*

⊜⊙ Weeting Castle

NORFOLK (p. 215, 9N)

The ruins of an early medieval manor house within a shallow rectangular moat.

Open *Any reasonable time.*
Entry *Free.*
🅿️
➲ *2m N of Brandon off B1106. (OS Map 144; ref TL 778891.)*
🚉 *Brandon 1½m.*

THE MIDLANDS

Arbor Low Stone Circle

The Midlands are home to the largest castle ruin in England – Kenilworth, a royal castle and palace for hundreds of years. At Boscobel House, discover the secret rooms and the Royal Oak in which King Charles II hid from Cromwell's troops. Stokesay Castle in the beautiful Welsh Marches is a delight-fully picturesque fortified manor house. And heritage from a more recent age can be seen at Iron Bridge in Shropshire – the birthplace of the Industrial Revolution, and the centrepiece of a World Heritage Site.

⊙ Abingdon County Hall

OXFORDSHIRE (p. 212, 6K)
A grand centrepiece for the market place at Abingdon, this 17th-century public building was built to house the Assize Courts.

Open *Museum 1 April–31 Oct: Tues–Sun, 11am–5pm (4pm outside British Summer Time). Closed Bank Holidays.*
Entry *Free.*
☎ **01235 523703**
✗ ⓜ
➲ *In Abingdon, 7m S of Oxford in Market Place.*
(OS Map 164; ref SU 497971.)
🚌 *Oxford 35/A, Thames Transit 30 from Oxford (passes BR Radley) (Tel: 01865 7855400).*
🚆 *Radley 2½m.*

⊙○ Acton Burnell Castle

SHROPSHIRE (p. 217, 9G)
The warm red sandstone shell of a fortified 13th-century manor house.

Open *Any reasonable time.*
Entry *Free.*
♿ ✗
➲ *In Acton Burnell, on unclassified road 8m S of Shrewsbury. (OS Map 126; ref SJ 534019.)*
🚌 *Boultons/Midland Red Church Stretton–Shrewsbury, Tues, Sat only (Tel: 0345 056 785).*
🚆 *Shrewsbury or Church Stretton, both 8m.*

⊘ Arbor Low Stone Circle and Gib Hill Barrow

DERBYSHIRE (p. 214, 11J)
A fine Neolithic monument, this 'Stonehenge of Derby-shire' comprises many slabs of limestone, surrounded by an unusually large ditch.

Open *Daily, 10am–6pm/dusk whichever is earlier. (Site managed by the Peak Park Joint Planning Board.)*
Entry *Farmer who owns right of way to site may levy a charge.*
✗
➲ *½m W of A515 2m S of Monyash. (OS Map 119; ref SK 161636.)*
🚌 *Mainline 181, Stagecoach E Midland 202, Bowers 442 from Buxton to Parsley Hay, thence 1m (Tel: 01332 292200).*
🚆 *Buxton 10m.*

⊘ Arthur's Stone

Dorstone, HEREFORD & WORCESTER (p. 217, 7F)
Impressive prehistoric burial chamber formed of large blocks of stone.

Open *Any reasonable time.*
Entry *Free.*

🚻

➲ *7m E of Hay-on-Wye off B4348 near Dorstone.*
(OS Map 148; ref SO 319431.)
🚌 *Stagecoach Red & White 39 Hereford–Brecon to within ¾m (Tel: 01633 266336).*

♡ Ashby de la Zouch Castle

LEICESTERSHIRE

(pp. 214/217, 10J)

The impressive ruins of this late-medieval castle are dominated by a magnificent 24-metre (80-foot) high tower, split in two during the Civil War, from which there are panoramic views of the surrounding countryside.

🌼 ***Attractive picnic spot.***
🌼 ***Explore the underground tunnels – remember to bring a torch!***
Open *22 March–31 Oct: daily, 10am–6pm (6pm/dusk in Oct). 1 Nov–31 March: Wed–Sun, 10am–4pm (closed 24–26 Dec). Closed 1–2pm in winter.*
Entry *£1.60/£1.20/80p.*
℘ *01530 413343*

🅿 ♿ *(grounds only)* 🚻 🛍 🍴
➲ *In Ashby de la Zouch, 12m S of Derby on A50.*
(OS Map 128; ref SK 363167.)
🚌 *Stevensons 9, 27 Burton-on-Trent–Ashby de la Zouch; Midland Fox/Stevensons 118, 218 Leicester-Swadlincote (Tel: 01332 292200).*
🚃 *Burton-on-Trent 9m.*

♋ Berkhamsted Castle

HERTFORDSHIRE

(p. 212, 6L)

The extensive remains of a large 11th-century motte and bailey castle.

Open *All year: daily, 10am–4pm. Please contact keykeeper, Mr Stevens, on 01442 871737.*
Entry *Free.*

🚻

➲ *By Berkhamsted station.*
(OS Map 165; ref SP 996083.)
🚌 *From surrounding areas (Tel: 0345 244344).*
🚃 *Berkhamsted, adjacent.*

Ashby de la Zouch Castle with the 80-foot Hasting's Tower

✝ Bishop's Old Palace

Lincoln, LINCOLNSHIRE
See Lincoln Bishop's Old Palace.

🅿 ♿ 🚃 Bolingbroke Castle

LINCOLNSHIRE

(p. 214, 11M)

Remains of a 13th-century hexagonal castle, birthplace of Henry IV in 1367 and besieged by Parliamentary forces in 1643.

Open *22 March–30 Sept: daily, 9am–9pm. 1 Oct–31 March: daily, 9am–7pm. (Site managed by Heritage Lincolnshire.)*
Entry *Free.*

🚻

➲ *In Old Bolingbroke, 16m N of Boston off A16.*
(OS Map 122; ref TF 349649.)
🚃 *Thorpe Culvert 10m.*

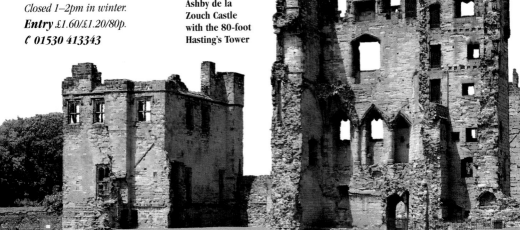

Bolsover Castle and the Pillar Chamber (right)

Bolsover Castle

DERBYSHIRE

(pp. 214/217, 11K)

An enchanting and romantic spectacle, situated high on a wooded hilltop dominating the surrounding landscape. Built on the site of a Norman castle, this is largely an early 17th-century mansion. Explore the 'Little Castle' or 'keep', a unique celebration of Jacobean romanticism with its elaborate fireplaces, panelling and wall paintings. There is also an impressive 17th-century indoor Riding School, built by the Duke of Newcastle, and ruins of great state apartments.

Winner of the 1995/6 NPI National Heritage Award, voted by the general public as one of Britain's favourite national treasures.

Free Children's Activity Sheet available.

Open *22 March–31 Oct: daily, 10am–6pm (6pm/dusk in Oct). 1 Nov–31 March: Wed–Sun, 10am–4pm (closed 24–26 Dec).*

Entry *£2.80/£2.10/£1.40.*

01246 822844 *or* ***823349***

P *(opposite main gate)*

(grounds only)

Off M1 at junction 29, 6m from Mansfield. In Bolsover, 6m E of Chesterfield on A632. (OS Map 120; ref SK 471707.)

Stagecoach E Midland 81/A, Chesterfield Transport 81–3, 282/3 Chesterfield–Bolsover (passes close to BR Chesterfield) (Tel: 01332 292200).

Chesterfield 6m.

Boscobel House and the Royal Oak

SHROPSHIRE

(p. 217, 9H)

Fully refurnished and restored, the panelled rooms, secret hiding places and pretty gardens lend this 17th-century timber-framed hunting lodge a truly romantic character. King Charles II hid in the house and the nearby Royal Oak after the Battle of Worcester in 1651 to avoid detection by Cromwell's troops. Today there is a farmhouse with dairy, farmyard and smithy, and an exhibition in the house.

See the Royal Oak and the secret places inside the house where Charles II hid.

Free Children's Activity Sheet available.

Open *22 March–31 Oct: daily, 10am–6pm (6pm/dusk in Oct). 1 Nov–31 Dec, 1 Feb–31 March: Wed–Sun, 10am–4pm (closed 24–26 Dec, 1–31 Jan). Last admission 3.30pm. Entry to house by guided tour only.*

Entry *£3.75/£2.80/£1.90.*

01902 850244

E P *(gardens only)*

('Boscobel House Tearoom'; normally open summer season only, Tues–Sun)

Boscobel House and the White Room

Boscobel House: portrait of Charles II

➲ *On minor road from A41 to A5, 8m NW of Wolverhampton. (OS Map 127; ref SJ 837083.)*
🚉 *Cosford 3m.*

🏛 Buildwas Abbey

SHROPSHIRE (p. 217, 9G)
Set beside the River Severn, against a backdrop of wooded grounds, are extensive remains of this Cistercian abbey begun in 1135.

Open *22 March–31 Oct: daily, 10am–6pm (6pm/dusk in Oct). Please telephone 01743 701101 for further details.*
Entry *£1.60/£1.20/80p.*
🚶 ♿
➲ *On S bank of River Severn on B4378, 2m W of Iron Bridge. (OS Map 127; ref SJ 642044.)*
🚌 *Williamsons X96*

Birmingham–Shrewsbury (passes close to BR Telford Central) (Tel: 0345 056 785).
🚉 *Telford Central 6m.*

🏛 Bushmead Priory

BEDFORDSHIRE (p. 214, 8M)
A rare survival of the medieval refectory of an Augustinian priory. Its original timber-framed roof is almost intact and contains interesting wall paintings and stained glass.

Bushmead Priory

Open *July–Aug: weekends only, 10am–6pm. Closed 1–2pm.*
Entry *£1.60/£1.20/80p.*
☎ *01234 376614*
🅿 ♿
➲ *On classified road near Colmworth, 2m E of B660.*

(OS Map 153; ref TL 115607.)
🚉 *St Neots 6m.*

⊜ Cantlop Bridge

SHROPSHIRE (p. 217, 9G)
Single-span cast-iron road bridge over the Cound Brook, designed by the great engineer Thomas Telford.

Open *Any reasonable time.*
Entry *Free.*
♿
➲ *¾m SW of Berrington on unclassified road off A458. (OS Map 126; ref SJ 517062.)*
🚉 *Shrewsbury 5m.*

🏛 Chichele College

NORTHAMPTONSHIRE (p. 214, 8L)
Parts of a quadrangle remain of this college for secular canons, founded in 1422.

Open *Quadrangle any reasonable time. For chapel please contact keykeeper, Mrs C. Jones, 22 Lancaster St., Higham Ferrers; tel. 01933 317182. (Site managed by East Northamptonshire District Council.)*
Entry *Free.*
♿
➲ *In Higham Ferrers, on A6. (OS Map 153; ref SP 960687.)*
🚌 *Stagecoach United Counties 46/A, X94 from Wellingborough (Tel: 01604 20077).*
🚉 *Wellingborough 5m.*

Buildwas Abbey from the west

Clun Castle

Clun Castle

SHROPSHIRE (p. 217, 8F)
The remains of a four-storey keep and other buildings of this border castle.

Open Any reasonable time.
Entry Free.

➡ *In Clun, off A488, 18m W of Ludlow.*
(OS Map 137; ref SO 299809.)
🚌 *Midland Red West 741–5, 773 from Ludlow (passes close to BR Ludlow) (Tel: 0345 056 785).*
🚉 *Hopton Heath 6½m; Knighton 6½m.*

✝ Croxden Abbey

STAFFORDSHIRE
(pp. 214/217, 10J)
Remains of a Cistercian abbey founded in 1176.

Open 10am–6pm/dusk, whichever is earlier.
Entry Free.

➡ *5m NW of Uttoxeter off A522.*
(OS Map 128; ref SK 065397.)
🚉 *Uttoxeter 6m.*

✝ De Grey Mausoleum

Flitton, BEDFORDSHIRE
(p. 214, 7L)
A remarkable treasure-house of sculpted tombs and monuments from the 16th to 19th centuries, dedicated to the de Grey family of Wrest Park.

Open Weekends only. Please contact keykeeper, Mr Stimpson, 3 Highfield Road, Flitton (Tel: 01525 860094). Access through Flitton Church.
Entry Free.
☎ 01799 522842

➡ *Flitton, attached to church, on unclassified road 1½m W of A6 at Silsoe.*
(OS Map 153; ref TL 059359.)
🚉 *Flitwick 2m.*

De Grey Mausoleum

🏰 Deddington Castle

OXFORDSHIRE
(pp. 214/217, 7K)
Extensive earthworks conceal the remains of a 12th-century castle.

Open Any reasonable time.
Entry Free.

➡ *S of B4031 on E side of Deddington, 17m N of Oxford on A423.*
(OS Map 151; ref SP 471316.)
🚌 *Midland Red X59 Oxford–Banbury to within ½m (Tel: 01788 535555).*
🚉 *King's Sutton 5m.*

✝ Edvin Loach Old Church

HEREFORD &
WORCESTER (p. 217, 8G)
Peaceful and isolated 11th-century church remains.

Open Any reasonable time.
Entry Free.
🅿

➡ *4m N of Bromyard on unclassified road off B4203.*
(OS Map 149; ref SO 663585.)

✝ Eleanor Cross

Geddington, NORTHAMP-
TONSHIRE (p. 214, 9L)
One of a series of famous crosses erected by Edward I to mark the resting places of the body of his wife, Eleanor, when brought for burial from Harby in Nottinghamshire to Westminster Abbey.

Gainsborough Old Hall

Open *Any reasonable time.*
Entry *Free.*
🚫

➲ *In Geddington, off A43
between Kettering and Corby.
(OS Map 141; ref SP 896830.)*
🚌 *Stagecoach United
Counties 8 Kettering–Corby.
(Tel: 01604 20077).*
🚃 *Kettering 4m.*

⊕ Gainsborough Old Hall

LINCOLNSHIRE (p. 214, 12L)
A large medieval house with a
magnificent Great Hall and
suites of rooms. A collection
of historic furniture and a
re-created medieval kitchen
are on display.

Open *Easter Sunday–31 Oct:
Mon–Sat, 10am–5pm,
Sun 2pm–5.30pm.
1 Nov–Easter Saturday,
Mon–Sat, 10am–5pm
(closed Good Friday, 24–26
Dec, 1 Jan). (Site managed by
Lincolnshire County Council.)*

Entry *£1.75/95p/95p
(no reduction for students/
unemployed). Small charge
on Special Event Days for
E.H. members.*
📞 *01427 612669*
🚻 🎧 ♿ *(most of ground floor)*
🚫 ⑪
➲ *In Gainsborough, opposite
the Library.
(OS Map 121; ref SK 815895.)*
🚌 *From surrounding areas
(Tel: 01522 553135).*
🚃 *Gainsborough Central ½m,
Gainsborough Lea Road 1m.*

✝ Geddington, Eleanor Cross

See Eleanor Cross.

Goodrich Castle

◐ ◑ Goodrich Castle

HEREFORD &
WORCESTER (p. 217, 7G)
Remarkably complete,
magnificent red sandstone
castle with 12th-century keep
and extensive remains from
the 13th and 14th centuries.

⊛ ***Free Children's Activity
Sheet available.***
Open *22 March–31 Oct: daily,
10am–6pm (6pm/dusk in Oct).
1 Nov–31 March: daily, 10am–
4pm (closed 24–26 Dec).*
Entry *£2.30/£1.70/£1.20.*
📞 *01600 890538*
🚻 🅿 🚫 🎧 *(also available for
the visually impaired and those
with learning difficulties)* ⑪
➲ *5m S of Ross-on-Wye
off A40.
(OS Map 162; ref SO 579199.)*
🚌 *Stagecoach Red & White
34 Monmouth-Gloucester
to within ½m (passes close
to BR Gloucester)
(Tel: 0345 125 436).*

Halesowen Abbey

✚ Halesowen Abbey
WEST MIDLANDS
(p.217, 8H)
Remains of an abbey founded
by King John in the 13th
century, now incorporated
into a 19th-century farm.

Open *July–August: weekends
only, 10am–6pm.*
Entry *£1.00/80p/50p.*
🅿 ✖ ♿ *(rough grass between
church and infirmary)*
➲ *Off A456 Kidderminster
road, 6m W of Birmingham
city centre.*
(OS Map 139; ref SO 975828.)
🚌 *West Midlands Travel 9,
19 Birmingham–Stourbridge
(Tel: 0121 200 2700).*
🚉 *Old Hill 2½m.*

♡ 🚷 Hardwick Old Hall
DERBYSHIRE
(pp. 214/217, 11K)
This large ruined house,
finished in 1591, still displays
Bess of Hardwick's innovative
planning and interesting

decorative plasterwork. The
views from the top floor over
the country park and 'New'
Hall are spectacular.

⊛ ***Ideal for children and
schools.***
Open *22 March–31 Oct:
Wed–Sun, 10am–6pm
(6pm/dusk in Oct).*
Entry *£1.60/£1.20/80p.
National Trust members admitted free, but small charge at
English Heritage events. (Site
maintained and managed by
English Heritage, and owned by
the National Trust. Joint ticket
available for the New Hall and
Gardens and the Old Hall.)*
☏ *01246 850431*
✖ 🅿 *(£2.00 vehicle entry
charge for access to National
Trust Estate, refundable on a
visit to Hardwick New Hall)*
🚻 *(in National Trust car park)*
➲ *9½m SE of Chesterfield, off
A6175, from J 29 of M1.
(OS Map 120; ref SK 463638.)*

🚌 *E Midland/Trent X2, 63
Chesterfield–Nottingham
to within 1½m
(Tel: 01332 292200).*
🚉 *Chesterfield 9½m.*

✚ Haughmond Abbey
SHROPSHIRE (p. 217, 9G)
The extensive remains of this
12th-century Augustinian
abbey include the Chapter
House, which retains its late-
medieval timber ceiling, and
some fine medieval sculpture.

Open *22 March–31 Oct: daily,
10am–6pm (6pm/dusk in Oct).
Closed 1–2pm.*
Entry *£1.60/£1.20/80p.*
☏ *01743 709661*
🅿 ♿ ✖ 🚻
➲ *3m NE of Shrewsbury
off B5062.
(OS Map 126; ref SJ 542152.)*
🚌 *Midland Red 519
Shrewsbury–Newport
(Tel: 0345 056 785).*
🚉 *Shrewsbury 3½m.*

Hardwick Old Hall

Haughmond Abbey: the Abbot's Chamber (top) and a detail of the Chapter House (above)

⚠🔄 Hob Hurst's House

DERBYSHIRE
(pp. 214/217, 11J)
A square prehistoric burial mound with an earthwork ditch and outer bank.

Open *Any reasonable time. (Site managed by the Peak Park Joint Planning Board.)*
Entry *Free.*
🚶
➲ *From unclassified road off B5057, 9m W of Chesterfield. (OS Map 119; ref SK287692.)*
🚌 *Stagecoach EAst Midland 58, 66, Hulleys X67, 170 from Chesterfield, to within 2m (Tel: 0132 292200).*
🚉 *Chesterfield 9m.*

♡⊕ Houghton House

BEDFORDSHIRE (p. 214, 7L)
Reputedly the inspiration for 'House Beautiful' in Bunyan's *Pilgrim's Progress*, the remains of this early 17th-century mansion still convey elements that justify the description, including work attributed to Inigo Jones.

Open *Any reasonable time.*
Entry *Free.*
🅿️ ♿ 🚶
➲ *1m NE of Ampthill off A421, 8m S of Bedford. (OS Map 153; ref TL 039394.)*
🚌 *Stagecoach United Counties 142/3 BR Flitwick– Bedford to within ½m (Tel: 01604 20077).*
🚉 *Flitwick or Stewartby, both 3m.*

⊖ Iron Bridge

SHROPSHIRE (p. 217, 9G)
The world's first iron bridge and Britain's best-known industrial monument. Cast in Coalbrookdale by local ironmaster Abraham Darby, it was erected across the River Severn in 1779.

Open *Any reasonable time.*
Entry *Free.*
🚶
➲ *In Ironbridge, adjacent to A4169. (OS Map 127; ref SJ 672034.)*
🚌 *Frequent from Telford (passes close to BR Telford Central or Wellington Telford West) (Tel: 0345 056 785).*
🚉 *Telford Central 5m.*

Iron Bridge

Jewry Wall

Leicester,
LEICESTERSHIRE
(p. 214, 9K)

One of the largest surviving lengths of Roman wall in the country. Over 9 metres (30 ft) high, it formed one side of the civic baths' exercise hall.

Open *Any reasonable time.*
Entry *Free.*

In St Nicholas St W of Church of St Nicholas.
(OS Map 140; ref SK 583044.)
From surrounding areas (Tel: 0116 251 1411).
Leicester ¾m.

Kenilworth Castle

WARWICKSHIRE (p. 217, 8J)
See pp 126–9 for full details.

Kirby Hall

NORTHAMPTONSHIRE
(p. 214, 9L)

Outstanding example of a large, stone-built Elizabethan mansion, begun in 1570 with 17th-century alterations. The fine gardens, currently being restored, are home to beautiful peacocks.

Come to "History in Action II" English Heritage's most spectacular special event of the year, 2–3 Aug.

Open *22 March–31 Oct: daily, 10am–6pm (6pm/dusk in Oct). 1 Nov–31 March: Wed–Sun, 10am–4pm (closed 24–26 Dec). Closed 1–2pm.*
Entry *£2.20/£1.70/£1.10.*
01536 203230
(grounds, gardens & ground floor only)
On unclassified road off A43 4m NE of Corby.
(OS Map 141; ref SP 926927.)

Kirby Hall: The Great Garden (bottom) and the "History in Action" spectacular (below)

Kirby Muxloe Castle

Kirby Muxloe Castle

LEICESTERSHIRE
(p. 214, 9K)

Picturesque, moated, brick-built castle begun in 1480 by William, Lord Hastings.

Open *22 March–31 Oct: weekends and Bank Holidays only, 10am–6pm (6pm/dusk in Oct). Closed 1–2pm.*
Entry *£1.60/£1.20/80p.*

4m W of Leicester off B5380.
(OS Map 140; ref SK 524046.)
Midland Fox 63, 152/3 from Leicester (Tel: 0116 251 1411).
Leicester 5m.

Langley Chapel

SHROPSHIRE
(p. 217, 9G)

This small chapel, standing alone in a field, contains a complete set of early 17th-century wooden fittings and furniture.

Open *Any reasonable time (closed 24–26 Dec).*
Entry *Free.*

1½m S of Acton Burnell, on unclassified road off A49, 9½m S of Shrewsbury. (OS Map 126; ref SJ 538001.) Boultons/Midland Red Church Stretton–Shrewsbury, Tues, Sat only, to within 1½m (Tel: 0345 056 785). Shrewsbury 7½m.

⊘ Leicester Jewry Wall

See Jewry Wall.

Leigh Court Barn

⊖⊘ Leigh Court Barn

HEREFORD &
WORCESTER (p. 217, 8H)
Magnificent 14th-century timber-framed barn, built for the monks of Pershore Abbey. It is the largest of its kind in Britain.

Open *1 April–30 Sept: Thurs–Sun, 10am–6pm.*
Entry *Free.*
✗
5m W of Worcester on unclassified road off A4103. (OS Map 150; ref 784534.) Midland Red West 417,

Langley Chapel

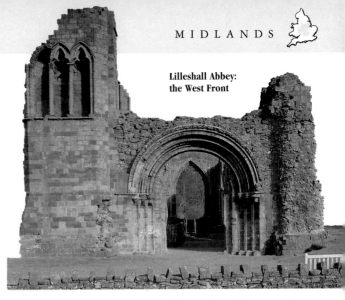

Lilleshall Abbey:
the West Front

421/2/3/5 from Worcester to within 1m (Tel: 0345 125 436). Worcester Foregate St 5m.

♰ Lilleshall Abbey
SHROPSHIRE
(p. 217, 9H)
Extensive and evocative ruins of an abbey of Augustinian canons, including remains of the 12th- and 13th-century church and the cloister buildings, surrounded by green lawns and ancient yew trees.

Open *22 March–31 Oct: week-ends and Bank Holidays only, 10am–6pm (6pm/ dusk in Oct). Closed 1–2pm.*
Entry *£1.10/80p/60p.*
🐾
On unclassified road off A518, 4m N of Oakengates. (OS Map 127; ref SJ 738142.) Midland Red/Timeline 80–3, 481 Telford–Stafford (passes close to BR Telford Central & Stafford) to within 1m (Tel: 0345 056 785). Oakengates 4½m.

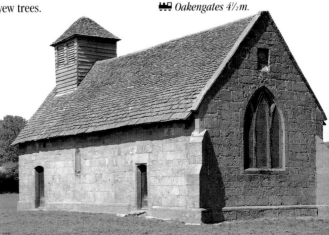

KENILWORTH CASTLE

Queen Elizabeth I *did* sleep here. The massive, red sandstone castle, which seems positively to glow in the early morning and evening light, was the Warwickshire power base of the best beloved of all her courtiers, Robert Dudley, Earl of Leicester. Among the buildings that remain are those that he built or rebuilt to entertain his queen and sustain his noble dignity. Other parts of Kenilworth, dating back to the

An arrow slit on Lunn's Tower

12th century, are powerful statements of its former strength and the way that it once dominated this part of the Midlands.

Kenilworth Castle has always been intimately linked with some of the most important names in English history. Today, with some of its Tudor gardens, its impressive Norman 'keep' and John of Gaunt's Great Hall, it is the largest castle ruin in England.

The first castle at Kenilworth was built about 50 years after the Norman conquest by Geoffrey de Clinton, chamberlain to Henry I. Henry II took over the castle – as well as nearby Warwick – 50 years later, to make both ready against attack from his son's rebel army, and it remained in royal hands when the rebellion ended. The castle was radically extended by King John in the 13th century, and he also transformed the surrounding mere (great lake) into one of its most glorious features.

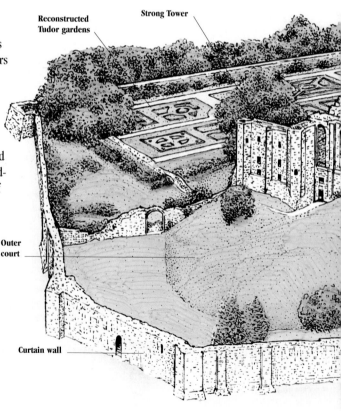

Artist's impression of Kenilworth Castle today

Reconstructed Tudor gardens

Strong Tower

Outer court

Curtain wall

George Gascoigne, Robert Dudley's pageant-master

TAM MARTI QVAM MERCVRIO.

Kenilworth was one of the four royal castles which were to be handed over to the barons under the terms of the Magna Carta. John, however, somehow managed to avoid surrendering the castle, which stayed in royal hands until 1253, when it was given to Simon de Montfort by Henry III. The de Montforts turned against the Crown in the Barons' War in 1266, and the castle was besieged. The defenders were well stocked with food and arms and had the added protection of the Great Mere, although a waterborne assault was attempted. They managed to hold out for almost nine months before disease took its toll and they were forced to surrender.

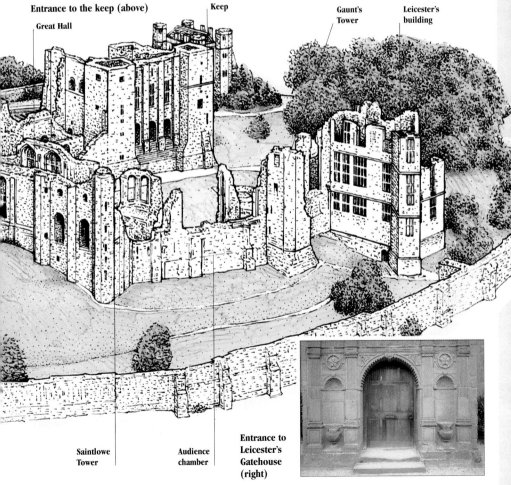

Entrance to the keep (above)

Great Hall

Keep

Gaunt's Tower

Leicester's building

Saintlowe Tower

Audience chamber

Entrance to Leicester's Gatehouse (right)

Kenilworth remained in royal hands. In a coup, Edward II was briefly imprisoned there, before being taken to Berkeley Castle and hideously murdered in 1326. John of Gaunt, a giant of English history, rebuilt the castle palatially in the 1390s. Henry V retired there after winning the Battle of Agincourt 20 years later. He built himself a banqueting house, The Pleasuance, on the other side

Leicester's building

A civil war pikeman (right)

of the lake. Henry VIII had it dismantled and moved the Pleasuance buildings back into the main castle.

The castle took centre stage again in the 16th century, when it was acquired by the Dudley family. John Dudley, Duke of Northumberland and effectively ruler of England in the reign of the boy-king Edward VI, was executed for trying to place his daughter-in-law Lady Jane Grey on the throne in 1553. Dudley's son Robert was a great favourite of Elizabeth I. Kenilworth was given back to him and he transformed it into a place fit for her to visit. Tales woven by Sir Walter Scott, in his novel *Kenilworth* (1821), around Dudley, his wife (who died in mysterious circumstances) and the Virgin Queen still give extra glamour to the castle.

Kenilworth never saw quite such glories again. Following the Battle of Edgehill in the Civil War it was partially demolished by Parliamentary troops to make it useless as a stronghold.

The castle from the south at sunset (below)

Over the years Kenilworth was allowed to fall into ruin, and the lake to drain away. The castle was saved for the nation in 1938. It remains a powerful reminder of great men, their glories, pleasures and rebellions, and offers glorious views over a countryside now at peace.

Re-enactment of life in the Civil War at Kenilworth

❧ Come and see 'Soldiers Through The Ages', with spectacular displays of soldiers from Romans to WWII, including the firing of a 25-pounder gun, 4–5 May.
❧ Family Discovery Pack and Free Children's Activity Sheet available.

Ornamental arrow slit on the water tower

Open 22 March–31 Oct: daily, 10am–6pm (6pm/dusk in Oct). 1 Nov–31 March: daily, 10am–4pm (closed 24–26 Dec).
Entry £2.75/£2.10/£1.40
☏ 01926 852078
Ⓔ ⋔ Ⓟ ⓖ (also available for the visually impaired and those with learning difficulties and in French, German and Japanese)
✖ ⬧ ⓜ ⬟ ♿
➲ In Kenilworth, Warwickshire (p. 217, 8J). (OS Map 140; ref SP 278723.)
🚌 Stagecoach Midland Red X16–9; Stagecoach G & G X12, West Midlands Travel 12A/C Coventry–Leamington Spa (passes close to BR Coventry & Leamington Spa) (Tel: 0121 200 2700).
🚆 Warwick 5m.

Medieval life, seen in a re-enactment at Kenilworth

Lincoln Bishop's Old Palace

✝ Lincoln Bishop's Old Palace

Lincoln, LINCOLNSHIRE
(pp. 214/219, 11L)
The remains of this medieval palace of the Bishops of Lincoln are in the shadow of Lincoln Cathedral. You can climb the stairs to the Alnwick Tower, explore the undercroft and see the recently established vineyard, which is one of the most northerly in Europe.

⊕ *Ideal for children and schools.*
⊕ *Exhibition on the history of the Bishops of Lincoln.*
Open *22 March–31 Oct: daily, 10am–6pm (6pm/dusk in Oct). 1 Nov–31 March: weekends only, 10am–4pm. Closed 1–2pm.*
Entry *£1.10/80p/60p.*
✆ *01522 527468*
✖ ♨
➲ *S side of Lincoln Cathedral. (OS Map 121; ref SK 981717.)*
🚌 *From surrounding areas*
(Tel: 01522 553135).
🚉 *Lincoln 1m.*

☻♡☻ Longtown Castle

HEREFORD & WORCESTER (p. 217, 7F)
An unusual cylindrical keep built *c.*1200, with walls 4.5 metres (15 feet) thick. There are magnificent views to the Black Mountains.

Open *Any reasonable time.*
Entry *Free.*
☻

Longtown Castle

➲ *4m WSW of Abbey Dore. (OS Map 161; ref SO 321291.)*

✝ Lyddington Bede House

LEICESTERSHIRE (p.214,9L)
Set among picturesque golden stone cottages, beside the handsome parish church of St Andrew, the Bede House (house of prayer) was originally a medieval palace of the Bishops of Lincoln. It was later converted into an almshouse.

Open *22 March–31 Oct: daily, 10am–6pm (6pm/dusk in Oct). Closed 1–2pm.*
Entry *£1.60/£1.20/80p.*
✆ *01572 822438*
✖ ♿ *(ground-floor rooms only).*
➲ *In Lyddington, 6m N of Corby, 1m E of A6003. (OS Map 141; ref SP 875970.)*
🚌 *Midland Fox 'Rutland Flyer' Corby–Melton Mowbray (passes close to BR Oakham) (Tel: 0116 251 1411).*

✝ Mattersey Priory

NOTTINGHAMSHIRE
(pp. 214/217/219, 11K)
Remains of a small Gilbertine monastery founded in 1185.

Open *Any reasonable time.*
Entry *Free.*
☻
➲ *Rough access down drive ¾m long, 1m E of Mattersey off B6045, 7m N of East Retford.*

Minster Lovell Hall

(OS Map 137; ref SO 306984.)
🚌 *Minsterley 553 Shrewsbury–Bishop's Castle (passes close to BR Shrewsbury) to within 1m (Tel: 0345 056 785)*
🚃 *Welshpool 10m.*

♡ ⓜ ⬁ Moreton Corbet Castle

SHROPSHIRE (p. 217, 10G)
A ruined medieval castle with the substantial remains of a splendid Elizabethan mansion.

Open *Any reasonable time.*
Entry *Free.*
🅿 ♿ ⊗
⬁ *In Moreton Corbet off B5063, 7m NE of Shrewsbury.*
(OS Map 126; ref SJ 562232.)
🚌 *Midland Red/PMT X64 Shrewsbury–Hanley (passes close to BR Shrewsbury & Stoke-on-Trent)*
(Tel: 0345 056 785).
🚃 *Yorton 4m.*

(OS Map 112; ref SK 704896.)
🚃 *Retford 7m.*

♡ Minster Lovell Hall and Dovecote

OXFORDSHIRE (p. 217, 6J)
The handsome ruins of Lord Lovell's 15th-century manor house stand in a lovely setting on the banks of the River Windrush.

Open *Any reasonable time.*
Dovecote – exterior only.
Entry *Free.*
🅿 ⊗
⬁ *Adjacent to Minster Lovell church, 3m W of Witney off A40*
(OS Map 164; ref SP 324114.)

🚌 *Thames Transit 102 Witney–Carterton with connections from BR Oxford (Tel: 01865 772250).*
🚃 *Charlbury 7m.*

⬁⬁ Mitchell's Fold Stone Circle

SHROPSHIRE (p. 217, 9F)
An air of mystery surrounds this Bronze Age stone circle, set on dramatic moorland and consisting of some 30 stones of which 15 are visible.

Open *Any reasonable time.*
Entry *Free.*
⊗
⬁ *16m SW of Shrewsbury W of A488.*

Lyddington Bede House

◉◔ Mortimer's Cross Water Mill

HEREFORD & WORCESTER (p. 217, 8G)
Intriguing 18th-century mill, still in working order, showing the process of corn milling.

Open *22 March–31 Oct: weekends only, 10am–6pm (6pm/dusk in Oct). Parties by appointment at other times.*
Entry *£1.50/£1.00/50p.*
✆ *01568 708820*
&. *(exterior & ground floor only)* ⊗
➔ *7m NW of Leominster on B4362.*
(OS Map 148; ref SO 426637.)
🚌 *Leominster 7½m.*

◉ Nine Ladies Stone Circle

Stanton Moor, DERBYSHIRE
(pp. 214/217, 11J)
Once part of the burial site for 300–400 people, this Early Bronze Age circle is 15 metres (50 feet) across.

Open *Any reasonable time. (Site managed by the Peak Park Joint Planning Board.)*
Entry *Free.*
⊛
➔ *From unclassified road off A6, 5m SE of Bakewell. (OS Map 119; ref SK 253635.)*
🚌 *Hulleys 170 Matlock–Bakewell (passes close to BR Matlock), to within 1m (Tel: 01332 292200).*
🚌 *Matlock 4½m.*

◉ North Hinksey Conduit House

OXFORDSHIRE (p. 217, 6K)
Roofed reservoir for Oxford's first water mains, built in the early 17th century.

Open *Any reasonable time (exterior only).*
Entry *Free.*
⊛
➔ *In North Hinksey off A34, 2½m W of Oxford. (OS Map 164; ref SP 494049.) Located off track leading from Harcourt Hill; use footpath*

Mortimer's Cross Water Mill

from Ferry Hinksey Lane (near station).
🚌 *Oxford 1½m.*

◉ North Leigh Roman Villa

OXFORDSHIRE
(pp. 214/217, 7J)
The remains of a large and well-built Roman courtyard villa. The most important feature is an almost complete mosaic tile floor, intricately patterned in reds and browns.

Open *Grounds – any reasonable time. Viewing window for mosaic. Pedestrian access only from main road (550 metres).*
Entry *Free.*
⊛
➔ *2m N of North Leigh, 10m W of Oxford off A4095. (OS Map 164; ref SP 397154.)*
🚌 *Thames Transit 11 Oxford–Witney to within 1½m (Tel: 01865 772250).*
🚌 *Handborough 3½m.*

Tiled floor at North Leigh Roman Villa

⚫⊖ Old Gorhambury House

HERTFORDSHIRE
(p. 212, 6M)
The remains of this Elizabethan mansion illustrate the impact of the Renaissance on English architecture.

Open *May–Sept: Thurs only, 2–5pm, or at other times by appointment. Call 01604 730320 for more information.* **Entry** *Free.*
⊛
➲ *¼m W of Gorhambury House & accessible only through private drive from A4147 at St Albans (2m).* *(OS Map 166; ref TL 110077.)* 🚌 *Sovereign 300, 734, Welwyn Hatfield 330, 340 St Albans–Hemel Hempstead to start of drive. (Tel: 0345 244344).* 🚉 *St Albans Abbey 3m, St Albans 3½m.*

⊙ Old Oswestry Hill Fort

SHROPSHIRE (p. 217, 10F)
An impressive Iron Age fort of 68 acres defended by a series of five ramparts, with an elaborate western entrance and unusual earthwork cisterns.

Open *Any reasonable time.* **Entry** *Free.*
⊛
➲ *1m N of Oswestry, accessible from unclassified road off A483.*

(OS Map 126; ref SJ 295310.) 🚌 *Midland Red 2, D53, D63 from BR Gobowen (Tel: 0345 056 785).* 🚉 *Gobowen 2m.*

⚪⊙ Peveril Castle

DERBYSHIRE
(pp. 214/217, 11J)
There are breathtaking views of the Peak District from this castle, perched high above the pretty village of Castleton. The great square tower stands almost to its original height.

⊛ *Picnic spot of exceptional beauty. Free Children's Activity sheet available.* **Open** *22 March–31 Oct: daily, 10am–6pm (6pm/dusk in Oct). 1 Nov–31 March: Wed–Sun, 10am–4pm (closed 24–26 Dec).*

Entry *£1.60/£1.20/80p.* ☎ **01433 620613** ⊛ Ⓘ 🚻 *(in town)* 🅿 *(in town)* ➲ *On S side of Castleton, 15m W of Sheffield on A625. (OS Map 110; ref SK 150827.)* 🚌 *Mainline/Hulleys 272, Stagecoach East Midlands 274 BR Sheffield-Manchester (Tel: 01332 292200).* 🚉 *Hope 2½m.*

Peveril Castle: a spectacular site for special events

⬟ Rollright Stones

OXFORDSHIRE
(pp. 214/217,7J)
Three groups of stones,
known as 'The King's Men',
'The Whispering Knights' and
'The King Stone', spanning
nearly 2,000 years of the
Neolithic and Bronze Ages.

Open *The King's Men any
reasonable time by courtesy
of the owner, who may levy
a charge. The Whispering
Knights & The King Stone any
reasonable time, by footpath.*
Entry *Free.*
P *(in layby)* ⊗
➲ *Off unclassified road
between A44 and A3400, 2m
NW of Chipping Norton near
villages of Little Rollright and
Long Compton.
(OS Map 185; ref SP 297308.)*

⊘ Roman Wall

St Albans, HERTFORD-
SHIRE (p. 212, 6M)
Several hundred yards of the
wall, built *c.*AD 200, which
enclosed the Roman city of
Verulamium. The remains of
towers and foundations of a
gateway can still be seen.

Open *Any reasonable time.*
Entry *Free.*
⊗
➲ *On S side of St Albans, ½m
from centre off A4147.
(OS Map 166; ref TL 135067.)*
🚌 *From surrounding areas
(Tel: 0345 244344).*

🚆 *St Albans Abbey ½m,
St Albans 1¼m.*

✠ Rotherwas Chapel

HEREFORD &
WORCESTER (p. 217, 7G)
This Roman Catholic chapel
dates from the 14th and 16th
centuries and features an
interesting mid-Victorian side
chapel and High Altar.

Open *Any reasonable time.
Keykeeper at nearby filling
station.*
Entry *Free.*
P ⅟ *(kissing gate)* ⊗
➲ *1½m SE of Hereford on
B4399.
(OS Map 149; ref SO 537383.)*
🚌 *Hereford Hopper
110/1/8 from City Centre
(Tel: 0345 125 436).*
🚆 *Hereford 3½m.*

✠ Rufford Abbey

NOTTINGHAMSHIRE
(pp. 214/217, 11K)
The remains of a 17th-century
country house, built on the
foundations of a 12th-century
Cistercian abbey, set in the
Rufford Country Park.

Open *22 March–31 Oct: daily,
10am–5pm. 1 Nov–31 March:
daily, 10am–4pm (closed
24–26 Dec).*
Entry *Free.*
✆ **01623 823148**
⑁ **P** ⑂ ⌂ *craft centre* ⅟ ⊗
➲ *2m S of Ollerton off A614.
(OS Map 120; ref SK 645646.)*

Rushton Triangular Lodge

🚌 *Stagecoach East Midland
33 Nottingham–Worksop,
Retford & District 36, 100
Nottingham–Retford
(Tel: 0115 924 0000).*

✠ Rushton Triangular Lodge

NORTHAMPTONSHIRE
(p. 214, 9L)
Extraordinary building built
by the Catholic Sir Thomas
Tresham on his return from
imprisonment for his
religious beliefs. Completed
in 1597, it symbolizes the
Holy Trinity – it has three
sides, three floors, trefoil
windows and three triangular
gables on each side.

Open *22 March–31 Oct: daily,
10am–6pm (6pm/dusk in Oct).
Closed 1–2pm.*
Entry *£1.10/80p/60p.*
✆ **01536 710761**
⊗

1m W of Rushton, on unclassified road 3m from Desborough on A6. (OS Map 141; ref SP 830831.) Stagecoach United Counties 19 Kettering–Market Harborough, alight Desborough, thence 2m (Tel: 01604 20077). *Kettering 5m.*

♠ Rycote Chapel
OXFORDSHIRE

(pp. 212/217, 6K)
This lovely 15th-century chapel, with exquisitely carved and painted wood-work, has many intriguing features, including two roofed pews and a musicians' gallery.

Open 22 March–30 Sept: Fri–Sun & Bank Holidays, 2–6pm.
Entry £1.50/£1.10/80p.
P ⊗ & *(assistance required)*
3m SW of Thame off A329. (OS Map 165; ref SP 667046.) Aylesbury and the Vale 260, 280 Oxford–Aylesbury (passes BR Haddenham & Thame Parkway) to within ¼m (Tel: 0345 382000). *Haddenham & Thame Parkway 5m.*

☺ Sibsey Trader Windmill
LINCOLNSHIRE

(pp. 214/219, 11M)
An impressive tower mill built in 1877, with its machinery and six sails intact. Flour milled on the spot can be bought there.

Rycote Chapel

Open Open for milling on 30 March; 6, 20 April; 4, 11, 25 May; 8, 22 June; 13, 27 July; 10, 24 Aug; 7, 14 Sept: 11am–5pm. (Site managed by Mr & Mrs Bent.)
Entry £1.60/£1.20/80p.
☎ 01205 820065
♦♦♦ P & *(exterior only)* ⊗ ♦♦
½m W of village of Sibsey, off A16 5m N of Boston. (OS Map 122; ref TF 345511.) Various services and operators from Boston to Sibsey, thence ½m (Tel: 01522 553135). *Boston 5m.*

⊘ St Albans Roman Wall
See Roman Wall.

♡ ⚙ ✿ Stokesay Castle
SHROPSHIRE (p. 217, 8G)
The finest medieval manor house in England, situated in peaceful countryside. The castle now stands in a picturesque group with its own splendid timber-framed Jacobean gate-house and the parish church.

● *Enjoy a fun day of Medieval Children's Entertainment, 4–5 May.*
Open 22 March–31 Oct: daily, 10am–6pm (6pm/dusk in Oct). 1 Nov–31 March: Wed–Sun, 10am–4pm (closed 24–26 Dec). Closed 1–2pm in winter.
Entry £2.75/£2.10/£1.40.
☎ 01588 672544
♦♦♦ P & *(gardens & great hall only)* ⊗ ♦ ☐ ■ (Refreshments, summer season only)
7m NW of Ludlow off A49. (OS Map 137; ref SO 436817.) Midland Red West 435 Shrewsbury–Ludlow (Tel: 0345 056 785). *Craven Arms 1m.*

Stokesay Castle

Sutton Scarsdale Hall

♡ ⊕ Sutton Scarsdale Hall

DERBYSHIRE
(pp. 214/217, 11K)
The dramatic hilltop shell of a great early 18th-century baroque mansion.

Open *10am–6pm/dusk, whichever is earlier.*
Entry *Free.*
🅿 ♿ ⊗
➲ *Between Chesterfield and Bolsover, 1½m S of Arkwright Town.*
(OS Map 120; ref SK 441690.)
🚌 *Stagecoach E Midland 48 Chesterfield–Bolsover (Tel: 01332 292200).*
🚉 *Chesterfield 5m.*

✝ Tattershall College

LINCOLNSHIRE
(p. 214, 11M)
Remains of a grammar school for church choristers, built in the mid-15th century by Ralph, Lord Cromwell, the builder of nearby Tattershall Castle.

Open *Any reasonable time. (Site managed by Heritage Trust of Lincolnshire.)*
Entry *Free.*
⊗
➲ *In Tattershall (off Market Place) 14m NE of Sleaford on A153.*
(OS Map 122; ref TF 213577.)
🚌 *Brylaine Boston–Woodhall Spa (passes close to BR Boston) (Tel: 01522 553135).*
🚉 *Ruskington 10m.*

⬆ Uffington Castle, White Horse and Dragon Hill

OXFORDSHIRE (p. 217; 6J)
A group of sites lying along the Ridgeway, an old prehistoric route. There is a large Iron Age camp enclosed within ramparts, a natural mound known as Dragon Hill and the spectacular White Horse, cut from turf to reveal chalk.

Open *Any reasonable time. (Site managed by the National Trust.)*
Entry *Free.*
🅿 ⊗
➲ *S of B4507, 7m W of Wantage. (OS Map 174; ref SU 301866.)*

⊘ Wall Roman Site (Letocetum)

STAFFORDSHIRE
(pp. 214/217, 9J)
The remains of a staging post, alongside Watling Street. Foundations of an inn and bath-house can be seen, and there is a display of finds in the site museum.

Open *22 March–31 Oct: daily, 10am–6pm (6pm/dusk in Oct). Closed 1–2pm.*
Entry *£1.50/£1.10/80p. National Trust members admitted free, but small charge on E.H. Special Events Days. (Site maintained and managed by English Heritage, and owned by the National Trust.)*
📞 *01543 480768*
🚹 🏠 ♿ ⊗ ♿ 🍴

Wall Roman Site: the bath-house

Off A5 at Wall near Lichfield.
(OS Map 139; ref SK 099067.)
🚃 *Shenstone 1½m.*

⏶ Wayland's Smithy

OXFORDSHIRE (p. 217, 6J)
Near to the Uffington White
Horse lies this evocative
Neolithic burial site,
surrounded by a small circle
of trees. It is an unusual site
in that two grave types lie one
upon the other.

Open Any reasonable time.
(Site managed by the
National Trust.)
Entry *Free.*
🐕

On the Ridgeway ¾m NE of
B4000 Ashbury–Lambourn road.
(OS Map 174; ref SU 281854.)

✝ Wenlock Priory
SHROPSHIRE
(p. 217, 9G)
The ruins of a large
Cluniac priory in an

A carved panel (above) from
Wenlock Priory (below)

attractive garden setting
featuring delightful topiary.
There are substantial
remains of the early
13th-century church and
Norman chapter house.

***Open** 22 March–31 Oct: daily,*
10am–6pm (6pm/dusk in Oct).
1 Nov–31 March: Wed–Sun,
10am–4pm (closed 24–26
Dec). Closed 1–2pm in winter.
***Entry** £2.20/£1.70/£1.10.*
✆ *01952 727466*

🅿 🎧 *(also available for the*
visually impaired, those with
learning difficulties, and in
French, German and Japanese)
🚻 🐕

In Much Wenlock.
(OS Map 127; ref SJ 625001.)
🚌 *Midland Red West 436/7*
Shrewsbury–Bridgnorth (passes
close to BR Shrewsbury)
(Tel: 0345 056 785).
🚃 *Telford Central 9m.*

✝ White Ladies Priory
SHROPSHIRE (p. 217, 9H)
The ruins of the late 12th-
century church of a small
priory of Augustinian
canonesses.

***Open** Any reasonable time.*
***Entry** Free.*
🐕

1m SW of Boscobel House
off unclassified road between
A41 and A5, 8m NW of
Wolverhampton.
(OS Map 127; ref SJ 826076.)
🚃 *Cosford 2½m.*

Wingfield Manor

⊙ Wigmore Castle

HEREFORD &
WORCESTER (p. 217, 8G)
Fortified since the 1060s, the
present ruins date from the
13th and 14th centuries. The
castle was dismantled during
the Civil War, and remains
very much as it was left then.

Open *The castle is undergoing
repairs and is not normally
open to the public. Any open
day will be announced in the
members' magazine,* Heritage
Today, *and the local press.*
Entry *Free.*
🚫

➡ *11m NW of Leominster,
14m SW of Ludlow off W
side of A4110.
(OS Map 137; ref SO 408693.)*
🚌 *Leominster 11m.*

♡✪⊙ Wingfield Manor

DERBYSHIRE
(pp. 214/217, 11J)
Huge, ruined, country mansion built in mid-15th century.
Mary Queen of Scots was
imprisoned here in 1569.
Though unoccupied since the
1770s, the late-Gothic Great
Hall and the 'High Tower' are
fine testaments to Wingfield in
its heyday. The manor has
been used as a film location
for *Peak Practice* and
Zeffirelli's *Jane Eyre.*

Open *22 March–31 Oct:
Wed–Sun, 10am–6pm*

*(6pm/dusk in Oct). 1 Nov–31
March: Wed–Sun, 10am–4pm
(closed 24–26 Dec). Closed
1–2pm. The manor incorpo-
rates a private working farm.
Visitors are requested to
respect the privacy of the owners and refrain from visiting
outside official opening hours.*
Entry *£2.75/£2.10/£1.40.*
🎧🏠♿🚫🔇 *(Great Hall and
grounds, steep approach 600
metres.* 🅿 *available by prior
arrangement only). Orientation leaflet available.*
☎ *01773 832060*
➡ *17m N of Derby, 11m S of
Chesterfield on B5035 ½m S of
South Wingfield. From M1
– Junc. 28, W on A38,
A615 (Matlock Road) at
Alfreton and turn onto
B5035 after 1½m.*

**Witley Court:
the Poseidon
fountain**

(OS Map 119; ref SK 374548.)
🚌 *Whites/Stagecoach
E Midland 140, 254 Matlock–
Alfreton (Tel: 01332 292200).*
🚉 *Alfreton 4m.*

♡✪ Witley Court

HEREFORD &
WORCESTER (p. 217, 8H)
Spectacular ruins of a once
great house. An earlier
Jacobean manor house was
converted in the 19th century
into a vast Italianate mansion
with porticoes by John Nash.
The adjoining church, by
James Gibbs, has a remarkable 18th-century baroque
interior. The gardens were
equally elaborate (William
Nesfield's 'Monster Work')
and contained immense stone
fountains, which still survive.
The largest, the Poseidon
Fountain, is being
restored to working
order.

Open 22 March–31 Oct: daily, 10am–6pm (6pm/dusk in Oct). 1 Nov–31 March: Wed–Sun, 10am–4pm (closed 24–26 Dec). Closed 1–2pm in winter. Special evening guided tours available during 1997; please telephone property for details.
***Entry** £2.75/£2.10/£1.40.*
01299 896636
(not managed by English Heritage) (exterior & grounds only, poor access up long, rough drive)
10m NW of Worcester on A443.
(OS Map 150; ref 769649.)
Yarranton 758 Worcester–Tenbury Wells (Passes close to BR Worcester Foregate Street) (Tel: 0345 125436)
Droitwich Spa 8½m.

Wrest Park Gardens

BEDFORDSHIRE (p.214, 7M)

Over 90 acres of wonderful gardens originally laid out in the early 18th century, including the Great Garden, with charming buildings and ornaments, and the delightfully intricate French Garden, with statues and fountain. The house, once the home of the de Grey family whose Mausoleum at Flitton is nearby, was inspired by 18th-century French chateaux. It now forms a delightful backdrop to the gardens.

Wroxeter Roman City

Commemorate Queen Victoria's Diamond Jubilee 100 years on at "Victoria's Glory", 21–22 June.
***Open** 22 March–31 Oct: weekends only, 10am–6pm (6pm/dusk in Oct). Last admission 5pm.*
***Entry** £2.75/£2.10/£1.40.*
01525 860152
¾m E of Silsoe off A6, 10m S of Bedford.
(OS Map 153; ref TL 093356.)
Stagecoach United Counties X1, X2, X52
BR Luton–Bedford to within ½m (Tel: 01604 20077).
Flitwick 4m.

Wroxeter Roman City

SHROPSHIRE (p. 217, 9G)

The excavated centre of the fourth largest city in Roman Britain, with impressive remains of the 2nd-century municipal baths.

Free Children's Activity Sheet available.
See "The Roman Army", legionary troops, artillery and cavalry, 17–18 May.
***Open** 22 March–31 Oct: daily, 10am–6pm (6pm/dusk in Oct). 1 Nov–31 March: Wed–Sun, 10am–4pm (closed 24–26 Dec). Closed 1–2pm in winter.*
***Entry** £2.75/£2.10/£1.40.*
01743 761330
At Wroxeter, 5m E of Shrewsbury on B4380.
(OS Map 126; ref SJ 568088.)
Williamsons X96, 96 Birmingham–Shrewsbury (passes close to BR Telford Central) (Tel: 0345 056 785).
Shrewsbury 5½m; Wellington Telford West 6m.

Wrest Park Gardens

THE NORTH

The wildness of the medieval North is reflected in the strength and vitality of its sites. Huge strongholds dominate the cities of York and Carlisle, while the region's breath-taking scenery can be seen best from mighty, imposing castle ruins at Beeston, Warkworth and Richmond. No less impressive are the monastic remains of Lindisfarne, Whitby and Rievaulx, all demonstrating the wealth and power of the ancient church. Most magnificent of all is Hadrian's Wall, the Roman defence that stretches across the country from the Solway Firth to the Tyne.

⊘ Aldborough Roman Town

NORTH YORKSHIRE
(p. 219, 14K)
The principal town of the Brigantes, the largest tribe in Roman Britain. The delight-fully located remains include parts of the Roman defences and two mosaic pavements. A museum displays Roman mosaic designs.

Aldborough Roman Town

Open 22 March–30 Sept: daily, 12–5pm.
Entry £1.40/£1.10/70p. Winter, grounds only, admission free.
(01423 322768
⍾⍾ (summer only) 🚻 🅿 🏧
➲ ¾m SE of Boroughbridge, on minor road off B6265 within 1m of junction of A1 and A6055. (OS Map 99; ref SE 405661.)
🚌 United 142 BR York–Ripon (Tel: 01325 468771).

⊘⛰ Ambleside Roman Fort

CUMBRIA (pp. 218/220, 15G)
The remains of this 1st- and 2nd-century fort were built to guard the Roman road from Brougham to Ravenglass.

Open Any reasonable time. (Site managed by the National Trust.)
Entry Free.
🚻
➲ 200 yds W of Waterhead car park, Ambleside. (OS Map 90; ref NY 376033.)
🚌 Stagecoach Cumberland 555, 599 W1 from BR Winder-mere (Tel: 01946 63222).
🚉 Windermere 5m.

⛰ Arthur's Round Table

CUMBRIA (pp. 218/220, 15G)
A prehistoric circular earthwork bounded by a ditch and an outer bank.

Open Any reasonable time.
Entry Free.
♿ 🚻
➲ At Eamont Bridge, 1m S of Penrith. (OS Map 90; ref NY 523284.)
🚉 Penrith 1½m.

⊘ Auckland Castle Deer House

Bishop Auckland, COUNTY DURHAM (pp. 218/220, 16J)
A charming building erected in 1760 in the park of the Bishops of Durham so that deer could shelter and find food.

Open Park opening times 22 March–30 Sept: daily,

Aydon Castle

10am–6pm. 1 Oct–31 March:
daily, 10am–4pm (closed
24–26 Dec).
Entry Free.

➲ In Auckland Park,
Bishop Auckland, N
of town centre on A68.
(OS Map 93; ref NZ 216305.)
From surrounding areas
(Tel: 0191 383 3337).
Bishop Auckland 1m.

◐ ♡ Aydon Castle
NORTHUMBERLAND
(p. 220, 17H)
One of the finest fortified
manor houses in England,
built in the late 13th century.
Situated in a position of great
natural beauty, its remarkably
intact state is due to its
conversion to a farmhouse
in the 17th century.

Open 22 March–31 Oct: daily,
10am–6pm (6pm/dusk in Oct).
Closed 1–2pm.
Entry £1.80/£1.40/90p.
✆ 01434 632450
☐ ♦♦ P ♿ (ground floor)

Barnard Castle

➲ 1m NE of Corbridge, on
minor road off B6321 or A68.
(OS Map 87; ref NZ 002663.)
Corbridge 4m – approach
by bridleparth from W side of
Aydon Road, immediately N of
Corbridge bypass.

◑ Baguley Hall
GREATER MANCHESTER
(pp. 217/218, 11H)
A medieval timber-framed
hall house dating from the
14th century, with 18th- and
19th-century additions. An
extensive programme of
repair is being carried out,
with access on advertised
open days only.

Open Please ring 0191 261
1585 for details.
Entry Free.

➲ 6m S of Manchester, in
Hall Lane, Baguley, near
Wythenshawe (E of junction 3
of M56, off A560).
(OS Map 109; ref SJ 815893.)
Frequent from surround-
ing areas (Tel: 0161 228 7811).
Gatley 2½m.

◎ Barnard Castle
COUNTY DURHAM
(pp. 218/220, 15H)
The substantial remains of
this large castle stand on a
rugged escarpment over-
looking the River Tees. You
can still see parts of the 14th-
century Great Hall and the
cylindrical 12th-century tower.

Open 22 March–31 Oct: daily,
10am–6pm (6pm/dusk in Oct).
1 Nov–31 March: Wed–Sun,
10am–4pm (closed 24–26
Dec). Closed 1–2pm in winter.
Entry £2.00/£1.50/£1.00.
✆ 01833 638212
♿ ⛟ ♦♦ (in town) ❀ ☐ ♫
➲ In Barnard Castle.
(OS Map 92; ref NZ 049165.)
United 75/A, X75
Darlington–Barnard Castle
(passes close to BR Darlington)
(Tel: 01325 468771).

Beeston Castle

☯♡ Beeston Castle

CHESHIRE (pp. 217/218, 11G)
Standing majestically on
sheer, rocky crags which
fall sharply away from the
castle walls, Beeston has
possibly the most stunning
views of the surrounding
countryside of any castle in
England and the rock has a
history which stretches back
over 2,500 years.

❋ *Experience the history*
of Viking and Saxon life
and see a re-enactment of a
ferocious battle between
them, 28–29 June.
❋ *Free Children's Activity*
Sheet available.
Open *22 March–31 Oct: daily,*
10am–6pm (6pm/dusk in Oct).
1 Nov–31 March: daily,

10am–4pm (closed 24–26 Dec).
Entry *£2.50/£1.90/£1.30.*
☏ *01829 260464*
🏻🅿️🐾♿🅣🅒🗓
➲ *11m SE of Chester on minor*
road off A49 or A41.
(OS Map 117; ref SJ 537593.)
🚌 *Cheshire Bus C83, L2 from*
Chester (Tel: 01244 602666).
🚉 *Chester 10m.*

☯☯❋♡ Belsay Hall, Castle and Gardens

NORTHUMBERLAND
(p. 220, 17J)
See pp 144–5 for full details.

☯ Berwick-upon-Tweed Barracks

NORTHUMBERLAND
(p. 220, 19H)
Among the earliest purpose-
built barracks, these have
changed very little since

1717. The barracks house
'By Beat of Drum', an exhibition which re-creates scenes
such as a British infantryman's
life in a barrack room, the
Museum of the King's Own
Scottish Borderers, the
Borough Museum with its
imaginative exhibitions and
part of the Burrell Collection.

❋ *A lively exhibition, 'By*
Beat of Drum'. Imaginative
and colourful display at
Borough Museum.
Open *22 March–31 Oct: daily,*
10am–6pm (6pm/dusk in Oct).
1 Nov–31 March: Wed–Sun,
10am–4pm (closed 24–26
Dec). Closed 1–2pm in winter.
(Museum of Kings Own Scottish
Borderers open Mon–Sat,
10am–4pm.)
Entry *£2.30/£1.70/£1.20.*
☏ *01289 304493*

Berwick Barracks: Ravensdown

† P *(in town)* 🐕 🅦 Ⓔ 🗂
➲ *On the Parade, off Church St,
Berwick town centre.
(OS Map 75; ref NT 994535.)*
🚌 *From surrounding areas
(Tel: 01670 533128).*
🚉 *Berwick-upon-Tweed ¼ m.*

Berwick-upon-Tweed Castle
NORTHUMBERLAND
(p. 220, 19H)
Remains of 12th-century castle.

Open *Any reasonable time.*
Entry *Free.*
🐕
➲ *Adjacent to Berwick railway
station, W of town centre,
accessible also from river bank.
(OS Map 75; ref NT 994535.)*
🚌 🚉 *see* **Berwick-upon-Tweed Barracks**.

Berwick-upon-Tweed Main Guard
NORTHUMBERLAND
(p. 220, 19H)
Georgian Guard House near
the quay. An exhibition cele-
brates the 150th anniversary
of the railway coming to
Berwick-upon Tweed. *The
Story of a Border Garrison
Town* is a permanent display
of the history of the town and
its fortifications.

Open *28–31 March, 3–5 May
24–26 May, 1 June–30 Sept:*

*daily, 1pm–5pm (closed Wed).
(Site managed by Berwick
Civic Society.)*
Entry *Free.*
♿
➲ *Surrounding Berwick town
centre on N bank of River Tweed.
(OS Map 75; ref NT 994535.)*
🚌 🚉 *see* **Berwick-upon-Tweed Barracks**.

Berwick Ramparts

Berwick-upon-Tweed Ramparts
NORTHUMBERLAND
(p. 220, 19H)
Remarkably complete,
16th-century town
fortifications, with gateways
and projecting bastions.

Open *Any reasonable time.*
Entry *Free.*
♿ († & P *in town centre*) 🐕
➲ *Surrounding Berwick
town centre on N bank
of River Tweed.
(OS Map 75; ref NT 994535.)*
🚌 🚉 *see* **Berwick-upon-Tweed Barracks**.

Berwick Barracks Museum

BELSAY HALL AND GARDENS

The beautiful honey-coloured stone from which Belsay Hall is built came from its own quarries in the grounds. Those quarries have since become the unusual setting for one of a series of spectacular gardens. They are the property's finest feature, deservedly listed Grade I in the Register of Gardens. The house itself was innovative, when built between 1810 and 1817 in a style derived directly from Ancient Greece.

The thirty acres of magnificent landscaped grounds and gardens are Belsay's particular glory. The quarry gardens and the Cragwood Walk are the most special features. Sir Charles Monck, who built the present hall, saw the potential of the stone quarries, and introduced many rare and fine specimens into them to make a garden.

Succeeding generations extended the quarry and added to its planting. They made a green gorge, its sheer walls hung with exotic plants and the floor dotted with ferns. It is an adventure in itself to explore its paths and shady corners. Rhododendrons are among Belsay's great delights; many beautiful examples grow in the quarry, as well as in the

A quiet corner of the garden

woodland and rhododendron gardens created later in the 19th century. These wilder areas are separated by a ha-ha ditch from the more formal

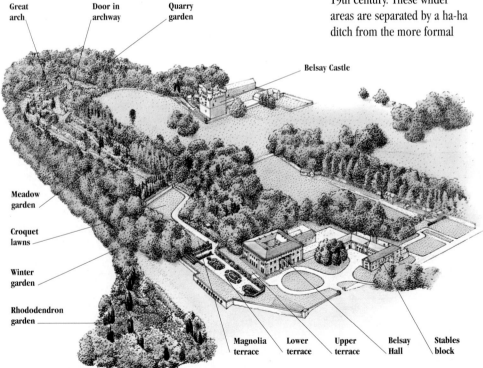

144

terraces at the front of the Hall, with their beds of roses, lilies, lavender and other fragrant and brightly-coloured plants.

English Heritage has made great efforts to return Belsay's gardens, which suffered from neglect after World War II, to their former state, to complement the great house.

Sir Charles Monck built the Hall to his own designs in 1810 after studying ancient Greek architecture. Inside and out, Belsay Hall has a severity that is softened by its garden setting. It resembles a Greek temple, raised on a podium with giant columns at the entrance and pilasters on the walls.

The castle preceded the house. Originally built in the 14th century, with a new range attached in 1614, its L-shaped plan provided special protection to the entrance staircase and it was crowned with a prominent roof display of defensive towers and battlements. The castle was abandoned by the family in 1817 when the new Hall was built.

Belsay has much to offer: the splendour of the ancient castle, a house of key importance in the Greek Revival of the 19th century, and the glorious gardens. Plants are on sale in summer.

The south side of Belsay Hall

The quarry garden in spring

The pure Greek Classicism of the present Hall

Open *22 March–31 Oct: daily, 10am–6pm (6pm/dusk in Oct). 1 Nov–31 March: daily, 10am–4pm (closed 24–26 Dec).*
Entry *£3.50/£2.60/£1.80*
✆ 01661 881636
(grounds, first floor only; toilets) ('Belsay Hall Tearoom'; normally open summer only)
In Belsay, Northumberland (p.220, 17J), 14m NW of Newcastle on A696. (OS Map 88; ref NZ 088785.)
Vasey's/Snaith's 808 from Newcastle (Tel: 01670 533128); Northumbria 508 from BR Newcastle (summer Suns only); National Express Newcastle–Edinburgh to within 1m. (Tel: any National Express agent).
Morpeth 10m.

⊕ Bessie Surtees House

TYNE & WEAR
(pp. 219/220, 16J)

Two 16th- and 17th-century merchants' houses. One is a remarkable and rare example of Jacobean domestic architecture. An exhibition about these buildings is on the first floor.

Open *Weekdays only 10am–4pm (closed Bank Holidays).*
Entry *Free.*
☏ *0191 261 1585*
⭗ ⊗
➲ *41–44 Sandhill, Newcastle. (OS Map 88; ref NZ 252639.)*
🚌 *From surrounding areas (Tel: 0191 232 5325).*
🚉 *Newcastle ½m.*
Metro: Central Station ½m.

⊚ Bishop Auckland Deer House

See Auckland Castle Deer House.

Bessie Surtees House

Brinkburn Priory

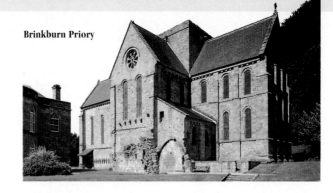

⊜⊚ Black Middens Bastle House

NORTHUMBERLAND
(p. 220, 17H)

A 16th-century two-storey defended farmhouse, set in splendid walking country.

Open *Any reasonable time.*
Entry *Free.*
🅿 ⚒ ⊗
➲ *200yds N of minor road 7m NW of Bellingham; access also along minor road from A68. (OS Map 80; ref NY 774900.)*

⊚⊜ Bow Bridge

Barrow-in-Furness,
CUMBRIA (p. 218, 14F)

Late medieval stone bridge across Mill Beck, carrying a route to nearby Furness Abbey.

Open *Any reasonable time.*
Entry *Free.*
⊗
➲ *½m N of Barrow-in-Furness, on minor road off A590 near Furness Abbey. (OS Map 96; ref SD 224715.)*
🚌 *Stagecoach Cumberland 6/A Barrow-in-Furness–*
Dalton, to within ¾m (Tel: 01946 63222).
🚉 *Barrow-in-Furness 1½m.*

⊙⊚ Bowes Castle

COUNTY DURHAM
(p. 218, 15H)

Massive ruins of Henry II's tower keep, three storeys high and set within the earthworks of a Roman fort.

Open *Any reasonable time.*
Entry *Free.*
⊗
➲ *In Bowes Village just off A66, 4m W of Barnard Castle. (OS Map 92; ref NY 992135.)*
🚌 *OK X74 Darlington–Carlisle, Primrose X69 from Newcastle, Burrell's/United 72/9 from Barnard Castle. (Tel: 0191 383 3337).*

✚ Brinkburn Priory

NORTHUMBERLAND
(p. 220, 17J)

This late 12th-century church is a fine example of early Gothic architecture, almost perfectly preserved, and is

set in a lovely spot beside
the River Coquet.

Open *22 March–30 Sept:*
daily, 12pm–5pm.
Entry *£1.40/£1.10/70p.*
(*01665 570628*
◫ ⬭ *(400 yds from* ◫ *)* ◉
➲ *4½m SE of Rothbury*
off B6344.
(OS Map 81; ref NZ 116984.)
▭▭ *Northumbria 516*
Morpeth–Rothbury to within
½m (Tel: 01670 533128).
▦ *Acklington 10m.*

◎ ⊛ Brodsworth Hall
SOUTH YORKSHIRE
(p. 214, 12K)
See pp 148–51 for full details.

◔ Brough Castle
CUMBRIA (p. 218/220, 15H)
Dating from Roman times,
the 12th-century keep
replaced an earlier stronghold destroyed by the Scots
in 1174. It was restored by
Lady Anne Clifford in the
17th century.

Open *Any reasonable time.*
Entry *Free.*
⊛ ◫
➲ *8m SE of Appleby S of A66.*
(OS Map 91; ref NY 791141.)
▭▭ *From BR Kirkby Stephen–*
Brough (Tel: 01228 606000).
▦ *Kirkby Stephen 6m.*

◑ Brougham Castle
CUMBRIA (pp. 218/220, 15G)
These impressive ruins on the
banks of the River Eamont
include an early 13th-century
keep and later buildings. Its
one-time owner Lady Anne
Clifford restored the castle in
the 17th century. There is an
exhibition of Roman tomb-
stones from the nearby fort.

Open *22 March–31 Oct: daily,*
10am–6pm (6pm/dusk in Oct).
Entry *£1.60/£1.20/80p.*
(*01768 862488*
◫ ⓖ *(excluding keep)* ⊛ ⬭
➲ *1½m SE of Penrith on minor*
road off A66.
(OS Map 90; ref NY 537290.)
▦ *Penrith 2m.*

◉ Burton Agnes Manor House
EAST RIDING OF
YORKSHIRE (p. 219, 14L)
Rare example of a Norman
house, altered and encased
in brick in the 17th and
18th centuries.

Open *Any reasonable time.*
(The adjoining Burton Agnes
Hall and Gardens are privately
owned and occupied, and not
managed by English Heritage.)
Entry *Free.*
⊛
➲ *In Burton Agnes village, 5m*
SW of Bridlington on A166.
(OS Map 101; ref TA 103633.)
▭▭ *E Yorkshire 744*
BR York–Bridlington
(Tel: 01482 327146).
▦ *Nafferton 5m.*

The Countess
Pillar (right)
at Brougham
Castle (below) –
see also p.153

BRODSWORTH HALL

One of England's most beautiful Victorian country houses, Brodsworth Hall has survived almost completely intact since the 1860s – an extraordinary time warp of richly marbled walls, Axminster carpets and family portraits. Opened for the first time in 1995, Brodsworth Hall and gardens offer visitors a breathtaking journey through the passage of time. When bequeathed to English Heritage, conservation policy was aimed at preserving the Hall's faded grandeur. In the long-abandoned kitchen, visitors can readily picture how meals were really made in the age of Mrs Beeton. And deep in the cluttered remains of the servants' wing, it is easy to imagine life below stairs, with all the benefits and drawbacks that such an insular Victorian existence brought.

Looking east towards the house from the flower garden (left)

When Charles Thellusson acquired Brodsworth in the early 1860s he immediately commissioned Chevalier Casentini, whom he had met in Italy, to build him a suitably impressive house. The result is formal, Italianate, four-square and lacks any fanciful detail. Casentini's designs were executed under the supervision of a little-known English architect, Philip Wilkinson. It is said that Casentini never came to Yorkshire to view what he had designed, fearing the cold, and a setting wholly different from the pastoral landscape and blue skies he had drawn.

At the same time, a new garden incorporating both formal and informal features was created, all contained within magnificent parkland. If the exterior of the house

One of the marble greyhounds that flank the steps down from the south front of the house (left)

Watercolour of the south front of Brodsworth showing only minor differences from the house as it was built (below)

The flower garden with its symmetrical beds cut into the turf (above). Marble statues (left) feature in the gardens as well as inside the house

seems a little pompous, the interior is Brodsworth's chief glory. The entrance hall, with its gold, red and marbled walls, is a prelude to the splendours of the inner halls and reception rooms.

The colours provide a dramatic backdrop to another of the house's remarkable features, the succession of white marble statues with typically Victorian themes. Casentini created a grand processional route through the house from the entrance hall, via the soaring height of the top-lit staircase, to the pillared south hall. The ceremonial feel is emphasized by the poise of the statues. Of all the sculptures, Argenti's 'Sleeping Venus' is particularly memorable, lying beneath the huge painted-glass internal window at the end of the hall which was inserted by Wilkinson in order to lighten what would otherwise have been the impenetrable

gloom of Casentini's original design. With its colourful garlands and playful cherubs, it provides a busy foil to the statue's lines.

Rich decorative schemes appear everywhere in the house: in the grand reception rooms, bedrooms and private quarters. The drawing room, with a dividing screen of Corinthian columns, red silk damask on the walls, chandeliers and gilding, is a grand monument to Thellusson's ambitions. The dining room, intended as much for show as for eating, contains some of the finest paintings in the house. Away from the finery of the reception rooms are the more intimate spaces of the library and morning room.

Nymph going to Bathe (left) by Giuseppe Lazzarini, in the South Hall (below)

The drawing room (left) with many of the original furnishings from Lapworths

Each has original wallpaper, a hand-painted pattern of roses and trellises resembling leather wallcoverings.

When Brodsworth was first built and occupied, it amply fulfilled its role as a grand residence. Parties were conducted in sumptuous style; and in the evenings the gentlemen would relax in the billiard room, which has survived remarkably intact. By the mid-19th century a billiard room was considered an essential part of a country house, and Brodsworth's retains its original massive table, along with the leather-bound book in which scores have been recorded since the 1880s.

The bedrooms have always been identified by a simple numbering system. Although much of their original decoration has been lost through frequent refurbishment, many pieces of mahogany furniture provided by Lapworths remain, including beds, marble-topped wash-stands, chests of drawers and armchairs.

The dining room (right) with many family portraits including one of Charles Thelluson's father and grandmother, Charles and Sabine, painted in 1807 (above)

The servants were housed in a wing abutting the house's main block. From the 1860s until about 1918 there were about ten female servants and several male. Their domain, the Victorian kitchen, is one of the most delightful features. Its 'Eagle Range' by Farr and Sons of Doncaster and its grained dressers still contain a vast range of cooking utensils.

Library with the 1725 picture of Peter Thelluson's mother (right)

Gradually, after World War I, with spiralling costs, parts of the house were shut away and, almost inadvertently, house and contents were preserved for the future. The kitchen too was gradually abandoned, although many of its original contents remain and can still be seen today. Brodsworth's history is written everywhere in its decoration: in the carpets in the library, laid one upon the other as each wore out; the High Victorian taste; the grandeur; the marbling; the painted decorative effects; and the sculptures. The gardens are now being coaxed from their very overgrown state. They include croquet lawns and a large formal flower garden; a quarry garden and a formal rose garden. The house itself has emerged from its slumber. Brodsworth, the grand Victorian sleeping beauty, has now awakened.

The billiard room

◉ *Exhibitions at Brodsworth include 'Family Life', 'Serving the House' and 'The Gardens'.*
◉ *Free Children's Activity Sheet available.*

Open 22 March–26 Oct: Tues–Sun & Bank Holidays, 1pm–6pm (6pm/dusk in Oct). Last admission 5pm. Gardens open 12 noon. 8 Nov–22 March: Sat–Sun: 11am–4pm (gardens, shop & tearooms only). Guided tours are available from 10am for pre-booked parties.

Entry £4.50/£3.40/£2.30. Gardens only £2.50/£1.90/£1.00; winter £1.50/£1.00/free
✆ *01302 722598*
Ⓘ *(colour)* 🛍 🍴 *('Brodsworth Hall Tearoom')* ♨ ♿ *(house and formal gardens)*
⚥ 🅿 Ⓔ ✗ *Pushchairs, prams and back carriers for babies are regrettably not permitted in the house.*
➲ *In Brodsworth, South Yorkshire (p. 214, 12K), off A635 Barnsley Road, from junction 37 of A1(M). (OS Map 111; ref SE 507071.)* 🚌 *Yorkshire Traction 211 Doncaster–Barnsley; Yorkshire Rider 497/8 Doncaster–Wakefield (Tel 0114 276 8688).* 🚃 *South Elmsall 4m; Moorthorpe 4½m; Doncaster 5½m*

The kitchen, abandoned since 1919, showing a part of the large collection of pots and pans

Byland Abbey

NORTH YORKSHIRE
(p. 219, 14K)
A hauntingly lovely ruin set in peaceful meadows in the shadow of the Hambleton Hills. It illustrates the later development of Cistercian churches, including the beautiful floor tiles.

Open *22 March–31 Oct: daily, 10am–6pm (6pm/dusk in Oct). Closed 1–2pm.*
Entry *£1.40/£1.10/70p.*
01347 868614
(including toilets)

2m S of A170 between Thirsk and Helmsley, near Coxwold village. (OS Map 100; ref SE 549789.)

Byland Abbey: the arch at the West front

Carlisle Castle

CUMBRIA (pp. 218/212, 16G)
See pp 154–5 for full details.

Castlerigg Stone Circle

Castlerigg Stone Circle

CUMBRIA (pp. 218/220, 15F)
Possibly one of the earliest Neolithic stone circles in Britain, its 33 stones stand in a beautiful setting.

Open *Any reasonable time. (Site managed by the National Trust.)*
Entry *Free.*

1½m E of Keswick. (OS Map 90; ref NY 293236.)
Stagecoach Cumberland X5 BR Penrith–Workington, to within ½m (Tel: 01946 63222).
Penrith 16m.

Chester Castle: Agricola Tower and Castle Walls

CHESHIRE (pp. 217/218, 11G)
Set in the angle of the city walls, this 12th-century tower contains a fine vaulted chapel.

Open *Castle walls open any reasonable time; cell block open 22 March–30 Sept: daily, 10am–6pm. 1 Oct–31 March: daily, 10am–4pm (closed 24–26 Dec).*
Entry *Free.*
(parts)
Access via Assizes Court car park on Grosvenor St. (OS Map 117; ref SJ 405658.)
From surrounding areas (Tel: 01244 602666).
Chester 1m.

Chester Roman Amphitheatre

CHESHIRE (pp. 217/218, 11G)
The largest Roman amphitheatre in Britain, partially excavated. Used for entertainment and military training by the 20th Legion, based at the fortress of Deva.

Open *Any reasonable time.*
Entry *Free.*
(no access to amphitheatre floor)

➲ *On Vicars Lane beyond Newgate, Chester.*
(OS Map 117; ref SJ 404660.)
🚌 *From surrounding areas (Tel: 01244 602666).*
🚉 *Chester ³⁄₄m.*

⊙ Clifford's Tower
CITY OF YORK (pp. 219,13K)
See pp 158–9 for full details.

⊖ Clifton Hall
CUMBRIA (pp. 218/220, 15G)
The surviving tower block of a 15th-century manor house.

Open *Any reasonable time (closed 24–26 Dec).*
Entry *Free.*
🐾

➲ *In Clifton next to Clifton Hall Farm, 2m S of Penrith on A6.*
(OS Map 90; ref NY 530271.)
🚉 *Penrith 2¹⁄₂m.*

⊙ Conisbrough Castle
SOUTH YORKSHIRE
(pp. 214/219, 12K)
The spectacular white circular keep of a 12th-century castle. It is the oldest circular keep in England and one of the finest medieval buildings. An exciting audio-visual presentation evokes a dramatic episode in the

Conisbrough Castle

castle's history. There is also a visitor centre and exhibition.

Open *22 March–30 Sept: daily, 10am–5pm (6pm weekends and Bank Holidays). 1 Oct–31 March: daily, 10am–4pm (5pm weekends, closed 24–25 Dec). (Castle managed by the Ivanhoe Trust.)*
Entry *£2.75/£1.75/£1.25/£6.25 (evening tours. English Heritage members admitted free. Concessionary rates for group bookings of over 25 people.)*
📞 *01709 863329*
🅿 ♿ *(limited access)* ✖
➲ *NE of Conisbrough town centre off A630, 4¹⁄₂m SW of Doncaster. (OS Map 111; ref SK 515989.)*
🚌 *From surrounding areas (Tel: 01709 515151).*
🚉 *Conisbrough ¹⁄₂m.*

⊖ Countess Pillar
Brougham, CUMBRIA
(pp. 218/220, 15G)
An unusual monument, bearing sundials and family crests, erected in 1656 by Lady Anne Clifford to commemorate her parting with her mother in 1616.

Open *Any reasonable time.*
Entry *Free.*
🐾

➲ *1m SE of Brougham on A66. (OS Map 90; ref NY 546289.)*
🚉 *Penrith 2¹⁄₂m.*

153

CARLISLE CASTLE

Sitting proudly on the highest point above the River Eden, Carlisle Castle has guarded the western end of the Anglo-Scottish border for over nine centuries. It was first built after William II relieved Carlisle of two centuries of Scottish domination in 1092. Since then it has often been the scene of turbulent conflict between the two nations, being fought over fairly constantly until the union of the crowns in 1603. It then fell into Scottish hands again during the Civil War and the Jacobite Rising 100 years later.

Henry I, who built the stone keep at Carlisle

Today, Carlisle Castle offers the visitor many insights into its violent past, including the legendary 'licking stones' in its dungeon, where parched Jacobite prisoners found enough moisture to stay alive, only to be barbarically executed on Gallow's Hill. The castle is now host to an exhibition about Bonnie Prince Charlie and the Jacobite Rising of 1745.

The views from the massive keep are magnificent, stretching from the Lakes to the Pennines, from the Solway Firth to the Grampians.

Carlisle Castle's military heritage stretches back to the forging of the English and Scottish nations. Briefly the seat of Royal government while Parliament met at Carlisle in 1306–7, it has played host to kings down the centuries, been attacked by both Robert the Bruce and Bonnie Prince Charlie, and acted as a prison for Mary Queen of Scots following her abdication in 1568.

The imposing Norman keep and curtain wall date from 1157, when Carlisle and its castle were handed back to Henry II by the Scots. The keep remains the nucleus of the castle to this day, while almost every other part has been remodelled, repaired or rebuilt.

A helmet (above) from the Civil War

The outer gatehouse (right), built about 1167, altered 1378–83

The outer gatehouse (above)

Throughout its long history, Carlisle has never lost its purpose as a fortress and today it remains the headquarters of the King's Own Royal Border Regiment and houses the Regimental Museum.

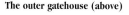

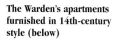

The Warden's apartments furnished in 14th-century style (below)

❦ *See Carlisle Castle as it was in 1542 with courtiers, soldiers and living history presentations, 19–21 Aug.*
❦ *Free Children's Activity Sheet available.*
❦ *Fine views from the keep and rampart walk.*
Open *22 March–31 Oct: daily, 9.30am–6pm (6pm/dusk in Oct). 1 Nov–31 March: daily, 10am–4pm (closed 24–26 Dec).*
Entry £2.70/£2.00/£1.40.
✆ *01228 591922*
🅿 *(disabled only). Car parking in nearby city car parks (sign-posted)* ♿ *(except interiors of buildings)* ♟⌂✗♨⊙
Guided tours available at a small extra charge. Tours are daily, June–Oct; weekends in May. Please telephone for times.
➲ *In Carlisle, Cumbria (pp. 218/212, 16G). (OS Map 85; ref NY 397563.)*
🚌 *From surrounding areas (Tel: 01228 606000).*
🚂 *Carlisle ½m.*

Graffiti by medieval prisoners

⊖ Derwentcote Steel Furnace

COUNTY DURHAM
(pp. 218/220, 16J)
Built in the 18th century, the earliest and most complete steel-making furnace to have survived. Closed in the 1870s, it has now been restored and opened to the public.

Open 22 March–30 Sept: 1st & 3rd Sunday of every month, 1pm–5pm.
Entry Free.
℃ 01207 562573
P ⊛
➲ *10m SW of Newcastle on A694 between Rowland's Gill and Hamsterley.*
(OS Map 88; ref NZ 131566.)
🚌 *Northern 745 Newcastle-upon-Tyne–Consett (Tel: 0191 232 5325).*
🚆 *Blaydon 7m.*

⊖♡ Dunstanburgh Castle

NORTHUMBERLAND
(p. 220, 18J)
An easy coastal walk leads to the eerie skeleton of this wonderful 14th-century castle, which is sited on a basalt crag more than 30 metres (100 feet) high. Dunstanburgh is noted for its seabirds, wildlife and flowers.

Dunstanburgh Castle

The surviving ruins include the large gatehouse, which later became the keep, and curtain walls.

Open 22 March–31 Oct: daily, 10am–6pm (6pm/dusk in Oct). 1 Nov–31 March: Wed–Sun, 10am–4pm (closed 24–26 Dec). Closed 1–2pm in winter.
Entry £1.60/£1.20/80p. National Trust members admitted free. (Site owned by the National Trust, maintained and managed by English Heritage.)
℃ 01665 576231
🖼 ⊛ P *(in Craster village – charge payable)*
➲ *8m NE of Alnwick, on foot-paths from Craster or Embleton. (OS Map 75; ref NU 258220.)*

Easby Abbey

Northumbria 501
Alnwick–Berwick-upon-Tweed
(passes close to BR Berwick-
upon-Tweed) with connections
from Newcastle (passing Tyne
& Wear Metro Haymarket),
alight Craster, 1½m
(Tel: 01670 533128).
Chathill 7m, Alnmouth 8m.

Easby Abbey
NORTH YORKSHIRE
(pp. 218/220, 15J)
Substantial remains of the
medieval abbey buildings stand
in a beautiful setting by the
River Swale near Richmond.
The abbey can be reached by
a pleasant riverside walk
from Richmond Castle.

Open 22 March–31 Oct: daily,
10am–6pm (6pm/dusk in Oct).
Entry £1.20/90p/60p. Please
ring regional office on 0191
261 1585 for further details.
➔ 1m SE of Richmond off B6271.
(OS Map 92; ref NZ 185003.)
United X27/8, 27/B, 28/A
BR Darlington–Richmond
(passes close to BR Darlington)
thence 1½m (Tel: 01325 468771).

Edlingham Castle
NORTHUMBERLAND
(p. 220, 18J)
Set in a beautiful valley, this
complex ruin has defensive
features spanning the
13th–15th centuries.

Etal Castle: the gatehouse
and keep (right) and
exhibition (below)

Open Any reasonable time.
Entry Free.
➔ At E end of Edlingham
village, on minor road off
B6341 6m SW of Alnwick
(OS Map 81; ref NU 115092).
Alnmouth 9m.

Egglestone Abbey
COUNTY DURHAM
(pp. 218/220, 15J)
Picturesque remains of a 12th-
century abbey. Substantial
parts of the church and abbey
buildings remain.

Open Any reasonable time.
Entry Free.
➔ 1m S of Barnard Castle on
minor road off B6277.
(OS Map 92; ref NZ 062151.)
United 75/A, X75 Darling-
ton–Barnard Castle (passes
close to BR Darlington), thence
1½m, or 79 Richmond–Barnard
Castle, thence ½m
(Tel: 01325 468771).

Etal Castle
NORTHUMBERLAND
(p. 220, 19H)
A 14th-century border castle
located in the picturesque
village of Etal. There is a
major award-winning exhibition about the castle, border
warfare and the Battle of
Flodden, which took place
nearby in 1513.

**A personal stereo tour
guides you through this
dramatic exhibition.**
Open 22 March–31 Oct: daily,
10am–6pm (6pm/dusk in Oct).
Entry £2.30/£1.70/£1.20.
(01890 820332
➔ In Etal village, 10m SW
of Berwick.
(OS Map 75; ref NT 925394.)
Peter Park 267
Berwick-upon-Tweed–Wooler
(Tel: 01670 533128).
Berwick-upon-Tweed 10½m.

CLIFFORD'S TOWER

Standing high on its mound in the city of York, Clifford's Tower is one of the few vestiges of the pair of castles built by William the Conqueror after his victory in 1066. William urgently needed to establish his control in the northern counties, where the local people had even welcomed a Danish force in 1069; in the ensuing struggle the city was set alight and the Norman garrisons overwhelmed. York's castles were the stepping stones for the Normans to terrorise the North. They both had wooden keeps, with Clifford's Tower being rebuilt in stone in the 13th century. York was often the seat of government in the 13th and 14th centuries, so the castle would have been magnificently appointed.

Today, the tower stands as a proud symbol of the might of the medieval English kings.

Part of a Viking sword found in York

The mound on which Clifford's Tower sits was constructed in 1069–70 from ingenious layers of gravel, clay, stone and timber to overcome the problems of waterlogged land. The original wooden keep was burnt down in 1190, when members of the Jewish community were sheltering there from a violent mob. Many of the Jews took their own lives; others died in the flames they lit; and those who finally surrendered were massacred.

The present tower, a rare and imaginative design of a quatrefoil of interlocking circles, was started in the mid-13th century by Henry III, but not completed until the early 14th century. It is thought to take its name from Roger Clifford, leader of the Lancastrian force defeated at Boroughbridge in 1322, who was hanged in chains from the keep.

The tower survived severe floods and fire during the following three centuries, and even an attempt by one of its gaolers, when it was used as a prison in the late 16th century, to demolish the tower and sell off the stone.

The south face and entrance of Clifford's Tower

A reconstruction of how Clifford's Tower may have looked in the late 13th century

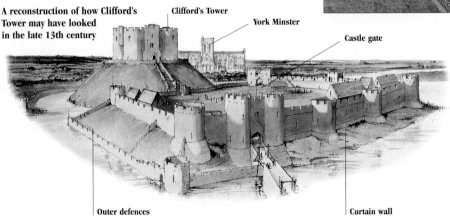

Clifford's Tower

York Minster

Castle gate

Outer defences

Curtain wall

An 1807 engraving of Clifford's Tower

Roman stone coffin from the York Castle site

The castle survived the first Civil War intact, being first garrisoned by Royalists and then falling into Parliamentary hands after the Battle of Marston Moor in 1644. The rightful owners claimed it back following the war, but it was only handed over after it had been partially destroyed by a fire, probably started deliberately, in 1648. It has remained a shell to this day, looking down from its steep mound and offering magnificent views of the city of York spread out below.

Plan of Clifford's Tower showing its innovative geometrical shape

⊕ *Tactile model with Braille text.*
Open *22 March–31 Oct: daily, 9.30am–6pm (6pm/dusk in Oct). 1 Nov–31 March: daily, 10am–4pm (closed 24–26 Dec)*
Entry *£1.60/£1.20/80p*
☎ *01904 646940*
🅿 *(city council; charge payable)* ⊗ ⓘ
➲ *In Tower St.*
(OS Map 105; ref SE 605515.)
🚌 *From surrounding areas (Tel: 01904 624161).*
🚉 *York 1m.*

The River Ouse (below) divided the sites of York's two castles

Furness Abbey

♿ 🅿 🅖 🅔 🅜
➲ 1½m N of Barrow-
in-Furness, on minor
road off A590.
(OS Map 96; ref SD 218717.)
🚌 Stagecoach Cumberland
6/A Barrow-in-Furness–
Dalton, to within ½m
(Tel: 01946 63222).
🚃 Barrow-in-Furness 2m.

🅶 ⊕ Gainsthorpe Medieval Village

NORTH LINCOLNSHIRE
(pp. 214/219, 12L)
Originally discovered and
still best seen from the air,
this hidden village comprises
earthworks of peasant
houses, gardens and streets.

Open Any reasonable time.
Entry Free.
🚽
➲ On minor road W of A15
S of Hibaldstow 5m SW of
Brigg (no directional signs).
(OS Map 112; ref SK 955012.)
🚃 Kirton Lindsey 3m.

✝ Gisborough Priory

REDCAR & CLEVELAND
(pp. 219/220, 15K)
An Augustinian priory. The
remains also include the
gatehouse and the east end
of an early 14th-century
church.

Open 22 March–30 Sept:
daily, 10am–5pm. 1 Oct–31
March: Tues–Sun, 10am–4pm

✝ Finchale Priory

 COUNTY DURHAM
(pp. 219/220, 16J)
These beautiful priory ruins,
dating from the 13th century,
are in a wooded setting
beside the River Wear.

Open 22 March–30 Sept:
daily, 12–5pm.
Entry £1.00/80p/50p.
📞 0191 386 3828
🅿 (on south side of river,
charge payable) 🚽
➲ 3m NE of Durham, on
minor road off A167.
(OS Map 88; ref NZ 29471.)
🚌 Gardiners 737
Durham–Chester-le-Street
(passes close to BR Durham)
(Tel: 01388 814417).
🚃 Durham 5m.

✝ Furness Abbey

CUMBRIA (p. 218, 14F)
In a peaceful valley, the red
sandstone remains of a
wealthy abbey founded in
1123 by Stephen, later King
of England, are at the end of
an ancient route from Bow
Bridge. There is an
exhibition and a museum
contains fine stone carvings.

Open 22 March–31 Oct:
daily, 10am–6pm (6pm/dusk
in Oct). 1 Nov–31 March:
Wed–Sun, 10am–4pm
(closed 24–26 Dec). Closed
1–2pm in winter.
Entry £2.50/£1.90/£1.30.
📞 01229 823420
🚻 🅿 🎧 (also available for the
visually impaired and those
with learning difficulties)

(closed 24 Dec–1 Jan).
Entry *80p/60p/40p. (Site managed by Langbaurgh Borough Council.)*
☎ *01287 633801*
& ⚐ ⚐ *(in town)* ⊗
➲ *In Guisborough town, next to parish church.*
(OS Map 94; ref NZ 618163.)
🚌 *Tees X56, 65, 93, from Middlesbrough (passes close to BR Middlesbrough) (Tel: 01642 210131).*
🚉 *Marske 4½m.*

🏛 Goodshaw Chapel

LANCASHIRE
(p. 218, 13H)
A recently restored 18th-century Baptist chapel with all its furnishings complete.

Open *Keykeeper. Tel: 0191 261 1585 for details.*
Entry *Free.*
⊗
➲ *In Crawshawbooth, 2m N*

Finchale Priory

of Rawtenstall, in Goodshaw Avenue off A682.
(OS Map 103; ref SD 815263.)
🚌 *Rossendale/Stagecoach Ribble 273 Burnley–Bolton; Stagecoach Ribble X43, 743 Burnley–Manchester. All pass BR Burnley Manchester Road (Tel: 01706 213677).*
🚉 *Burnley Manchester Road 4½m.*

⊘ Hadrian's Wall
(pp. 162–163)
See pp 162–173 for full details and for details on the following sites on Hadrian's Wall.

Banks East Turret

Benwell Roman Temple

Benwell Vallum Crossing

Birdoswald Fort, Wall and Turret

Black Carts Turret

Brunton Turret

Cawfields Roman Wall and Milecastle

Chesters Bridge, Chesters Fort and Museum (Cilurnum)

Corbridge Roman Site (Corstopitum)

Denton Hall Turret and West Denton

Hare Hill

Harrow's Scar

Heddon-On-The-Wall

Housesteads Roman Fort (Vercovicium)

Leahill Turret

Pike Hill Signal Tower

Piper Sike Turret

Planetrees Roman Wall

Poltross Burn

Sewingshields Wall, Turrets and Milecastle

Temple of Mithras

Vindolanda Fort and Roman Milestone

Walltown Crags Wall and Turret

Willowford Wall, Turrets and Bridge

Winshields Wall and Milecastle

HADRIAN'S WALL

Stretching across northern England from the Solway Firth in the west to the Tyne in the east, Hadrian's Wall divided the 'civilized' world of the Romans, from the northern tribes beyond. Emperor Hadrian, who came to Britain in 122, was unusual in that he believed consolidation to be more glorious than new conquest. The Wall was the physical manifestation of his strategy, a defensive barrier linking the existing system of forts and watchtowers along the Stanegate

Head of Hadrian, emperor from AD117 to 138

road. Fortified lines once marked many of the Roman Empire's boundaries – along the Rhine and the Danube, on North Africa's desert edge, and in the Middle East. These, along with Hadrian's Wall and the Antonine Wall in Britain, were the outposts of the empire. Of them all, Hadrian's Wall, a World Heritage Site, is by far the best-preserved and being there still invokes a sense of standing on the edge of the world.

The original Wall was built from AD122–23. From coast to coast 73 miles (80 Roman miles), it was punctuated by small forts a mile apart ('milecastles') with turrets positioned between them. In front of the Wall was a deep ditch running in parallel and, behind it, a great earthwork or Vallum stretching along its entire length.

Building tools found at Corbridge (below and right)

Looking west along the wall

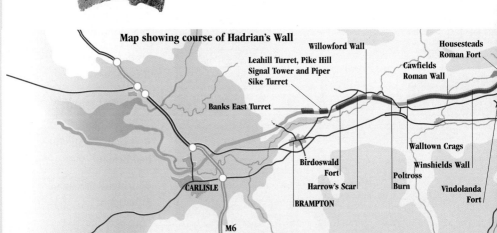

Map showing course of Hadrian's Wall

Willowford Wall
Housesteads Roman Fort
Leahill Turret, Pike Hill Signal Tower and Piper Sike Turret
Cawfields Roman Wall
Banks East Turret
Walltown Crags
Birdoswald Fort
Winshields Wall
Poltross Burn
Harrow's Scar
Vindolanda Fort
CARLISLE
BRAMPTON
M6

Illustration of a typical milecastle

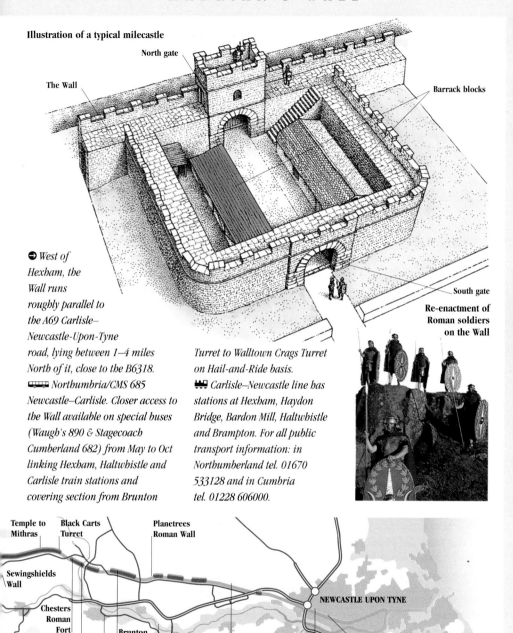

North gate

The Wall

Barrack blocks

South gate

Re-enactment of Roman soldiers on the Wall

➲ West of Hexham, the Wall runs roughly parallel to the A69 Carlisle–Newcastle-Upon-Tyne road, lying between 1–4 miles North of it, close to the B6318. 🚌 Northumbria/CMS 685 Newcastle–Carlisle. Closer access to the Wall available on special buses (Waugh's 890 & Stagecoach Cumberland 682) from May to Oct linking Hexham, Haltwhistle and Carlisle train stations and covering section from Brunton Turret to Walltown Crags Turret on Hail-and-Ride basis. 🚃 Carlisle–Newcastle line has stations at Hexham, Haydon Bridge, Bardon Mill, Haltwhistle and Brampton. For all public transport information: in Northumberland tel. 01670 533128 and in Cumbria tel. 01228 606000.

Temple to Mithras

Black Carts Turret

Planetrees Roman Wall

Sewingshields Wall

Chesters Roman Fort

Brunton Turret

CORBRIDGE

Heddon-on-the-Wall

NEWCASTLE UPON TYNE

Benwell Roman Temple and Vallum Crossing

HEXHAM

Denton Hall

Chesters Bridge

Corbridge Roman Site

A1(M)

Banks East Turret

Well-preserved turret with adjoining stretches of Wall and fine views.

Open Any reasonable time. (Site managed by Cumbria County Council.)
Entry Free.

🅿 ♿

➲ *On minor road E of Banks village, 3½m NE of Brampton. (OS Map 86; ref NY 575647.)*
🚌 ♿ *see p. 163.*

Benwell Roman Temple

Remains of small temple, surrounded by modern housing.

Open Any reasonable time.
Entry Free.

♿

➲ *Immediately S off A69 at Benwell in Broomridge Ave. (OS Map 88; ref NZ 217646.)*
🚌 *Frequent from centre of Newcastle (Tel 0191 232 5325).*
♿ *Newcastle 2m.*

Benwell Vallum Crossing

The sole remaining example of an original stone-built causeway across the ditch of the Vallum earthwork that ran parallel to the Wall.

Open Any reasonable time.
Entry Free.

♿

➲ *Immediately S off A69 at Benwell in Broomridge Ave. (OS Map 88; ref NZ 217646.)*

Centurion stone at Birdoswald

🚌 *Frequent from centre of Newcastle (Tel 0191 232 5325).*
♿ *Newcastle 2m.*

Birdoswald Fort

Almost on the edge of the Irthing escarpment, there is visible evidence of the granaries, the west gate and, most importantly, the east gate, which is among the best-preserved on the Wall.

Open Easter–31 Oct: daily 10am–5.30pm. Winter season, by arrangement only.

Entry £1.95/£1.45/ £1.00.
(Site managed by Cumbria County Council on behalf of English Heritage.)
♿ 🅿 🏠 ♿ 🍴
☎ *01697 747602*
➲ *2¾m W of Greenhead, on minor road off B6318. (OS Map 86; ref NY 615663).*
🚌 ♿ *see p. 163.*

Black Carts Turret

A 460 metre (500 yard) length of Wall and turret foundations, with magnificent views to the north.

Black Carts Turret

Open Any reasonable time.
Entry Free.

♿

➲ *2m W of Chollerford on B6318. (OS Map 87; ref NY 884712.)*
🚌 ♿ *see p. 163.*

Earring and statue of Fortuna found at Birdoswald

Brunton Turret

Well-preserved 2.5 metre (8 foot) high turret with a 20 metre (70 yard) stretch of Wall.

Open *Any reasonable time.*
Entry *Free.*
🅿 ☞

➲ *¼m S of Low Brunton on A6079.*
(OS Map 87; ref NY 922698.)
🚌 *Waugh's 890; also Tyne Valley 880/2 from BR Hexham (Tel: 01670 533128).*
🚃 *Hexham 4m.*

Cawfields Roman Wall

A concentration of Roman sites – camps, turrets, a fortlet, and Milecastle 42 –

Cawfields Milecastle

Brunton Turret

along with a particularly fine, consolidated stretch of the Wall, and one of the best-preserved sections of the Vallum earthwork and ditch.

Open *Any reasonable time.*
Entry *Free.*
☞ 🅿 🚻

➲ *1¼m N of Haltwhistle off B6318.*
(OS Map 87; ref NY 716667.)
🚌 🚃 *see p. 163.*

Chesters Bridge

Fragments of the bridge that carried Hadrian's Wall across the North Tyne are visible on each bank. The most impressive remains are on the east side, across from Chesters Fort, where a short stretch of the Wall itself leads from the broad splay of the bridge's east abutment, and ends at a gatehouse tower.

Open *Any reasonable time.*
Entry *Free.*
☞

➲ *¼m S of Low Brunton on A6079.*
(OS Map 87; ref NY 922698.)
🚌 *Waugh's 890; also Tyne Valley 880/2 from BR Hexham (Tel: 01670 533128).*
🚃 *Hexham 4m.*

Chesters Bridge abutment

Chesters Roman Fort

Throughout the Empire, Roman forts were built to a very similar pattern. Chesters, located between the 27th and 28th milecastles, is one of the best-preserved examples. Laid out in a rectangle but with rounded corners, it had two gates on the shorter sides, with a main road running between them, and two gates in each of the longer sides.

Bath-house statue of Neptune

Chesters from the north

An artist's reconstruction of Chesters Roman Fort (below)

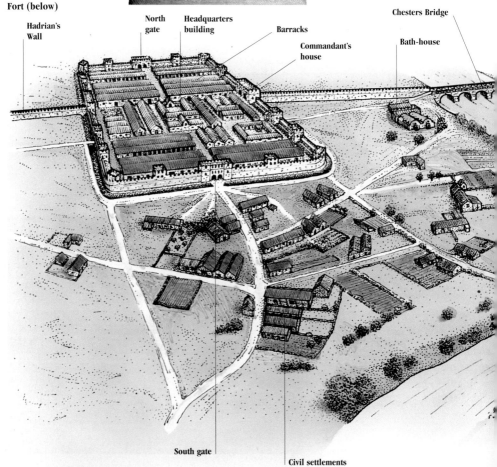

Hadrian's Wall

North gate

Headquarters building

Barracks

Commandant's house

Chesters Bridge

Bath-house

South gate

Civil settlements

The administrative buildings were placed in the centre, including the headquarters of the legion or garrison and the commanding officer's house. The complete plan is not exposed at Chesters, but many parts are visible above ground: the four principal gates, the headquarters building, commandant's house and barracks for the troops.

A glass flask from the bath-house

River Tyne

The Wall's line ran through the fort and down to cross the River Tyne. The finely preserved bath-house is sited between the fort and the river. Originally an aqueduct brought water from the river to serve both fort and baths. Large changing rooms led to a welcoming sequence of hot, steam, warm (and cold) baths. An altar to the goddess Fortuna (Luck), found in the bath-house, suggests that gambling and bathing co-existed.

So much is known about this early fort because of the pioneering archaeological work of John Clayton, who inherited the local estate in 1832. The museum, built

The goddess Juno Dolichena standing on a heifer

in 1896 soon after his death, houses many of the important finds from the site, and still contains its original displays.

Open *22 March–31 Oct: daily, 9.30am– 6pm (6pm/dusk in Oct). 1 Nov–31 March: daily, 10am–4pm (closed 24–26 Dec).* ***Entry*** *£2.50/£1.90/£1.30* ***(01434 681379*** *🏠 🚻 🅿 ♿ ⊙ ⊘ 💻 (not managed by English Heritage).* ➡ *1½m W of Chollerford on B6318. (OS Map 87; ref NY 913701.)* 🚌 *Waugh's 890, also Tyne Valley 880/2 from BR Hexham to within ½m (Tel: 01670 533128).* 🚂 *Hexham 5½m.*

A re-creation of Roman Auxiliaries by the bathhouse at Chesters

Corbridge Roman Site

Originally the site of a fort on the former patrol road, Corbridge evolved into a principal town of the Roman era, flourishing until the 5th century. The large granaries, with their ingenious ventilation system, are among its most impressive remains. Corbridge is an excellent starting point to explore the Wall.

🌐 **Activity book for children available**.

Open *22 March–31 Oct: daily, 10am–6pm (6pm/dusk in Oct). 1 Nov–31 March: Wed–Sun, 10am–4pm (closed 24–26 Dec). (Closed 1–2pm in winter.)*
Entry *£2.50/£1.90/£1.30*
☎ **01434 632349**

🚪 👬 🅿 ♿ ⊕ ⑫ 🎧 *(also available for the visually impaired and those with learning difficulties)*
➲ *½m NW of Corbridge on minor road, signed Corbridge Roman Site. (OS Map 87; ref NY 983649.)*
🚌 *Northumbria 602, 685 Newcastle-upon-Tyne–Hexham to within ½m (Tel: 0191 212 3000).*
🚃 *Corbridge 1¼m*

The Corbridge Lion

Altar to Jupiter and other gods

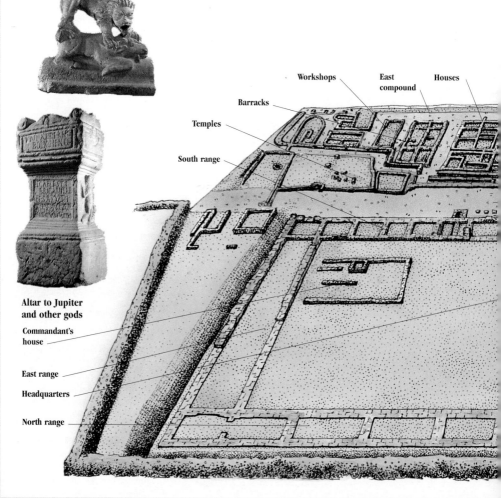

Workshops
East compound
Houses
Barracks
Temples
South range
Commandant's house
East range
Headquarters
North range

Corbridge Roman site

Denton Hall Turret

Foundations and 65 metre (70 yard) section of Wall. The turret retains the base of the platform on which rested the ladder to the upper floor.

Open *Any reasonable time.*
Entry *Free.*

➲ *4m W of Newcastle city centre on A69.*
(OS Map 88; ref NZ 195656.)
🚌 *Frequent from centre of Newcastle (Tel: 0191 232 5325).*
🚆 *Blaydon 2m.*

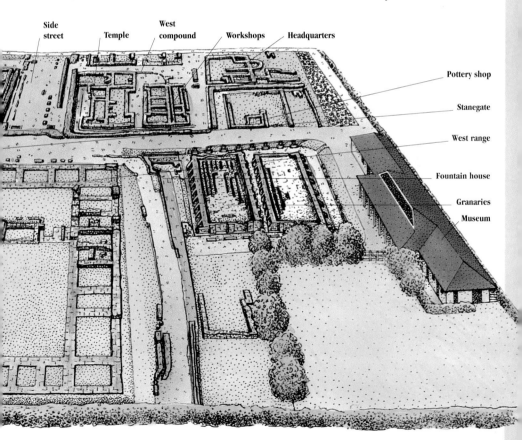

Side street · Temple · West compound · Workshops · Headquarters · Pottery shop · Stanegate · West range · Fountain house · Granaries · Museum

Housesteads Roman Fort

Housesteads occupies a commanding position on the basalt cliffs of the Whin Sill.

Sculpture of Victory which once adorned the east gate at Housesteads and is now in Chesters Museum

The latrines today (above) and an artist's reconstruction of how they would have looked (right)

One of the twelve permanent forts built by Hadrian *c.* 124, between milecastles 36 and 37, Housesteads is the most complete example of a Roman fort to be seen in Britain. Its visible remains include four gates, with towers at intervals between, and their curtain walls, as well as examples of the principal types of buildings within an auxiliary fort: military headquarters: commandant's house, barracks, granaries, a hospital and latrines. There are also remains of the civilian settlement that clustered at Housesteads' gates, while standing sections of Hadrian's Wall run to the east.

From the archaeological record of Housesteads, we can glimpse at the type of people who lived at the edge of the Empire.

A view of Housesteads from the south, with the civil settlement outside the fort walls in the foreground

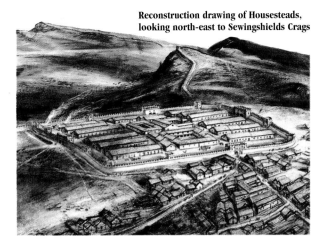

Reconstruction drawing of Housesteads, looking north-east to Sewingshields Crags

We know that cavalry from Frisia, in what is now the north-eastern Netherlands, were stationed here in the third century – the pottery found at the site, mainly flat-bottomed dishes and larger cooking pots, is Frisian in origin. A child's shoe was also found in the wet ground alongside. Deities represented in carvings from a shrine wear the hooded cape raingear, byrrus

Britannicus, that was one of the famed exports of Roman Britain and an important garment for life on Hadrian's Wall.

To the east of Housesteads, Knag Burn Gate, constructed in the third century, was an alternative way through the wall when the north gate in the fort itself fell out of use. It is one of only two isolated gates – all the rest are found at forts and milecastles. This gate and some of the Wall have been

partially reconstructed, and much has been consolidated, to give one of the most coherent pictures of the Romans and their great works in Britain.

⊕ Activity book for children available.
Open *22 March–31 Oct: daily, 10am–6pm (6pm/dusk in Oct). 1 Nov–31 March: daily, 10am–4pm (closed 24–26 Dec).*
Entry *£2.50/£1.90/£1.30. National Trust members admitted free. (Site owned by the National Trust, and maintained and managed by English Heritage.)*
☏ 01434 344363
⚦ P (both on main road, ½m walk to S) ♿ (car park at site; enquire at information centre on main road) ⊛ ⊘ Ⓔ
➲ 2¾m NE of Bardon Mill on B6318.
(OS Map 87; ref NY 790687.)
🚌 🚂 see p. 163.

Third-century hooded deities found in a shrine at Housesteads (left)

Looking towards Housesteads along the Wall (right)

Hare Hill

A short length of Wall standing nine feet high.

Open *Any reasonable time. (Site managed by Cumbria County Council.)*
Entry *Free.*
🦽
➲ *¾m NE of Lanercost, off minor road.*
(OS Map 86; ref NY 562646.)
🚌 🦽 *see p. 163.*

Harrow's Scar Milecastle

Remains linked to Birdoswald Fort by probably the most instructive mile section on the whole length of Hadrian's Wall.

Open *Any reasonable time. (Site managed by Cumbria County Council.)*
Entry *Free.*
🦽
➲ *¼m E of Birdoswald, on minor road off B6318.*
(OS Map 86; ref NY 621664.)
🚌 🦽 *see p. 163.*

Heddon-on-the-Wall

A fine stretch of the Wall up to three metres (ten feet) thick, with the remains of a medieval kiln near the west end.

Open *Any reasonable time.*
Entry *Free.*
🦽
➲ *Immediately E of Heddon village, S of A69.*
(OS Map 88; ref NZ 136669.)
🚌 *Blue Bus 83, OK 684,*

Northumbria 685 from Newcastle-upon-Tyne (Tel: 0191 232 5325).
🚃 *Wylam 3m.*

Housesteads Roman Fort

see pp. 170-1 for full details

Leahill Turret and Piper Sike Turret

Turrets in the section of Wall west of Birdoswald, originally constucted for the turf wall.

Open *Any reasonable time. (Site managed by Cumbria County Council.)*
Entry *Free.*
🦽
➲ *On minor road 2m W of Birdoswald Fort.*
(OS Map 86; ref NY 585653.)
🚌 🦽 *see p. 163.*

Pike Hill Signal Tower

Remains of a signal tower joined to the Wall at an angle of 45 degrees.

Open *Any reasonable time. (Site managed by Cumbria County Council.)*
Entry *Free.*
🦽
➲ *On minor road E of Banks village.*
(OS Map 86; ref NY 597648.)
🚌 🦽 *see p. 163.*

Planetrees Roman Wall

A 15-metre (50-foot) length of narrow wall on broad

foundations, showing extensive rebuilding in Roman times.

Open *Any reasonable time.*
Entry *Free.*
🦽
➲ *1m SE of Chollerford on B6318.*
(OS Map 87; ref NY 928696.)
🚌 🦽 *see p. 163.*

Poltross Burn Milecastle

One of the best-preserved milecastles, with part of a flight of steps to the top of the Wall and the remains of the gates, enclosing walls and barrack blocks.

Poltross Burn Milecastle

Open *Any reasonable time. (Site managed by Cumbria County Council.)*
Entry *Free.*
🅿 *(near Station Hotel)* 🦽
➲ *Immediately SW of Gilsland village by old railway station.*
(OS Map 86; ref NY 634662).
🚌 🦽 *see p. 163.*

Sewingshields Wall

Largely unexcavated section of Wall. Remains of Sewingshields

Milecastle and Turret and Grindon and Coesike Turrets.

Open *Any reasonable time.*
Entry *Free.*

➲ *N of B6318, 1½m E of Housesteads Fort.*
(OS Map 87; ref NY 813702.)
🚌 ♨ *see p. 163.*

Walltown Craggs

Temple of Mithras, Carrawburgh
Remains of a third-century temple and facsimiles of altars found during excavations.

Open *Any reasonable time.*
Entry *Free.*
🅿 ✆
➲ *3¾m W of Chollerford on B6318.*
(OS Map 87; ref NY 869713.)
🚌 ♨ *see p. 163.*

Vindolanda Fort
A fort and well-excavated civil settlement. A museum there contains many unusual artefacts from everyday Roman life.

Open *April and Sept: daily, 10am–5.30pm. May and June: daily, 10am–6pm. July and Aug: daily, 10am–6.30pm. March and Oct: daily, 10am–5pm. Nov–Feb: daily, 10am–4pm (closed 25 Dec) (usually site open at reduced charge and museum closed during this period). Site owned and managed by Vindolanda Trust*

Entry *£3.50/£2.75/£2.25. (10% discount for English Heritage members and groups of 15 or more.)*
✆ *01434 344277*
🚐 ♙ 🅿 ✆
➲ *1¼m SE of Twice Brewed, on minor road off B6318.*
(OS Map 87; ref NY 771664.)
🚌 ♨ *see p. 163.*

Walltown Crags
One of the best-preserved sections of the Wall, snaking over the crags to the turret on its summit.

Open *Any reasonable time.*
Entry *Free.*
🅿 *(nearby)* ✆
➲ *1m NE of Greenhead off B6318.*
(OS Map 87; ref NY 674664).
🚌 ♨ *see p. 163.*

Willowford Wall, Turrets and Bridge
One thousand yards of Wall, including two turrets, leading to bridge abutment remains.

Open *Any reasonable time. (Access to bridge controlled by Willowford Farm; small charge levied.)*
Entry *Free but see above.*
✆
➲ *W of minor road ¾m W of Gilsland.*
(OS Map 86; ref NY 629664.)
🚌 ♨ *see p. 163.*

Winshields Wall
Very rugged section of the Wall, including the highest point at Winshields Crag.

Open *Any reasonable time.*
Entry *Free.*
✆
➲ *W of Steel Rigg car park, on minor road off B6318.*
(OS Map 87; ref NY 745676).
🚌 ♨ *see p. 163.*

Bronze terrier found at Coventina's Well near the Temple of Mithras

⊘ Hardknott Roman Fort

CUMBRIA (pp. 218/220, 15F)
One of the most dramatic Roman sites in Britain, with stunning views across the Lakeland fells. The fort, built between AD120 and 138, controlled the road from Ravenglass to Ambleside. There are visible remains of granaries, the head-quarters building and the comman-dant's house, with a bath house and parade ground outside the fort.

Open *Any reasonable time. Access may be hazardous in winter. (Site managed by the National Trust.)*
P ⊛
➡ *9m NE of Ravenglass, at W end of Hardknott Pass. (OS Map 96; ref NY 218015.)*
🚌 *Eskdale (Dalegarth) (Ravenglass & Eskdale Railway) 3m.*

⊙ Helmsley Castle

NORTH YORKSHIRE
(p. 219, 14K)
This 12th-century castle lies close to the market square,

Helmsley Castle

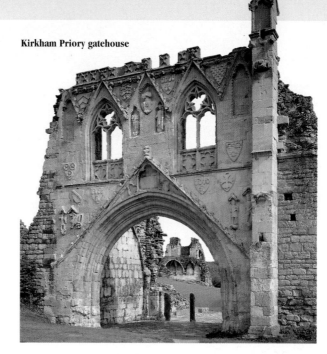

Kirkham Priory gatehouse

with a view of the town. Spectacular earthworks sur-round a great ruined Norman keep. There is an exhibition on the history of the castle in Elizabethan buildings.

Open *22 March–31 Oct: daily, 10am–6pm (6pm/dusk in Oct). 1 Nov–31 March: Wed–Sun, 10am–4pm (closed 24–26 Dec). Closed 1–2pm.*
Entry *£2.00/£1.50/£1.00.*
☎ *01439 770442*
P *(large car park N of*

castle; charge payable)
⊙ ⊕ ♦♦♦ *(in car park and in town centre)*
➡ *Near town centre. (OS Map 100; ref SE 611836.)*
🚌 *Scarborough & District 128 from BR Scarborough (Tel: 01723 375463); Stephensons from BR York (Tel: 01347 838990).*

⊕ Howden Minster

EAST RIDING OF YORKSHIRE (p. 219, 13L)
A large, cathedral-like church dating from the 14th century, which belonged to the Bishop of Durham. The ruined chan-cel and octagonal chapter house are in the care of English Heritage, and managed by Howden Minster

Parochial Church Council. They may be viewed from the outside only.

Open *Any reasonable time (closed 24–26 Dec).*
Entry *Free.*
🅿 *(street parking nearby)*
➲ *In Howden, 23m W of Kingston Upon Hull, 25m SE of York, near junction of A63 & A614. (OS Map 106; ref SE 748283.)*
🚌 *East Yorkshire 155 Goole–Hull (Tel: 01432 327146).*
🚆 *Howden 1½m.*

⊙ Hylton Castle
TYNE & WEAR
(pp. 219/220, 16J)
A 15th-century keep-gatehouse, with a fine display of medieval heraldry adorning the facades.

Open *Any reasonable time (access to grounds only). (Site managed by Sunderland City Council.)*
Entry *Free.*
🅿 ♿ *(grounds only)* 🐕
➲ *3¾m W of Sunderland. (OS Map 88; ref NZ 358588.)*
🚌 *From surrounding areas (Tel: 0191 232 5325).*
🚆 *Seaburn 2½m.*

✚ Kirkham Priory
NORTH YORKSHIRE
(p. 219, 14K)
The ruins of this Augustinian priory, including a magnificent

carved gatehouse, are set in a peaceful and secluded valley by the River Derwent.

Open *22 March–30 Sept: daily, 12pm–5pm.*
Entry *£1.40/£1.10/70p.*
☎ *01653 618768*
🅿 ♿ 🐕 🛍
➲ *5m SW of Malton on minor road off A64. (OS Map 100; ref SE 735657.)*
🚌 *Yorkshire Coastliner 840/2/3 Leeds–Scarborough (passes BR York and Malton) to within ¾m (Tel: 01653 692556).*
🚆 *Malton 6m.*

✚ Lanercost Priory
CUMBRIA (p. 220, 17G)
Augustinian priory founded c.1166. The church's nave contrasts with the ruined chancel, transepts and priory buildings.

Open *22 March–31 Oct: daily, 10am–6pm (6pm/dusk in Oct). (Parish church not managed by English Heritage.)*
Entry *£1.20/90p/60p.*
☎ *01697 73030*
🛍 🅿 🐕

➲ *Off minor road S of Lanercost, 2m NE of Brampton. (OS Map 86; ref NY 556637.)*
🚌 *Stagecoach Cumberland/ Northumbria 685 Carlisle–Newcastle-upon-Tyne to within 1½m (Tel: 01946 63222).*
🚆 *Brampton 3m.*

✚ Lindisfarne Priory
NORTHUMBERLAND
(p. 220, 19J)
See pp 176–7 for full details.

⊙ Marmion Tower
NORTH YORKSHIRE
(p. 219, 14J)
A medieval gatehouse with a fine oriel window.

Open *Any reasonable time (closed 24–26 Dec).*
Entry *Free.*
🐕
➲ *N of Ripon on A6108 in West Tanfield. (OS Map 99; ref SE 267787.)*
🚆 *Thirsk 10m.*

Lanercost Priory: the undercroft and tomb of Elizabeth Dacre Howard

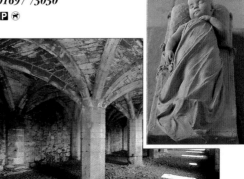

LINDISFARNE PRIORY

One of the holiest sites of Anglo-Saxon England, Lindisfarne was renowned as the original burial place of St Cuthbert, and for being founded by St Aidan, who came from Iona, the centre of Christianity in Scotland.

ENGLAND'S CHRISTIAN HERITAGE

ENGLISH HERITAGE

The island of Lindisfarne, with its wealthy monastery, was easy prey for Viking raiders from the end of the 8th century. Only in the 12th century did monks from Durham, Cuthbert's final resting place, re-establish a religious house on Lindisfarne, now more commonly known as Holy Island. The priory was a victim of the dissolution of monastic houses in 1537 and seems to have been disused by the early 18th century.

Lindisfarne, with its ancient associations, is still a holy site and place of pilgrimage. Today, going to Lindisfarne requires prior knowledge of the tide tables (see ➲ opposite). At high tide the causeway linking Holy Island to the Northumberland coast is submerged under water and the island is cut off from the mainland.

St Aidan founded Lindisfarne in 635. Austerity was the watch-word of the community – a few monks and a simple wooden church. It was, however, to become a shrine when the corpse of the former bishop St Cuthbert was dug up 11 years after his burial in 698 and found undecayed. Cuthbert was an exceedingly holy man

A modern sculpture of St Aidan, founder of Lindisfarne (below)

The priory ruins with Lindisfarne Castle in the distance

who earlier withdrew to be a hermit on the lonely Farne Islands and later returned there to die. His relics survive in Durham Cathedral, taken there after the monks fled the plundering Vikings at the end of the 8th century. Lindisfarne was a treasure house of jewels and manuscripts, including incomparable illuminated Gospels (now in

Grave-marker (c. 900) with a procession of armed soldiers

A modern version of Lindisfarne's Madonna and Child

The priory's 'Rainbow Arch' (top) and Norman arcading (above)

◉ *Free Children's Activity Sheet available.*
Open *22 March–31 Oct: daily, 10am–6pm (6pm/dusk in Oct). 1 Nov–31 March: daily, 10am–4pm (closed 24–26 Dec)*
Entry *£2.50/£1.90/£1.30*
✆ *01289 389200*
🏛 👪 🅿 ♿ ⊙ ⓦ

➲ *On Holy Island, Northumberland (p. 220, 19J),* **only reached at low tide across causeway (tide tables at each end).** *(OS Map 75; ref NU 126418.)*
🚌 *Northumbria 477 from Berwick-upon-Tweed (passes close to BR Berwick-upon-Tweed). Times vary with tides (Tel: 01670 533128).*
🚉 *Berwick-upon-Tweed 14m via causeway.*

Lindisfarne Museum (below)

the British Library). Today, in the award-winning museum, Anglo-Saxon carvings are displayed in a lively, atmospheric exhibition. The dramatic ruins of the medieval priory express its lasting power and beauty.

⬣ Mayburgh Earthwork

CUMBRIA (pp. 218/220, 16G)

An impressive prehistoric circular earthwork, with banks up to 4.5 metres (15 feet) high, enclosing a central area of one and a half acres containing a single large stone.

Open *Any reasonable time.*
Entry *Free.*
🌫
➡ *At Eamont Bridge, 1m S of Penrith off A6. (OS Map 90; ref NY 519285.)*
🚉 *Penrith 1½m.*

⬤ Middleham Castle

NORTH YORKSHIRE
(p. 218, 14J)

This childhood home of Richard III stands controlling the river that winds through Wensleydale. There is a

massive 12th-century keep with splendid views of the surrounding countryside from the battlements.

Open *22 March–31 Oct: daily, 10am–6pm (6pm/dusk in Oct). 1 Nov–31 March: Wed–Sun, 10am–4pm (closed 24–26 Dec). Closed 1–2pm in winter.*
Entry *£1.60/£1.20/80p.*
☎ **01969 623899**
📋 🖼 🚫 ♿ *(except tower)* 🅿
🚹 *(in town centre)*
➡ *At Middleham, 2m S of Leyburn on A6108. (OS Map 99; ref SE 128875.)*

✠ Monk Bretton Priory

SOUTH YORKSHIRE
(pp. 214/219, 12K)

Sandstone ruins of a Cluniac monastery founded in 1153. There are extensive remains

Norham Castle

of the fully restored 14th-century gatehouse.

Open *Any reasonable time.*
Entry *Free.*
🅿 ♿ 🖼 🚫
➡ *1m E of Barnsley town centre off A633. (OS Map 111; ref SE 373065.)*

Middleham Castle

🚌 *from surrounding areas
(Tel: 01709 515151).*
🚃 *Barnsley 2½m.*

🏰 Mount Grace Priory
NORTH YORKSHIRE
(pp. 219/220, 15K)
See pp 180–1 for full details.

⦿⊖ Norham Castle
NORTHUMBERLAND
(p. 220, 19H)
Set on a promontory in a curve of the River Tweed, this was one of the strongest of the border castles, built *c*.1160.

Open *22 March–31 Oct: daily, 10am–6pm (6pm/dusk in Oct).*
Entry *£1.40/£1.10/70p.*
✆ **01289 382329**
&. *(excluding keep)* 🍴 🚭 📱
⊖ *Norham village, 6½m SW of Berwick-upon-Tweed on minor road off B6470 (from A698).
(OS Map 75; ref NT 907476.)*
🚌 *Swan/Northumbria/ Lowland 23 BR Berwick-upon-Tweed–Kelso (Tel: 01670 533128).*
🚃 *Berwick-upon-Tweed 7½m.*

⊖ Penrith Castle
CUMBRIA (pp. 218/220, 16G)
A 14th-century castle set in a park on the edge of the town.

Open *Park: summer, 7.30am–9pm; winter, 7.30am–4.30pm.*
Entry *Free.*

Pickering Castle: Colemans Tower, the motte and keep (above) and an aerial view (right).

🚻 🚭
⊖ *Opposite Penrith railway station.
(OS Map 90; ref NY 513299.)*
🚃 *Penrith, adjacent.*

⦿ Pickering Castle
NORTH YORKSHIRE
(p. 219, 14L)
A splendid motte and bailey castle, once a royal hunting lodge. It is well preserved, with much of the original walls, towers and keep, and spectacular views over the surrounding countryside. There is an exhibition on the castle's history.

❂ **Witness the clash of cold steel and the thunder of cannons at a re-enactment of a Tudor siege, 24–26 Aug.**

❂ **Free Children's Activity Sheet available.**
Open *22 March–31 Oct: daily, 10am–6pm (6pm/dusk in Oct). 1 Nov–31 March: Wed–Sun, 10am–4pm (closed 24–26 Dec). Closed 1–2pm.*
Entry *£2.00/£1.50/£1.00.*
✆ **01751 474989**
🅿 🚭 &. *(except motte)*
🍴 Ⓔ 📱 ⓘ
⊖ *In Pickering 15m SW of Scarborough.
(OS Map 100; ref SE 800845.)*
🚌 *Yorkshire Coastliner 840/2 from BR Malton (Tel: 01653 692556). Scarborough & District 128 from BR Scarborough (Tel: 01723 37563).*
🚃 *Malton 9m; Pickering (N York Moors Rly) ¼m.*

MOUNT GRACE PRIORY

ENGLAND'S

CHRISTIAN

HERITAGE

ENGLISH HERITAGE

Mount Grace Priory is the best-preserved of the ten Carthusian monasteries in Britain. Founded in 1398, it is beautifully situated under the steep slopes of the Hambleton Hills, nestled amongst attractive woodlands. The Carthusian monks each lived as a virtual hermit in his own cell, only congregating when it was time for a service in the monastery's small church. Today, you can see what life must have been like there in the 15th century by viewing the specially reconstructed cell, and wandering through the remains of the Great Cloister, church and outer court, as well as the extensive gardens with herb garden and fish pond.

There is also the guest house which was first transformed into a splendid manor house in the 17th century and later adapted in 1900–01 into a larger house using the style of the Arts and Craft movement.

The layout of Mount Grace Priory, with its Great Cloister surrounded by individual two-storey cells is practically unique. Known as 'Christ's Poor Men', the Carthusians alone among the monastic

The Manor House (left) and the monk's fish pond (below)

orders of western Europe practised as hermits, living in a community only for protection and to share a sound economy. The reconstructed cell at Mount Grace gives a fascinating insight into their solitary but highly ordered life, and contains hand-carved replica cabinets, beds and chests. Apart from their

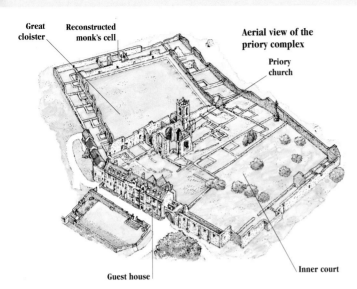

Great cloister

Reconstructed monk's cell

Aerial view of the priory complex

Priory church

Guest house

Inner court

❀ *Picnic spot of exceptional beauty. Nature trail.*

❀ *Free Children's Activity Sheet and nature trail leaflet available.*

Open *22 March–31 Oct: daily, 10am–6pm (6pm/dusk in Oct). Last admission 5.30pm. 1 Nov–31 March: Wed–Sun, 10am–4pm. Last admission 3.30pm. Closed 1–2pm in winter.*

Entry *£2.50/£1.90/£1.30. National Trust members admitted free. (Site owned by the National Trust, maintained and managed by English Heritage.)*

℡ *01609 883494*

♿ 🅿 ♿ 🍴 ⊗ ♿ ⊙

➲ *12m N of Thirsk, 7m NE of Northallerton on A19. (OS Map 99; ref SE 453982.)*

🚌 *Tees 90, 190 Northallerton–Middlesbrough (passes close to BR Northallerton) to within ½m (Tel: 01642 210131).*

🚆 *Northallerton 6m.*

The living room of a reconstructed monk's cell

cells, the Priory included a guest house and small church, which are part of the Inner Court. The monks would only leave their solitary lives of contemplation and scholarship to congregate in the small church for communal services.

After the Reformation Mount Grace fell into decline. The buildings disintegrated until Thomas Lascelles built himself a manor house from the remains of the Priory guest house in the 17th century. This in turn was extended at the beginning of the 20th century in the prevalent Arts and Crafts style, including wallpapers by William Morris.

Today, the monastery itself is a vivid reminder of the extreme lifestyle of the Carthusians in medieval England, while the gardens are a perfect spot to relax and enjoy the beautiful surrounding countryside.

Mount Grace from the south

Prudhoe Castle

➲ ○ Piel Castle

CUMBRIA (p. 218, 14F)
The ruins of a 14th-century
castle, accessible by boat from
Roa Island, with the massive
keep, inner and outer baileys,
and curtain walls and towers.

*Open Any reasonable time.
Access by small boat from Roa
Island during summer, subject
to tides and weather. For
information tel. 01229 833609
or 870156.*
Entry Free.
🐾
➲ *On Piel Island, 3¼m
SE of Barrow.
(OS Map 96; ref SD 233636.)*
🚌 *Stagecoach Cumberland
11/2 Barrow-in-Furness–Roa
Island (Tel: 01946 63222).*
🚉 *Barrow-in-Furness 4m
to Roa Island.*

❼ Piercebridge Roman Bridge

NORTH YORKSHIRE
(pp. 218/220, 15J)
Remains of the stone piers and
abutment of a Roman timber
bridge over the River Tees.

Open Any reasonable time.
Entry Free.
🐾
➲ *At Piercebridge, 4m W of
Darlington on B6275.
(OS Map 93; ref NZ 214154.)*
🚌 *United 75/A, X75
BR Darlington–Barnard Castle
(passes close to BR Darlington)
(Tel: 01325 468771).*
🚉 *Darlington 5m.*

❶ Prudhoe Castle

NORTHUMBERLAND
(pp. 218/220, 16J)
Set on a wooded hillside
overlooking the River Tyne

are the extensive remains of a
12th-century castle, with gatehouse, curtain wall and keep.
There is a small exhibition
and video presentation.

🎡 *Picnic spot; brass rubbing.*
*Open 22 March–30 Sept:
daily, 12pm–5pm.*
Entry £1.60/£1.20/80p.
☎ *01661 833459*
🅿 🚻 ⊕ 🛍 Ⓔ 🛒
➲ *In Prudhoe, on minor
road off A695.
(OS Map 88; ref NZ 092634.)*
🚌 *From surrounding areas
(Tel: 01670 533128).*
🚉 *Prudhoe ¼m.*

❼ Ravenglass Roman Bath House

CUMBRIA (p. 218, 15F)
The walls of the bathhouse
are among the most complete
Roman remains in Britain.

Open *Any reasonable time.*
Entry *Free.*

⮕ *¼m E of Ravenglass, off minor road leading to A595. (OS Map 96; ref NY 088961.)*
🚉 *Ravenglass, adjacent.*

✪ Richmond Castle

NORTH YORKSHIRE
(pp. 218/220, 15J)
Hugely dramatic Norman fortress, built by William the Conqueror in his quest to quell the rebellious North. William's close ally, Alan of Brittany, chose the site for his principal castle and residence. The 11th-century remains of the curtain wall and domestic buildings are combined with the 100ft high keep with its hugely thick walls, which was added in the 12th century. There are magnificent views over the River Swale from the keep.

Richmond Castle keep and curtain wall

⚘ **Free Children's Activity Sheet available.**
Open *22 March–31 Oct: daily, 10am–6pm (6pm/dusk in Oct). 1 Nov–31 March: daily, 10am–4pm (closed 24–26 Dec). Closed 1–2pm in winter.*
Entry *£1.80/£1.40/90p.*
✆ **01748 822493**

👬 👦 🚗 ⓘ ⊗ 🛇
⮕ *In Richmond.*
(OS Map 92; ref NZ 174006.)
🚌 *United X27/8, 27/B, 28/A Darlington–Richmond (passes close to BR Darlington) (Tel: 01325 468771).*

Richmond Castle from the River Swale

Roche Abbey

✠ Rievaulx Abbey
NORTH YORKSHIRE
(p. 219, 14K)
See pp 186–9 for full details.

✠ Roche Abbey
SOUTH YORKSHIRE
(pp. 214/219, 11K)
A Cistercian monastery, founded in 1147. Excavation has revealed the complete layout of the abbey.

Open *22 March–31 Oct: daily, 10am–6pm (6pm/dusk in Oct). Closed 1–2pm.*
Entry *£1.40/£1.10/70p.*
☎ 01709 812739
🚹 🅿 📷 ♿ 🍴 🐕 ⑳
➲ *1½m S of Maltby off A634. (OS Map 111; ref SK 544898.)*
🚌 *Main Line 100–2, Powell 122 Rotherham–Maltby, thence 1½m (Tel: 01709 515151).*
🚆 *Conisbrough 7m.*

✠ St Mary's Church
Studley Royal, NORTH YORKSHIRE (p. 219, 14J)
Magnificent Victorian church, designed by William Burges in the 1870s, with a highly decorated interior. Coloured marble, stained glass, gilded and painted figures and a splendid organ remain in their original glory.

Open *22 March–30 Sept: daily, 1–5pm. (English Heritage site managed by the National Trust as part of Studley Royal estate.)*
Entry *Free.*
☎ 01765 608888
🅿 *(free at visitor centre)* ♿ 🐕
➲ *2½m W of Ripon off B6265, in grounds of Studley Royal estate. (OS Map 99; ref SE 278703.)*
🚌 *Angloblue 802 Bradford–Ripon (connections from BR Harrogate), Sun, June–Aug only (Tel: 01609 780780); otherwise United 145 from Ripon (with connections from BR Harrogate), Thurs and Sat only (Tel: 01325 468771).*

St. Mary's Church

St Paul's Monastery and Bede's World Museum

Jarrow, TYNE & WEAR
(p. 220, 16J)

The home of the Venerable Bede, partly surviving as the chancel of the parish church. The monastery has become one of the best-understood Anglo-Saxon monastic sites. The museum tells the story of St Paul's Monastery and displays excavated finds. There is an Anglo-Saxon landscape with fields, crops, animals and timber buildings on land next to the museum. Phase One of the new museum building is now open.

Open Monastery ruins, any reasonable time. Museum, 22 March–31 Oct: Tues–Sat and Bank Holidays, 10am–5.30pm. Sun 2.30–5.30pm; 1 Nov– 31 March: Tues–Sat 11am– 4.30pm, Sun 2.30–5.30pm (closed Christmas–New Year). Entry £2.50/£1.25/£1.25, family ticket £6.00, UB40 family ticket £4.00. Free to monastery ruins.
☎ *0191 489 2106*
🅰 ¶ ♯ ♿ 🛇 ♻ ⊗ *(monastery only; only guide dogs allowed into museum)* ⑫
➲ *In Jarrow, on minor road N of A185. (OS Map 88; ref NZ 339652.)*
🚌 *VFM 527 Newcastle-upon-Tyne–South Shields (Tel: 0191 460 5144). Metro: Bede ¾m, Jarrow ¾m.*
🚃 *Brockley Whins 2½m.*

St Peter's Church

Barton-upon-Humber, NORTH LINCOLNSHIRE
(p. 219, 12L)

A fine 15th-century former parish church, with an Anglo-Saxon tower and baptistry.

Open Daily, 2–4pm (closed 24–26 Dec). Entry Free.
☎ *01652 632516*
⊗
➲ *In Barton-upon-Humber. (OS Map 112; ref TA 034220.)*
🚌 *Road Car/E Yorks/ Applebys/Hornsby 350 Hull–Scunthorpe (Tel: 01522 532424).*
🚃 *Barton-upon-Humber ½m.*

Salley Abbey

LANCASHIRE
(p. 218, 13H)

The remains of a Cistercian abbey founded in 1147.

Open Any reasonable time. (Site managed by Lancashire Heritage Trust.) Entry Free.
♿ ⊗
➲ *At Sawley 3½m, N of Clitheroe off A59. (OS Map 103; ref SD 776464.)*
🚃 *Clitheroe 4m.*

Sandbach Crosses

CHESHIRE
(pp. 217/218, 11H)

Rare Saxon stone crosses from the 9th century, carved with animals, dragons and biblical scenes, in the centre of the market square.

Open Any reasonable time. Entry Free.
♿ ⊗
➲ *Market square, Sandbach. (OS Map 118; ref SJ 758608.)*
🚌 *North Western K33/7 from BR Sandbach (Tel: 01244 602666).*
🚃 *Sandbach 1½m.*

Sandbach Crosses

RIEVAULX ABBEY

'Everywhere peace, everywhere serenity, and a marvellous freedom from the tumult of the world'. Those words could easily be taken to describe Rievaulx today, one of the most atmospheric of all the ruined medieval abbeys of the North. In fact, they were written over eight centuries ago by St Aelred, the monastery's third abbot. A long line of Cistercian monks lived in the beautiful River Rye valley from the 12th century until the 16th. The Cistercians, with their ascetic lifestyle and their capacity for hard work, wanted to be isolated from the world. Although much of what was built by the monks is destroyed or ruined, most of the spectacular presbytery, the great eastern part of the abbey church, stands virtually to its full height. Built in the 13th century to contain the shrine of St Aelred (to whom an exhibition is now devoted), its soaring beauty conveys a sense of the glory and splendours that Rievaulx once possessed.

Rievaulx was founded directly by the great and holy St Bernard of Clairvaux, as part of the missionary effort to bring Christianity to western Europe. Twelve Clairvaux monks came to Rievaulx in 1132, and from these modest beginnings sprang one of the wealthiest monasteries of medieval England and the first Cistercian monastery in the North.

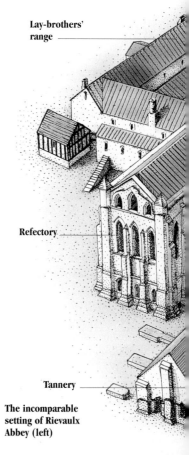

Lay-brothers' range

Refectory

Tannery

The incomparable setting of Rievaulx Abbey (left)

A reconstruction of how Rievaulx Abbey might have appeared at the end of the 15th century

A view through the arcades of the abbey church

Cloister

The 12th-century nave

Crossing and transepts

13th-century presbytery

Chapter house

Infirmary hall and abbot's house

Infirmary cloister

Monks' dormitory

Monks' latrine

In the Middle Ages, wealthy families vied with each other in founding churches. Rievaulx enjoyed the protection and endowment of Walter Espec, who provided much of the abbey's land. The monks of Byland Abbey, over the river, cooperated with the Cistercians in agreeing to divert the course of the River

The ruins in 1841 drawn by William Richardson

Rye. You can still make out traces of the old river, and the channels dug by the monks.

A steady stream of monks came to Aelred, author and preacher, who was regarded then, and since, as a wise and saintly man. After his death in 1167 the monks sought his canonisation and, in the 1220s, rebuilt the east part of their church in a much more elaborate style for his tomb. Rievaulx was still a vibrant

A medieval carving depicting the abbey's mill (above)

community when Henry VIII dissolved it in 1538. Its new owner, Thomas Manners, first Earl of Rutland, swiftly began the systematic destruction of the buildings. What he left was one of the most eloquent of all monastic sites, free 'from the tumult of the world', as Aelred once said.

Ruins of the monastic buildings

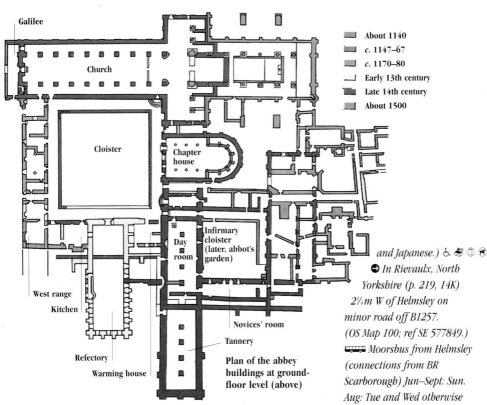

Galilee

Church

About 1140
c. 1147–67
c. 1170–80
Early 13th century
Late 14th century
About 1500

Cloister

Chapter house

Day room

Infirmary cloister (later, abbot's garden)

West range

Kitchen

Novices' room

Tannery

Refectory

Warming house

Plan of the abbey buildings at ground-floor level (above)

and Japanese.) ♿ 🏪 📖 🛍️
➲ *In Rievaulx, North Yorkshire (p. 219, 14K) 2¼m W of Helmsley on minor road off B1257. (OS Map 100; ref SE 577849.)*
🚌 *Moorsbus from Helmsley (connections from BR Scarborough) Jun–Sept: Sun. Aug: Tue and Wed otherwise Scarborough & District 128 from Scarborough (Tel: 01723 375463), Stephensons 57 from BR York (Tel: 01347 838990), alighting Helmsley, thence 2½m.*

Open *22 March–31 Oct: daily, 10am–6pm (6pm/dusk in Oct). 1 Nov–31 March: daily, 10am–4pm (closed 24–26 Dec).*
Entry *£2.70/£2.00/£1.40.*

✆ *01439 798228*
📱 👫 🅿 ♿ *(also available for the visually impaired, those with learning difficulties and in French, German, Swedish*

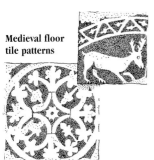

Medieval floor tile patterns

A corner of the cloister arcade reconstructed (left)

A fragment of an abbot's tomb (above)

Scarborough Castle and a decorated 16th-century slipware plate found there

◷ Scarborough Castle

NORTH YORKSHIRE
(p. 219, 14L)

There are spectacular coastal views from the walls of this enormous 12th-century castle. The buttressed castle walls stretch out along the cliff edge and the remains of the great rectangular stone keep still stand to over three storeys high. There is also the site of a 4th-century Roman signal station. The castle was often attacked, but despite being blasted by cannons of the Civil War and bombarded during World War I, it is still a spectacular place to visit.

⊕ Free Children's Activity Sheet available.
Open *22 March–31 Oct: daily, 10am–6pm (6pm/dusk in Oct).*

1 Nov–31 March: Wed–Sun, 10am–4pm (closed 24–26 Dec). Closed 1–2pm in winter.
Entry *£1.80/£1.40/90p.*
☎ 01723 372451
🚶🏻 🎧 *(also available for the visually impaired and those with learning difficulties)*
♿ *(except keep)* 🛍 ⓘ ⊛
➡ *Castle Rd, E of town centre.*
(OS Map 101; ref TA 050893.)
🚌 *From surrounding areas (Tel: 01723 375463).*
🚉 *Scarborough 1m.*

✟ Shap Abbey

CUMBRIA
(pp. 218/220, 15G)

The striking tower and other remains of this Premonstratensian abbey stand in a remote and isolated location.

Open *Any reasonable time.*
Entry *Free.*
🅿 ♿ ⊛
➡ *1½m W of Shap on bank of River Lowther.*

(OS Map 90; ref NY 548153.)
🚌 *Stagecoach Cumberland 107 Penrith–Shap, to within 1½m (Tel: 01946 63222).*
🚉 *Penrith 10m.*

◷ Skipsea Castle

EAST RIDING OF YORKSHIRE (p. 219, 13M)
The remaining earthworks of a Norman motte and bailey castle.

Open *Any reasonable time.*
Entry *Free.*
⊛

➡ *8m S of Bridlington, W of Skipsea village.*
(OS Map 107; ref TA 163551.)
🚉 *Bridlington 9m.*

◷◷ Spofforth Castle

NORTH YORKSHIRE
(p. 219, 13J)

This manor house has some fascinating features including an undercroft built into the rock. It was once owned by the Percy family.

Open *22 March–30 Sept: daily, 10am–6pm. 1 Oct–31 March: daily, 10am–4pm (closed 24–26 Dec). Keykeeper.*
Entry *Free.*
⊛

➡ *3½m SE of Harrogate, off A661 at Spofforth.*
(OS Map 104; ref SE 360511.)
🚌 *Harrogate & District 78/A, 79 Harrogate–York (Tel: 01423 566061).*
🚉 *Pannal 4m.*

⬤ Stanwick Iron Age Fortifications

NORTH YORKSHIRE
(pp. 218/220, 15J)
The tribal stronghold of the Brigantes, whose vast earthworks cover some 850 acres. Today you can see an excavated section of the ditch, cut into the rock, and the rampart.

Open *Any reasonable time.*
Entry *Free.*
🐾

➲ *On minor road off A6274 at Forcett Village.*
(OS Map 92; ref NZ 178124.)
🚌 *Barnard Castle Coaches 78 from Darlington (Passes close to BR Darlington), Sat only (Tel: 01833 621302).*
🚉 *Darlington 10m.*

⊙ Steeton Hall Gateway

NORTH YORKSHIRE
(p. 219, 13K)
A fine example of a small, well-preserved 14th-century gatehouse.

Open *Daily, 10am–5pm (exterior only).*
Entry *Free.*
☎ *Regional Office 0191 261 1585*
♿ 🐾
➲ *4m NE of Castleford,*

Thornton Abbey

Stott Park Bobbin Mill

on minor road off A162 at South Milford.
(OS Map 105; ref SE 484314.)
🚉 *South Milford 1m.*

⊙ Stott Park Bobbin Mill

CUMBRIA (p. 218, 14G)
Working mill, built in 1835. It is typical of the mills in the Lake District which supplied the spinning and weaving industry in Lancashire.

⊛ See a real working Victorian bobbin mill.
Open *22 March–31 Oct: daily, 10am–6pm (6pm/dusk in Oct). Guided tours lasting 45 minutes included in admission charge, last tour starts 1 hour before closure. Steam engine*

operates Tues, Weds and Thurs.
Entry *£2.70/£2.00/£1.40.*
☎ *01539 531087*
👥 🅿 ♿ *(ground floor only)*
🍴 ✖ 🐕 📷

➲ *½m N of Finsthwaite near Newby Bridge.*
(OS Map 96; ref SD 373883.)
🚌 *Stagecoach Cumberland 518 Ulverston–Ambleside to within 1½m (Tel: 01946 63222).*
🚉 *Grange-over-Sands 8m.*

✝ Thornton Abbey and Gatehouse

NORTH LINCOLNSHIRE
(p. 219, 12M)
Ruined Augustinian priory with magnificent brick gatehouse.

Open *Abbey grounds, any reasonable time. Gatehouse, 22 March–30 Sept: 1st & 3rd Sun, 12–6pm. 1 Oct–31 March: 3rd Sun, 12–4pm.*
Entry *Free.*
🅿 ♿ *(except interior of gatehouse and part of chapter house ruins)*
🐕 ⊛
➲ *18m NE of Scunthorpe on minor road N of A160; 7m SE of Humber Bridge on minor road E of A1077.*
(OS Map 113; ref TA 115190.)
🚉 *Thornton Abbey ¼m.*

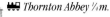

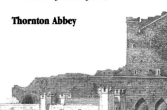

Stott Park Bobbin Mill

WARKWORTH CASTLE AND HERMITAGE

The magnificent eight-towered keep of Warkworth Castle stands on its hill above the River Coquet, dominating all around it. A

The keep from the south

large and complex stronghold, it was home to the Percy family who at times wielded more power in the North than the King himself. Most famous of

them all was Harry Hotspur (Sir Henry Percy), immortalised in Northumbrian ballads and Shakespeare's *Henry IV*, several scenes of which were set at Warkworth. He dominated the Borders in the 15th century with his father, the Earl of Northumberland, and fought off the Scots on behalf of the King before being instrumental in the removal of Richard II from the throne.

As headquarters and home to the region's most powerful family, Warkworth needed to be an impressive castle and it remains so to this day.

Warkworth is one of the most outstanding examples of an aristocratic fortified residence. It was not only a mighty defence against the sieges and attacks prevalent in medieval England but also the home of the most powerful family in the vicinity, the Percys. Along with their castle at Alnwick, some eight miles away, Warkworth allowed them to influence the entire region. As the largest landowners in an area far from London, local society revolved around the Percy family and Warkworth was a regional court quite as much as it was a military stronghold.

The huge defences that make up the original castle

were begun in the 12th century, when the area was regained from the Scots. But it was the granting of the castle to the Percy family in the early

A medieval mummers' play

The Lion Tower and the remains of the Great Hall

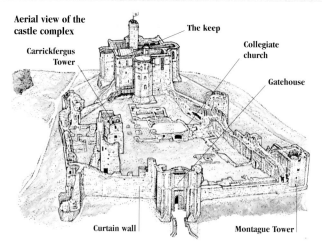

Aerial view of the castle complex

Carrickfergus Tower

The keep

Collegiate church

Gatehouse

Curtain wall

Montague Tower

❀ *Many chambers, passageways and dark staircases to explore.*
❀ *Free Children's Activity Sheet available.*
Open *Castle: 22 March–31 Oct: daily, 10am–6pm (6pm/dusk in Oct). 1 Nov–31 March: daily, 10am–4pm (closed 24–26 Dec). Closed 1–2pm in winter. Hermitage: 1 April–30 Sept: Wed, Sun & Bank Holidays.*
Entry *£2.20/£1.70/£1.10.*
✆ *01665 711423*
🕴 🅿 *(at castle)* 🎧 ♿ *(castle, excluding keep)* ♨ ❀
➲ *In Warkworth, Northumberland (p. 220, 18J), 7½m S of Alnwick on A1068. (OS Map 81; Castle ref NU 247057, Hermitage ref NU 242060.)*
🚌 *Northumbria X18 Newcastle–Alnwick (Tel: 01670 533128).*
🚉 *Alnmouth 3½m.*

14th century that ensured its stature. Their power built a castle strong enough to withstand the mightiest enemy, protected by a huge curtain wall surmounted with towers at each corner which dominate

The entrance hall in the keep

the surrounding countryside to this day. Like many castles it was built piece by piece, being adapted as time and money permitted. The curtain wall with its gatehouse enclosed the outer bailey and

included the living quarters for the garrison as well as the Percys and their retinue.

The great keep was added in the late 14th century, and this more than anything indicates the family's power. It was in effect a second castle, built to a single plan, as the new residence for a family who could justify their permanence and importance in the locality. Today you can still get lost in its maze of passages and rooms.

The Hermitage is cut into the rock of the river cliff, hidden away underneath the wooded bank, a short walk upstream from the castle. It remains very much as a 14th-century recluse would remember. Visit by taking a short ferry trip across the river after the walk from the village.

Steps leading to the Hermitage

✚ Tynemouth Priory and Castle

TYNE & WEAR (p. 220, 17J)
The castle walls and gate-house enclose the substantial remains of a Benedictine priory founded *c*.1090 on a Saxon monastic site.

☉ *Explore underground chambers beneath the World War I gun batteries.*
Open *22 March–31 Oct: daily, 10am–6pm (6pm/dusk in Oct). 1 Nov–31 March: Wed–Sun, 10am–4pm (closed 24–26 Dec). Closed 1–2pm in winter. Gun battery April–Sept: Sat, Sun and Bank Holidays 10am–6pm.*
Entry *£1.60/£1.20/80p.*
☎ **0191 257 1090**

🗎 ❖ *(nearby; local council)*
♿ *(priory)* ☐ ☐
➲ *In Tynemouth, near North Pier.*
(OS Map 88; ref NZ 374695.)
🚌 *From surrounding areas (Tel: 0191 232 5325).*
Metro: Tynemouth ½m.

♡☉☐ Warkworth Castle and Hermitage

NORTHUMBERLAND
(p. 220, 18J)
See pp 192–3 for full details.

Tynemouth Castle Barbican (below) and Priory (bottom)

Warton Old Rectory

LANCASHIRE (p. 218, 14G)
Rare medieval stone house with remains of the hall, chambers and domestic offices.

Open *Any reasonable time (closed 24–26 Dec).*
Entry *Free.*

➲ *At Warton, 1m N of Carnforth on minor road off A6. (OS Map 97; ref SD 499723.)*
 Stagecoach Ribble 55/A Lancaster–Warton (passes BR Carnforth) (Tel: 01524 841656).
 Carnforth 1m.

Wetheral Priory Gatehouse

CUMBRIA (pp. 218/220, 16G)
A Benedictine priory gatehouse, preserved after the Dissolution by serving as the vicarage for the parish church.

Open *Any reasonable time (closed 24–26 Dec).*
Entry *Free.*

➲ *On minor road in Wetheral village, 6m E of Carlisle on B6263. (OS Map 86; ref NY 469542.)*
 Stagecoach Cumberland 74/5 Carlisle–Wetherall (Tel: 01946 63222).
 Wetherall ½m.

Whalley Abbey Gatehouse

LANCASHIRE (p. 218, 13H)
The outer gatehouse of the nearby Cistercian abbey. There was originally a chapel on the first floor.

Open *Any reasonable time. (Site managed by Lancashire Heritage Trust.)*
Entry *Free.*

➲ *In Whalley, 6m NE of Blackburn on minor road off A59. (OS Map 103; ref SD 730360.)*
 Stagecoach Ribble 225 BR Blackburn–Clitheroe (Tel: 01254 681120).
 Whalley ½m. Rishton 5½m.

 Wharram Percy Deserted Medieval Village

NORTH YORKSHIRE (p. 219, 14L)
One of over 3,000 deserted villages to have been identified from faint outlines of walls and foundations. The remains of the medieval church still stand.

Open *Any reasonable time.*
Entry *Free.*
 (at Bella Farm, ¾m walk to site)
➲ *6m SE of Malton, on minor road from B1248 ½ S of Wharram le Street. (OS Map 100; ref SE 859645.)*
 Malton 8m.

The deserted medieval village at Wharram Percy

Wheeldale Roman Road

N. YORKSHIRE (p. 219, 15L)
This mile-long stretch of Roman road, still with its hardcore and drainage ditches, runs across isolated moorland.

Open *Any reasonable time. (Site managed by North York Moors National Park.)*
Entry *Free.*

➲ *S of Goathland, W of A169, 7m S of Whitby. (OS Map 94; ref SE 805975.)*
 Goathland (N York Moors Rly) 4m.

 Whitby Abbey

N. YORKSHIRE (p. 219, 15L)
See pp 196–7 for full details.

WHITBY ABBEY

Pilgrims badge

Set high on a North Yorkshire clifftop, the remains of the Abbey overlook a picturesque town and harbour with associations ranging from Victorian jewellery and whaling to Count Dracula. Whitby Abbey is a magnificent reminder of the early church's power and dedication; it contained the shrine of St

ENGLAND'S
CHRISTIAN
HERITAGE

ENGLISH HERITAGE

Hilda, the foundress who died in 680, and it symbolized the continuing Christian tradition in the north.

Destroyed by Viking invaders, rebuilt by Normans, embellished by later generations and dismantled under Henry VIII, the abbey is today a gaunt and moving ruin. Those who choose to approach it up the 199 steps from Whitby town also know the meaning of dedication.

St Hilda brought nuns and monks, including the poet Caedmon, to found a religious house on the coastal headland in 657. Because of her reputation, the Synod of 664 was held there and the two branches of early English Christianity, the Celtic and Roman churches, buried many differences in practice and doctrine. The matter that had principally divided them was the date of Easter and the Synod decided in favour of the Roman tradition. When the Vikings invaded Northumbria in 867, the abbey was destroyed and its wealth pillaged.

A Norman invader, Reinfrid, revived Whitby Abbey in the late 1070s; he also resettled Jarrow, home of Bede, whose writings had kept alive the memory of the early holy places, and refounded Whitby.

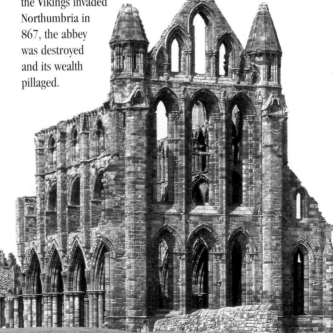

Surviving tracery (above) and the towering mass of the largely standing east end (right)

The abbey ruins in 1789

The Norman church proved inadequate under the pressure of pilgrims, and in the 1220s rebuilding commenced.
Since its dissolution in 1538, Whitby's dramatic location has attracted 18th-century painters and engravers. They helped begin the appreciation of the grandeur of these ruins, which has led to their continued preservation.

✦ *The town is the setting of famous scenes from Bram Stoker's novel* Dracula.
✦ *Activity book for children available.*

Open *22 March–31 Oct: daily, 10am–6pm (6pm/dusk in Oct). 1 Nov–31 March: daily, 10am–4pm (closed 24–26 Dec).*
Entry *£1.60/£1.20/80p.*

☎ *01947 603568*
� 🅿 *(both local council; charge payable)* 🍴 ⓘ ✉ 🛍
(We regret access unsuitable for wheelchairs.)
➲ *On cliff top E of Whitby in North Yorkshire (p. 219, 15L). (OS Map 94; ref NZ 904115.)*
🚌 *From surrounding areas (Tel: 01947 602146).*
🚃 *Whitby ½ m.*

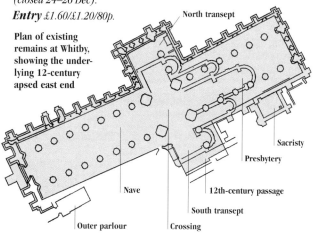

Plan of existing remains at Whitby, showing the underlying 12-century apsed east end

North transept
Sacristy
Presbytery
12th-century passage
South transept
Crossing
Nave
Outer parlour

Sculpted decoration around the north transept windows (above)

The abbey and parish church, perched above the town and harbour

Other historic sites to see in England

As well as giving you free entry to our own properties, becoming a member of English Heritage opens up many other opportunities for enjoying England's past. You can enjoy half- or reduced-price admission to numerous other historic attractions across the country, including the Weald and Downland Museum in the South Downs, Pendle Heritage Centre at the start of the Pendle Way and the six historic attractions in the care of Sussex Past. *These benefits are only available to members of English Heritage.*

For further information about these sites and discounted entry, please contact the relevant organisations:

 Sussex Past,
Bull House,
92 High Street, Lewes,
East Sussex, BN7 1XH.
Tel: 01273 486260.
English Heritage members receive 50% off all full adult & child tickets.

Anne of Cleves House and Museum

LEWES (p. 213, 3M)
This picturesque timber-framed house contains wide-ranging collections of Sussex interest and features a small, formal garden.
Open 25 Mar–10 Nov: Daily, 10am–5.30pm (Sun, opens 12pm). 11 Nov–24 Mar: Tues, Thur & Sat, 10am–5.30pm.
Entry £2.00/£1.00, joint ticket with Lewes Castle: £4.25/£2.20.
✆ 01273 474610. ♦♿🏠🅿🎧🍴❌
➲ *In Southover High Street, Lewes, off A27. (OS Map 198; ref TQ 412097.)*

Fishbourne Roman Palace

CHICHESTER (p. 212, 3C)
The remains of the largest Roman residence yet discovered north of the Alps, featuring some of the finest mosaics in northern Europe.
Open 8 Feb–13 Dec: Daily, 10am–5pm (6pm in Aug, 4pm in Feb, Nov & Dec). 14 Dec–7 Feb: Sunday only, 10am–4pm.

Entry £3.80/£1.80.
✆ 01243 785859.
🅿♿🏠🎧🅴🍴❌
➲ *In Fishbourne village, 1½m W of Chichester, off A27/A259. (OS Map 197; ref SZ 839048.)*

Lewes Castle

LEWES (p. 213, 4M)
A splendid Norman castle with superb views across the Sussex countryside. The adjacent Barbican House is home to the Museum of Sussex Archaeology.
Open All year: Mon–Sat, 10am–5.30pm, Sun & Bank Holidays, 12pm–5.30pm. (Closed 25–26 Dec.)
Entry £3.25/£1.75, joint ticket with Anne of Cleves House: £4.25/£2.20.
✆ 01273 486290.
🏠🎧🅴❌
➲ *In Lewes town centre, off A27, A26 and A275. (OS Map 198; ref TQ 413102.)*

Marlipins Museum

SHOREHAM (p. 212, 3M)
Dedicated to the history of Shoreham, with its long maritime tradition, the building dates back to Norman times.
Open 1 May–30 Sept: Tues–Sat, 10am–4.30pm (closed 1–2pm), Sun, 2pm–4.30pm.
Entry £1.00/50p.

✆ 01273 462994. 🏠🍴❌
➲ *In town centre of Shoreham-by-Sea on A259 and off A27. (OS Map 198; ref TQ 214051.)*

Michelham Priory

HAILSHAM (p. 213, 3N)
An Elizabethan country house in a tranquil moated setting and spacious gardens. The house incorporates parts of the medieval priory.
Open 15 March–31 July: Wed–Sun, 11am–5pm (4pm in March). 1–31 Aug: daily, 10.30am–5.30pm. 1 Sep–31 Oct: Wed–Sun, 11am–5pm (4pm in Oct).
Entry £4.00/£2.00.
✆ 01323 844224.
🅿♿🏠🎧🅴🍴❌
➲ *Nr Hailsham, off A22/A27. (OS Map 198; ref TQ 558093.)*

Priest House

WEST HOATHLY (p. 213, 4M)
A 15th-century timber-framed house, containing a fine collection of 17th- and 18th-century furniture.
Open 1 Mar–31 Oct: daily, 11am–5.30pm (Sun, opens 2pm).
Entry £2.00/£1.00.
✆ 01342 810479.
🏠🎧❌
➲ *West Hoathly, 4 miles W of Wych Cross off A22. (OS Map 187; ref TQ 810479.)*

Weald & Downland Open Air Museum

Singleton, Chichester, West Sussex PO18 0EU.
Tel: 01243 811348
WEST SUSSEX (p. 212, 4L)
A museum of historic buildings rescued from destruction and re-built on a beautiful 40-acre site in the South Downs.

🅿 ♦♦ ♿ *(limited facilities)* ⛽🍴♟️⚙️⏱️ⓔ
➲ *In Singleton, 6 miles N of Chichester off A286.*
(OS map 197, ref SU 875128.)

Flag Fen Excavations

Fourth Drove, Fengate, Peterborough PE1 5UR.
Tel: 01733 313414.
CAMBRIDGESHIRE (p. 214, 9M)
One of Europe's most important ongoing archaeological sites. The Bronze Age museum contains the earliest wheel in England. See also 3,000-year-old timbers, a re-created fen landscape and primitive breeds of pig and sheep.
🎖️ *Award-winning exhibition hall and Bronze Age farm.*
Open *All year: daily, 10am–5pm (last entry 4pm). Closed 25–26 Dec.*
⏱️ ♦♦ ♿ *(toilets)* ❌🚻🍴⚙️ 💷 🅿
➲ *Signposted from A47 and A1139, 2m from Peterborough city centre.*

Pendle Heritage Centre

Park Hill, Barrowford, Nelson, Lancashire BB9 6JQ.
Tel. 01282 695366
LANCASHIRE (p. 218, 13H)
Situated in a group of historic buildings representing several centuries of architectural styles, the Museum contains displays about the house and its families and the Pendle area.

Open *All year: daily, 10am–5pm.*
Entry *£2.75/£1.50 (50% discount to English Heritage members).*
♦♦ ♿ *(toilets)* 🅿🏠⏱️🍴❌ 💷
➲ *In Barrowford at junction of A682 and B6247.*
🚌 *9/10 from Nelson.*
🚂 *Nelson 1½m.*

Jorvik Viking Centre

Coppergate, York YO1 1NT.
Tel: 01904 643211.
YORK (p. 219, 13K)
A time-car journey back 1,000 years to a bustling street in Jorvik – Viking age York – reconstructed on the site of extensive excavations beneath Coppergate in the heart of the city. A wharf, houses and work-shops, merchants and fisherfolk, have been recreated in accurate detail complete with sounds and smells evocative of the time. Many of the magnificent objects found during the excavations are on dis-play in an exhibition at the centre.
Open *1 April–31 Oct: daily, 9am–7pm. 1 Nov–31 March: daily, 9am–5.30pm.*
Entry *10% discount to English Heritage members. Discount not applicable on Family or PASTport tickets or other reduced admission promotions. Jorvik Viking Centre is a project of the York Archaeological Trust.*
♦♦ ♿ *(toilets provided)* 🏠⏱️❌
✆ *Information Hotline 01904 653000.*
➲ *In Coppergate, York city centre.*
🚌 *From surrounding areas (Tel. 01904 624161).*
🚂 *York ¾m.*

The Archae-ological Resource Centre (ARC)

St Saviour's Church, St Saviourgate, York YO1 2NN.
Tel: 01904 654324.
YORK (p. 219, 13K)
Visit the ARC and touch the past. Meet real archaeologists, learn to sort and identify finds, try out ancient crafts and use computers to learn the value of technology in uncovering the past. Hands-on archaeology for all ages.
Open *All year: Mon–Fri, 10am–4pm, Sat, 1–4pm (last admission 3.30pm). Closed Suns and last 2 weeks of December.*
Entry *25% discount for English Heritage members. Discount not applicable on Family or PASTport tickets or other reduced admission promotions. The ARC is a project of the York Archaeological Trust, registered charity 509 060.*
♦♦ ♿ *(toilets provided)* ❌
✆ *Information Hotline 01904 653000.*

Merchant Adventurers' Hall

Fossgate, York YO1 2XD.
Tel: 01904 654818.
YORK (p. 219, 13K)
Finest remaining guild hall in Europe today, little altered since its 14th-century origin. It houses furniture, paintings, archives, silver and other objects used by the merchants of York.
Entry *£1.90/£1.60/60p*
♦♦ ⏱️❌🏠⚙️
➲ *In York, from Piccadilly near Clifford's Tower.*
(OS map 105, ref SE 605517.)

199

Free or half-price admission to historic sites throughout Britain

English Heritage members planning to spend some time across England's borders will benefit from our long-standing arrangement with our sister organizations in Scotland, Wales and the Isle of Man. Entry to these properties, totalling over 100 sites, is half-price in the first year of membership and free in the following years. *These benefits are only available to members of English Heritage.*

For further information about these sites, please contact our sister organizations:

HISTORIC SCOTLAND

Historic Scotland, Longmore House, Salisbury Place, Edinburgh EH9 1SH. Tel: 0131 668 8800.

Aberdour Castle

FIFE & CENTRAL (p. 220, 20F)
A 14th-century castle, extended in the 16th and 17th centuries with splendid residential accommodation and a terraced garden and bowling green. There is a fine circular dovecote.
✆ *01383 860519.* ➲ *In Aberdour.*

Arbroath Abbey

TAYSIDE (p. 220, 21G)
The substantial ruins of a Tironensian monastery, founded by William the Lion in 1178. Parts of the abbey church and domestic buildings remain. This was the scene of the Declaration of Arbroath of 1320, which asserted Scotland's independence from England.
✆ *01241 878756.* ➲ *In Arbroath.*

Balvenie Castle

GRAMPIAN (p. 220, 24G)
A castle of enclosure first owned by the Comyns with a curtain wall of 13th-century date. Added to in the 15th and 16th centuries and visited by Mary Queen of Scots in 1562.
✆ *01340 820121.* ➲ *At Dufftown.*

Bishop's and Earl's Palaces

ORKNEY (p. 220, 29G)
The Bishop's palace is a 12th-century hall-house, later much altered, with a round tower begun by Bishop Reid in 1541. A later addition was made by the notorious Patrick Stewart, Earl of Orkney, who built the adjacent Earl's Palace between 1600 and 1607 in a splendid Renaissance style.
✆ *01856 875461.*
➲ *In Kirkwall.*

Black House

Arnol, HIGHLANDS & WESTERN ISLES (p. 220, 27A)
A traditional Lewis thatched house, with byre, attached barn and stackyard, complete and furnished.
✆ *01851 710395.*
➲ *In Arnol village, Lewis.*

Blackness Castle

FIFE & CENTRAL (p. 220, 20F)
Built in the 1440s, and massively strengthened in the 16th century as an artillery fortress, Blackness was an ammunition depot in the 1870s. It was restored by the Office of Works in the 1920s.
✆ *01506 834807.*
➲ *4m N of Linlithgow, on a promontory in the Forth estuary.*

Bonawe Iron Furnace

ARGYLL & BUTE & ARRAN (p. 220, 21C)
Founded in 1753 by a Lake District partnership, this is the most complete charcoal-fuelled ironworks in Britain. Displays illustrate how iron was made here.
✆ *01866 2432.*
➲ *Close to the village of Taynuilt.*

Bothwell Castle

SOUTH STRATHCLYDE (p. 220, 19E)
The largest and finest 13th-century stone castle in Scotland, much fought over during the Wars of Independence. Part of the original circular keep survives, but most of the castle dates from the 14th and 15th centuries.
✆ *01698 816894.*
➲ *In Bothwell, approached from Uddingston, off the B7071.*

Broch of Gurness

ORKNEY (p. 220, 30G)
Protected by three lines of ditch and rampart, the base of the broch is surrounded by a warren of Iron Age buildings.
✆ *01856 841815.*
➲ *At Aikerness, about 14m NW of Kirkwall.*

Caerlaverock Castle

DUMFRIES & GALLOWAY
(p. 220, 17F)

One of the finest castles in Scotland, on a triangular site surrounded by moats. Its special features are the twin-towered gatehouse and the Nithsdale Lodging, a Renaissance range dating from 1638.

☎ *01387 770244*.

➲ *8m SE of Dumfries.*

Cardoness Castle

DUMFRIES & GALLOWAY
(p. 220, 16D)

The well-preserved ruin of a tower house of 15th-century date, the ancient home of the McCullochs.

☎ *01557 814427*.

➲ *1m SW of Gatehouse of Fleet.*

Castle Campbell

FIFE & CENTRAL (p. 220, 20E)

Traditionally known as the 'Castle of Gloom'. The oldest part is a well-preserved 15th-century tower, around which other buildings were constructed, including an unusual loggia.

☎ *01259 742408*.

➲ *At the head of Dollar Glen.*

Corgarff Castle

GRAMPIAN (p. 220, 23F)

A 16th-century tower house converted into a barracks for Hanoverian troops in 1748. Its last military use was to control the smuggling of illicit whisky between 1827 and 1831. Still complete and with star-shaped fortification.

☎ *01975 651460*. ➲ *8m W of Strathdon village.*

Craigmillar Castle

LOTHIAN (p. 220, 19F)

Built round an L-plan tower house of the early 15th century,

Craigmillar was much expanded in the 15th and 16th centuries. It is a handsome ruin, and includes a range of private rooms.

☎ *0131 661 4445*.

➲ *2½m SE of central Edinburgh, to E of Edinburgh–Dalkeith road.*

Craignethan Castle

SOUTH STRATHCLYDE
(p. 220, 19E)

The oldest part is a tower house built by Sir James Hamilton of Finnart in the 16th century, defended by an outer wall pierced by gun ports, and by a wide and deep ditch with a most unusual 'caponier' – a stone vaulted chamber for artillery.

☎ *01555 860364*.

➲ *5½m NW of Lanark.*

Crichton Castle

LOTHIAN (p. 220, 19G)

A large and sophisticated castle, of which the most spectacular part is the range erected by the Earl of Bothwell between 1581 and 1591.

☎ *01875 320017*.

➲ *2½m SW of Pathhead.*

Crossraguel Abbey

SOUTH STRATHCLYDE
(p. 220, 18D)

The 13th-century remains, which are remarkably complete and of high quality, include the church, cloister, chapter house and much of the domestic premises.

☎ *01655 883113*. ➲ *2m S of Maybole.*

Dallas Dhu Distillery and Visitor Centre

GRAMPIAN (p. 220, 25F)

A perfectly preserved time capsule of the distiller's art. Built in 1898 to supply malt whisky for Wright and Greig's 'Roderick Dhu' blend.

Video presentation and a glass of whisky to end your visit.

☎ *01309 676548*. ➲ *About 1m S of Forres off the Grantown Road.*

Dirleton Castle and Gardens

LOTHIAN (p. 220, 20G)

The oldest part of this romantic castle dates from the 13th century. It was rebuilt in the 14th century and extended in the 16th century, when the gardens were established.

☎ *01620 850330*. ➲ *In the village of Dirleton.*

Doune Castle

FIFE & CENTRAL (p. 220, 20E)

A late 14th-century courtyard castle built for the Regent Albany. Its most striking feature is the combination of keep, gatehouse and hall, with its kitchen in a massive frontal block.

☎ *01786 841742*. ➲ *In Doune.*

Dryburgh Abbey

BORDERS (p. 220, 18G)

Both beautifully situated and of intrinsic quality, the ruins of Dryburgh Abbey are remarkably complete. Much of the work is of the 12th and 13th century. Sir Walter Scott and Field Marshal Earl Haig are buried in the abbey.

☎ *01835 822381*.

➲ *5m SE of Melrose, near St Boswells.*

Dumbarton Castle

SOUTH STRATHCLYDE
(p. 220, 20D)

Spectacularly sited on a volcanic rock, this was the site of the ancient capital of Strathclyde. The most interesting features are the 18th-century artillery fortifications, with 19th-century guns.

☎ *01389 732167*. ➲ *At Dumbarton.*

Dundonald Castle

SOUTH STRATHCLYDE
(p. 220, 18D)
A fine 13th-century tower built
by Robert II incorporating part of
an earlier building. The king used
the castle as a summer residence
until his death in 1390.
☏ 01563 850201.
➲ *In Dundonald, off the A759.*

Dundrennan Abbey

DUMFRIES & GALLOWAY
(p. 220, 16E)
The beautiful ruins of a Cistercian
abbey founded by David I. Mary
Queen of Scots spent her last night
on Scottish soil here.
☏ 01557 500262.
➲ *6½m SE of Kirkcudbright.*

Dunfermline Abbey and Palace

FIFE & CENTRAL
(p. 220, 20F)
The remains of a Benedictine
abbey which was founded by
Queen Margaret in the 11th
century. The foundations of her
church are under the superb,
Romanesque nave, built in the
12th century. Robert the Bruce
was buried in the choir, now the
site of the present parish church.
☏ 01383 739026.
➲ *In Dunfermline.*

Dunstaffnage Castle and Chapel

ARGYLL & BUTE & ARRAN
(p. 220, 21B)
A very fine 13th-century castle
enclosure, built on a rock,
with nearby ruins of a chapel
of exceptional architectural
refinement.
☏ 01631 562465.
➲ *By Loch Etive, 3½m from Oban.*

Edinburgh Castle

LOTHIAN (p. 220, 20F)
The most famous of Scottish castles
has a complex history. The oldest
part dates from the Norman period;
there is a Great Hall built by the
James IV; the Half Moon battery was
built by Regent Morton in the late
16th century; the Scottish National
War Memorial was formed after
World War I. The castle also houses
the crown jewels (Honours) of
Scotland, the history of which is
described in a new exhibition. Also
see the famous 15th-century gun,
Mons Meg. Attractive restaurant
with spectacular views over the city.
☏ 0131 225 9846.
➲ *In the centre of Edinburgh.*

Edzell Castle and Garden

TAYSIDE (p. 220, 22G)
Very beautiful complex with a late-
medieval tower house incorporated
into a 16th-century courtyard mansion. The carved decoration of the
garden walls is unique in Britain.
☏ 01356 648631.
➲ *At Edzell, 6m N of Brechin.*

Elgin Cathedral

GRAMPIAN (p. 220, 25F)
The superb ruin of what many
think was Scotland's most beautiful
cathedral. Much of the work is in a
rich late 13th century style, much
modified after the burning of the
church by the Wolf of Badenoch in
1390. The octaganol chapter
house is the finest in Scotland.
☏ 01343 547171. ➲ *In Elgin.*

Fort George

HIGHLANDS & WESTERN ISLES
(p. 220, 25E)
A vast site and one of the most outstanding artillery fortifications in

Europe. It was planned in 1747 as
a base for George II's army, and
was completed in 1769. Since then
it has served as a barracks. There
are reconstructions of barrack
rooms in different periods and a
display of muskets and pikes.
☏ 01667 462777.
➲ *11m NE of Inverness, by
the village of Ardersier.*

Glenluce Abbey

DUMFRIES & GALLOWAY
(p. 220, 16C)
Cistercian abbey founded in 1192.
The remains include a handsome
early 16th-century chapter house.
☏ 01581 300541.
➲ *2m N of Glenluce village.*

Hermitage Castle

BORDERS (p. 220, 17G)
A vast and eerie ruin in a lonely
situation, of the 14th and 15th
centuries. Mary Queen of Scots
made her famous ride there to
meet the Earl of Bothwell.
☏ 013873 76222.
➲ *In Liddesdale, 5½m NE of
Newcastleton, off the B6399.*

Huntingtower Castle

TAYSIDE (p. 220, 21F)
Two fine and complete towers, of
the 15th and 16th centuries, now
linked by a 17th-century range.
There are fine painted ceilings.
☏ 01738 627231.
➲ *2m W of Perth.*

Huntly Castle

GRAMPIAN (p. 220, 24G)
A magnificent ruin consisting
mainly of a palace block erected
in the 16th and 17th centuries by
the Gordon family.
☏ 01466 793191.
➲ *In Huntly.*

Inchcolm Abbey

FIFE & CENTRAL (p. 220, 20F)
The best-preserved group of monastic buildings in Scotland, founded in about 1123, and including a 13th-century octagonal chapter house.
℅ *0131 331 4857.*
➲ *On an island on the Firth of Forth, opposite Aberdour. Ferries from South Queensferry and North Queensferry.*

Inchmahome Priory

FIFE & CENTRAL (p. 220, 20D)
A beautifully situated Augustinian monastery founded in 1238, with much of the original 13th-century building surviving.
℅ *01877 385294.* ➲ *On an island in the Lake of Menteith, approached by boat from Port of Menteith.*

Jarlshof Prehistoric and Norse Settlement

SHETLAND (p. 220, INSET)
An very important site with a complex of ancient settlements within three acres. The oldest is a Bronze Age village of oval stone huts. There is an Iron Age broch and an entire Viking settlement. The visitor centre has new displays on Iron Age life and a history of the site.
℅ *01950 460112.* ➲ *At Sumburgh Head, about 22m S of Lerwick.*

Jedburgh Abbey and Visitor Centre

BORDERS (p. 220, 18G)
One of the abbeys founded by David I and the Bishop of Glasgow in about 1138 for Augustinian canons. The church is mostly in Romanesque and early Gothic styles and is remarkably complete.
℅ *01835 863925.*
➲ *In Jedburgh.*

Kildrummy Castle

GRAMPIAN (p. 220, 24G)
Though ruined, the best example in Scotland of a 13th-century castle, with a curtain wall, four round towers, hall and chapel. The seat of the Earls of Mar, it was dismantled after the 1715 Jacobite Rising.
℅ *01975 571331.* ➲ *10m W of Alford.*

Kinnaird Head Lighthouse

GRAMPIAN (p. 220, 25H)
Built in 1787 within a 16th-century tower house, Kinnaird Head was the first lighthouse built by the Northern Lighthouse Company.
℅ *01346 511022.*
➲ *On a promontory in Fraserburgh.*

Linlithgow Palace

LOTHIAN (p. 220, 20E)
Magnificent ruin of a great royal palace, set in its own park. All the Stewart kings lived here, and work commissioned by James I, III, IV, V and VI can be seen. The great hall and the chapel are particularly fine.
℅ *01506 842896.* ➲ *In Linlithgow.*

Lochleven Castle

TAYSIDE (p. 220, 21F)
Late 14th-century tower on one side of an irregular courtyard. Mary Queen of Scots was imprisoned here in 1567 and escaped in 1568.
℅ *01786 450000.*
➲ *On an island in Loch Leven, accessible by boat from Kinross.*

Maclellan's Castle

DUMFRIES & GALLOWAY (p. 220, 16E)
A castellated town house built by the then provost of Kirkcudbright from 1577, with particularly good architectural details.
℅ *01557 331856.*
➲ *In the centre of Kirkcudbright.*

Maes Howe Chambered Cairn

ORKNEY (p. 220, 29G)
The finest megalithic tomb in the British Isles, with a large mound covering a stone-built passage and a large burial chamber with cells in the walls. Of Neolithic date, broken into during Viking times, with Viking runes carved on the walls.
℅ *01856 761606.*
➲ *About 9m W of Kirkwall.*

Meigle Sculptured Stone Museum

TAYSIDE (p. 220, 22F)
A magnificent collection of 25 sculptured monuments of the Celtic Christian period, one of the finest collections of Dark Age sculpture in Western Europe.
℅ *01828 640612.* ➲ *In Meigle.*

Melrose Abbey

BORDERS (p. 220, 19G)
Probably the most famous ruin in Scotland, founded around 1136 as a Cistercian abbey by David I, and repeatedly wrecked in the Wars of Independence. The surviving remains of the church are 15th century and of an elegance unique in Scotland. The Commendator's house contains displays relating to the abbey's history and to the Roman fort at Newstead.
℅ *01896 822562.* ➲ *In Melrose.*

New Abbey Corn Mill

DUMFRIES & GALLOWAY (p. 220, 17E)
A carefully renovated water-powered oatmeal mill, in working order, and demonstrated regularly to visitors in the summer.
℅ *01387 850260.*
➲ *In New Abbey village.*

Newark Castle

SOUTH STRATHCLYDE
(p. 220, 20D)
The oldest part of the castle is a tower built soon after 1478, with a detached gatehouse. The main part was added in 1597–9 by Patrick Maxwell.
(01475 741858.
➲ *In Port Glasgow.*

Rothesay Castle

ARGYLL & BUTE & ARRAN
(p. 220, 20C)
A remarkable 13th-century, circular castle of enclosure. A favourite residence of the Stewart kings.
(01700 502691.
➲ *In Rothesay, Isle of Bute.*

St Andrews Castle and Visitor Centre

FIFE & CENTRAL
(p. 220, 21G)
Ruins of the castle of the Archbishops of St Andrews, dating in part from the 13th century. Features include a 'bottle dungeon', and mine and counter-mine tunnelled during the siege that followed the murder of Cardinal Beaton in 1546. Visitor Centre with shop and major exhibition depicting the history of the castle and cathedral.
(01334 477196.
➲ *In St Andrews.*

St Andrews Cathedral

FIFE & CENTRAL (p. 220, 21G)
Remains of the largest cathedral in Scotland, and of the priory's domestic ranges. The precinct walls are particularly well-preserved.
(01334 472563.
➲ *In St Andrews.*

Seton Collegiate Church

LOTHIAN (p. 220, 20G)
The chancel and apse of this lovely building date from the 15th century, and the transepts and steeple were built by the widow of Lord Seton, who was killed at Flodden in 1513.
(01875 813334.
➲ *1m SE of Cockenzie off Edinburgh–North Berwick Road.*

Skara Brae Prehistoric Village

ORKNEY (p. 220, 29F)
The best-preserved group of Stone Age houses in Western Europe. The houses contain hearths, stone furniture and drains, and give a remarkable picture of life in Neolithic times.
(01856 841815.
➲ *19m NW of Kirkwall.*

Smailholm Tower

BORDERS (p. 220, 19G)
A simple rectangular tower in a good state of preservation. It houses costume figures and tapestries relating to Sir Walter Scott's 'Minstrelsy of the Scottish Borders'.
(01573 460365.
➲ *Near Smailholm village, 6m NW of Kelso.*

Spynie Palace

GRAMPIAN (p. 220, 25F)
Residence of the Bishops of Moray from the 14th century to 1686. The site is dominated by the massive tower built by Bishop David Stewart (1461–77).
(01343 546358.
➲ *2m N of Elgin, off the A941.*

Stirling Castle

FIFE & CENTRAL
(p. 220, 20E)
The grandest of all Scottish castles. The Great Hall and the Gatehouse of James IV, the marvellous Palace of James V, the Chapel Royal remodelled by James VI, and the artillery fortifications of the 16th and 18th centuries, are all of outstanding interest. Medieval kitchens and introductory display now open.
(01786 50000. ➲ *In Stirling.*

Sweetheart Abbey

DUMFRIES & GALLOWAY
(p. 220, 17E)
Splendid ruin of a late 13th- and early 14th-century Cistercian abbey founded by Dervorgilla, Lady of Galloway.
(01387 850397. ➲ *In New Abbey village, 7m S of Dumfries.*

Tantallon Castle

LOTHIAN (p. 220, 20G)
Remarkable fortification with earthwork defences, and a massive 14th-century curtain wall with towers. Interpretive displays include replica guns.
(01620 892727.
➲ *3m E of North Berwick.*

Threave Castle

DUMFRIES & GALLOWAY
(p. 220, 17E)
Massive tower built in the late 14th century. Round its base is an artillery fortification built before 1455, when the castle was besieged by James II. It is on an island, approached by boat, followed by a long walk.
(0831 168512.
➲ *3m W of Castle Douglas.*

Tolquhon Castle

GRAMPIAN

(p. 220, 24H)

Built for the Forbes family, Tolquhon has an early 15th-century tower. It is noted for its highly ornamented gatehouse.

✆ 01651 851286.

➲ *15m from Aberdeen off the Pitmedden–Tarves Road.*

Urquhart Castle

HIGHLANDS & WESTERN ISLES

(p. 220, 24D)

Standing above Loch Ness, this was one of the largest castles in Scotland, having fallen into decay after 1689. Most of the existing buildings date from after the 16th century.

✆ 01456 450551.

➲ *On Loch Ness, near Drumnadrochit.*

Whithorn Priory and Museum

DUMFRIES & GALLOWAY

(p. 220, 16D)

Site of the first Christian church in Scotland, founded as 'Candida Casa' by St Ninian in the early 5th century. The priory was built over the church for remonstratensian canons in the 12th century and became the cathedral church of Galloway. In the museum is a fine collection of early Christian stones.

✆ 01988 500508. ➲ *In Whithorn.*

 Cadw: Welsh Historic Monuments, CADW **Crown Building,** Cathays Park, Cardiff CF1 3NQ. Tel: 01222 500200.

Beaumaris Castle

ANGLESEY (p. 216, 11D)

Begun in 1295, this unfinished castle was the last and largest of King Edward I's Welsh fortifications. Formidable defences survive, surrounded by a partly restored moat.

✆ 01248 810361.

➲ *In Beaumaris, off A545.*

(OS Map 114; ref SH 607762.)

Blaenavon Ironworks

TORFAEN (p. 217, 6F)

Substantial remains of five early blast furnaces and associated workers' housing, dating in part from 1788–89.

➲ *6m N of Pontypool, off A4043.*

(OS Map 161; ref SO 249092.)

Caerleon Roman Fortress

NEWPORT (p. 217, 6F)

Site of the 50-acre Roman legionary fortress of Isca, dating from *c*. AD75. Impressive remains of the Fortress Baths, amphitheatre ('King Arthur's Round Table'), barracks and fortress wall.

✆ 01633 422518.

🚪⊗🅿

➲ *B4596 to Caerleon, from M4.*

(OS Map 171; ref ST 337906.)

Caernarfon Castle

GWYNEDD (p. 216, 11D)

With its nine polygonal towers (including the great Eagle Tower), two gatehouses and walls of colour-banded stone, the castle was intended by King Edward I to

be a royal residence and seat of government for North Wales.

✆ 01286 677617. 🚪 �♦♦

➲ *In Caernarfon town centre.*

(OS Map 115; ref SH 477626.)

Caerphilly Castle

CAERPHILLY (p. 216, 6F)

One of the largest medieval fortresses in Britain, begun in 1268 by the Anglo-Norman Marcher lord, Gilbert de Clare. Famous for its 'leaning tower'. Impressive great hall, now used for various functions.

✆ 01222 883143.

🚪♦♦🎧

➲ *In Caerphilly town centre.*

(OS Map 171; ref ST155870.)

Carreg Cennen Castle

CARMARTHENSHIRE (p. 216, 7E)

Magnificently located castle, high on a limestone precipice. Surviving remains date from the late 13th and early 14th centuries, including an underground passage and cave.

✆ 01558 822291. 🅿🚪

➲ *Near Trapp, off A484, 4m SE of Llandeilo.*

(OS Map 159; ref SH 668191.)

Castell Coch

CARDIFF (p. 216, 6F)

A unique, late 19th century fairytale-style castle, which was designed for the third Marquess of Bute by William Burges. It is lavishly decorated and furnished in the Victorian Gothic style; a 'romantic' vision of the Middle Ages.

✆ 01222 810101.

🅿♦♦🚪🎧

➲ *Near Tongwynlais, off A470, 5m NW of Cardiff.*

(OS Map 171; ref ST 131826.)

Chepstow Castle

MONMOUTHSHIRE (p. 217, 6G)
Substantial remains of one of the earliest stone-built castles in Britain and the centre of the medieval Marcher lordship of Chepstow. The castle was modified and developed in successive stages throughout the Middle Ages and again following the Civil War.
℡ 01291 624065. 🅿️ 🖂
➤ *In Chepstow town centre, off A48 or M4. (OS Map 162; ref ST 533941.)*

Cilgerran Castle

CEREDIGION (p. 216, 7C)
Picturesque remains that date from the early 13th century.
➤ *In Cilgerran, 3m S of Cardigan, off A478. (OS Map 145; ref SN 195431.)*

Conwy Castle

CONWY (p. 216, 11E)
Built for King Edward I between 1283 and 1287, Master James of St George's design at Conwy remains one of the most outstanding achievements of medieval military architecture.
℡ 01492 592358. 🖂 👫
➤ *In Conwy town centre. (OS Map 115; ref SH 783774.)*

Criccieth Castle

GWYNEDD (p. 216, 10D)
Perched in an imposing position, the castle is still dominated by the twin-towered gatehouse built by Prince Llywelyn ab Iorwerth ('the Great'). Later remodelled by Edward I and Edward II.
℡ 01766 522227. 👫 ➤ *On coastal bluff, near Criccieth town centre. (OS Map 123/124; ref SH 500377.)*

Cymer Abbey

GWYNEDD (p. 216, 10E)
Remains of a simple abbey church, founded in 1198 by Maredudd ap Cynan for the Cistercian order.
℡ 01341 422854. ➤ *Near Llanelltyd, off A470, 1½m N of Dolgellau. (OS Map 124; ref SH 721195.)*

Dolwyddelan Castle

CONWY (p. 216, 10E)
A square stone keep, dating from the 13th century, remains of this castle built by Llywelyn ab Iorwerth. The site was later remodelled by King Edward I.
℡ 01690 750366. ➤ *1m W of Dolwyddelan, on A470. (OS Map 115; ref SH 721523.)*

Harlech Castle

GWYNEDD (p. 216, 10D)
Built between 1283 and 1289 by Master James of St George for King Edward I. The castle is designed on a concentric plan. Seized by Owain Glyndŵr and held successfully by him for four years.
℡ 01766 780552. 🅿️ 👫 🖂
➤ *Harlech town centre. (OS Map 124; ref SH 581312.)*

Kidwelly Castle

CARMARTHENSHIRE (p. 216, 6D)
Impressive remains of a castle established as a huge earthwork in the early 12th century. The stone castle was raised by the de Chaworths in the 13th century, and was much modified later by the Earls of Lancaster.
℡ 01554 890104. 🅿️ 👫 🖂 🎧
➤ *In centre of Kidwelly. (OS Map 159; ref SN 409701.)*

Laugharne Castle

CARMARTHENSHIRE (p. 216, 6D)
Established during the 12th century, Laugharne underwent many transformations under a long series of occupiers, which included the Anglo-Norman de Brian family and, in the 16th century, Sir John Perrot
℡ 01994 427906. ➤ *In Laugharne on A4066, 14m SW of Carmarthen. (OS Map 159; ref SN 302107.)*

Oxwich Castle

SWANSEA (p. 216, 6D)
Remains of a sumptuous courtyard house built by the Mansel family during the 16th century.
℡ 01792 390359. 🅿️
➤ *In Oxwich, off A4118, Gower peninsula, 8m SW of Swansea. (OS Map 159; ref SS 497862.)*

Plas Mawr

CONWY (p. 216, 11E)
Possibly the best-preserved Elizabethan townhouse in Great Britain. Built by Robert Wynn between 1576 and 1585 and now faithfully restored, it dominates the town with its gatehouse, stepped gables and lookout tower. The interior, with its elaborately decorated plasterwork and fine timber screens, has been refurnished to illustrate its occupation by the Wynn family in the 16th and 17th centuries.
🎧 🖂 ➤ *In High Street, Conwy. (OS Map 115, ref SH 781776.)*

Raglan Castle

MONMOUTHSHIRE (p. 217, 6G)
Remains of impressive 15th-century castle built by Sir William ap Thomas and his son William Herbert, and later remodelled by William, Earl of Worcester. Despite demolition attempts during the Civil War, much survives.
℡ 01291 690228. 🅿️ 👫 ➤ *½m N of Raglan, 7m SW of Monmouth, off A40. (OS Map 161; ref S414083.)*

Rhuddlan Castle

DENBIGHSHIRE (p. 216, 11F)
Begun in 1277, this was the
second of King Edward I's great
Welsh fortifications. A protected
river dock forms one side of the
defences of this concentrically
planned castle.

(01745 590777. ▣ ⋔
➲ *In Rhuddlan, 3m S of Rhyl.*
(OS Map 116; ref SJ 026777.)

Rug Chapel and Llangar Church

DENBIGHSHIRE (p. 216, 7B)
Built in 1637, Rug is best described
as 'the painted chapel' with its
glorious interior roof carried on
the wings of wooden angels, which
adorn the trusses. Just a mile or so
from Rug you will find the former
parish church of All Saints,
Llangar. The wall paintings are of
immense importance, dating from
the 14th to 18th centuries.

(01490 412025. ▣ ⋔
➲ *W of Corwen, off A5(T).*
(OS Map 125; ref SJ 055442.)

St Davids Bishop's Palace

PEMBROKESHIRE (p. 216, 7B)
Imposing palace within the defended perimeter of the cathedral
precincts. The surviving buildings
date chiefly from the 14th century,
particularly the work of Bishop
Henry de Gower. It is de Gower's
celebrated arcaded parapet that is
one of the glories of the site.

(01437 720517.
➲ *Near centre of St Davids.*
(OS Map 157; ref SM 750254.)

Strata Florida Abbey

CEREDIGION (p. 216, 8E)
Initially founded in 1164 on a
nearby site, the present buildings
were erected under the patronage
of the Lord Rhys. The Cistercians
at Strata Florida were loyal
supporters of the Welsh princes.
Burial place of the poet Dafydd
ap Gwilym.

(01974 831261.
➲ *1¼m SE of Pontrhydfendigaid, off
B4343, 14m SE of Aberystwyth.*
(OS Map 135; ref SN 746657.)

Talley Abbey

CARMARTHENSHIRE
(p. 216, 7D)
Founded for the Premon-
stratensian order by the Lord Rhys,
between 1184 and 1189, parts of
the abbey church survive.
➲ *In Talley, on B4302, 6m
N of Llandeilo.*
(OS Map 146; ref JN 632327.)

Tintern Abbey

MONMOUTHSHIRE
(p. 217, 6G)
This beautifully located Cistercian
abbey, founded in 1131 in the
stunning Wye Valley, has a remarkably complete abbey church
rebuilt in the later 13th century.

(01291 689251. ▣ ⋔ ⛶ ⌾
➲ *In Tintern, on A466, 5m
N of Chepstow.*
(OS Map 162; ref SO 533000.)

Tretower Castle

POWYS (p. 217, 7F)
Motte and bailey castle established
during the Norman conquest of
Brycheiniog. The shell-keep was
raised on the mound about 1150,
and a round tower added in the
early 13th century.

(01874 730279. ▣ ⋔ ⌾
➲ *In Tretower, off A40, 3m
NW of Crickhowell.*
(OS Map 161; ref SO 185212.)

Tretower Court

POWYS (p. 217, 7F)
Restored courtyard house with
origins in the 15th century.
Magnificent timberwork survives
in the northern and western
ranges, with later classical-style
windows dating from the 1630s.

(01874 730279. ▣ ⋔ ⌾
➲ *In Tretower, off A40, 3m
NW of Crickhowell.*
(OS Map 161; ref SO 185212.)

Valle Crucis Abbey

DENBIGHSHIRE (p. 217, 10F)
There are extensive remains of
this Cistercian abbey founded in
1201. The church dates from the
13th century, and the east range
of the cloister was remodelled
around 1400.

(01978 860326. ▣ ⋔
➲ *1½m NW of Llangollen, on A542.*
(OS Map 117; ref SJ 205442.)

Weobley Castle

SWANSEA (p. 216, 6D)
Picturesque medieval fortified
manor house. There are
substantial remains dating
principally from the later 13th
and 14th centuries.

(01792 390012. ▣
➲ *2m W of Llanrhidian, off B4271,
11m W of Swansea.*
(OS Map 159; ref SS 478927.)

White Castle

MONMOUTHSHIRE (p. 217, 7G)
Imposing moated remains of a
12th-century castle, probably the
work of Henry II. It was
substantially remodelled in the
later 13th century.

(01600 780380. ➲ *6m NE of
Abergavenny, off B4233.*
(OS Map 161; ref SO 379167.)

The Manx Museum, Douglas, Isle of Man IM1 3LY. Tel: 01624 648000.

Castle Rushen

Castletown (p. 216, INSET)
This impressive limestone fortress is one of Britain's most complete medieval castles. The castle has its origins in the Norse period and the last Viking King, Magnus, died here in 1265. The settlement that grew up to serve the castle became the main governmental centre and island capital until the major port of Douglas took over in 1869.
℡ 01624 648000. ● *In Castletown.*

Cregneash Village Folk Museum

Creagneash (p. 216, INSET)
Nestling under Meayll Hill, with stunning views of the Calf of Man. Cregneash is a unique illustration of 19th-century life in a Manx upland crofting community. The distinctive white-washed and thatched buildings include a weaver's shed, a turner's workshop and a smithy.
℡ 01624 648000.
● *Near Port St Mary, Cregneash.*

Grove Museum

Ramsey (p. 216, INSET)
A perfectly preserved Victorian house, the Grove Museum was developed as a summer retreat for Duncan Gibb, a shipping merchant from Liverpool. The rooms house displays of toys and costumes, whilst the outhouses hold a fascinating collection of vehicles and agricultural implements.
℡ 01624 648000. ● *In Ramsey.*

Laxey Wheel

Laxey (p. 216, INSET)
The great Laxey Wheel was built in 1854. Designed to pump water from the Laxey Mining Company's mines, the wheel has a diameter of 22 metres, and is the largest working watermill in the world.
℡ 01624 648000. ● *In Laxey.*

Manx Museum

Douglas (p. 216, INSET)
The visitor can walk through a sequence of newly designed galleries depicting art, historic maps, natural history, prehistoric, Viking and early medieval archaeology and social history bringing the chronological story of island life up to the present day.
℡ 01624 648000. ● *In Douglas.*

Nautical Museum

Castletown (p. 216, INSET)
Situated at the mouth of Castletown harbour, the museum contains an 18th-century armed yacht, 'The Peggy', built by George Quayle in 1791. It is shown in its original boathouse, where it remained undisturbed for a century after its owner's death, being rediscovered in 1935. Exhibits and photographs bring alive maritime life on the Isle.
℡ 01624 648000. ● *In Castletown.*

Old Grammar School

Castletown (p. 216, INSET)
Built c.1200 as Castletown's first church, St Mary's chapel played an important role in the history of Manx education. A school was first recorded in the chapel in 1570. Saved from destruction by the Manx Museum in 1950, its displays recount its history and include a Victorian period school room.
℡ 01624 648000. ● *In Castletown.*

Peel Castle

Peel (p. 216, INSET)
Situated on the important site of St Patrick's Isle at Peel, the castle's wall encircles the ruins of many buildings, including the 11th-century church and round tower and the 13th-century Cathedral of St German. In the 11th century the castle became the ruling seat of the Norse Kingdom of Man and the Isles. Recent archaeological excavation has uncovered artefacts from the Norse period, now on display at the Manx Museum in Douglas.
℡ 01624 648000. ● *In Peel.*

A guide to maps

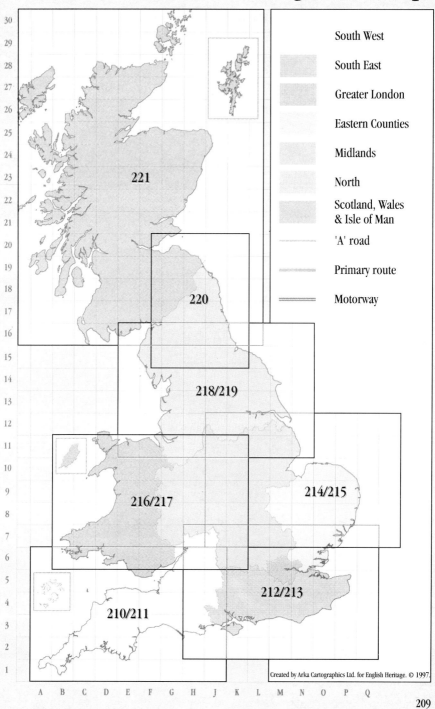

	South West
	South East
	Greater London
	Eastern Counties
	Midlands
	North
	Scotland, Wales & Isle of Man
	'A' road
	Primary route
	Motorway

221

220

218/219

216/217

214/215

212/213

210/211

Created by Arka Cartographics Ltd. for English Heritage. © 1997.

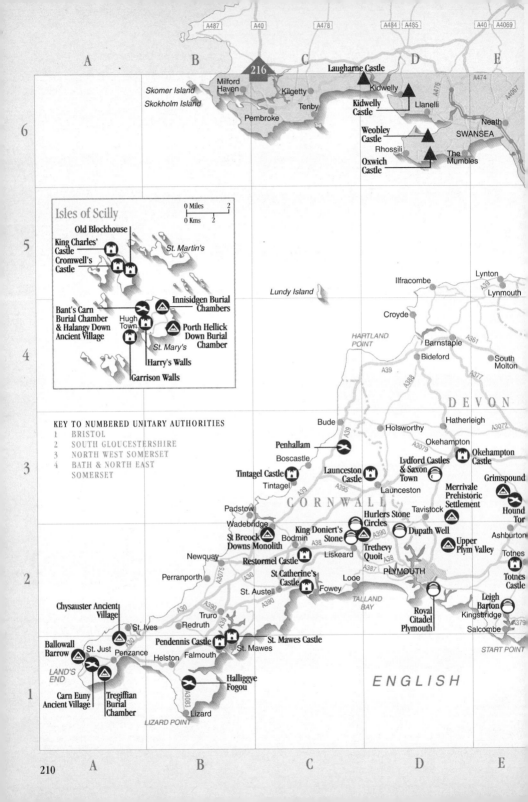

Map labels

A487   A40   A478   A484 A485   A40 A4069

A474

Laugharne Castle

216

Skomer Island
Skokholm Island

Milford Haven
Kilgetty
Tenby
Pembroke

Kidwelly
Kidwelly Castle
Llanelli
A476

Neath

Weobley Castle
SWANSEA

Rhossili

Oxwich Castle
The Mumbles

6

Isles of Scilly

0 Miles 2
0 Kms 2

Old Blockhouse
King Charles' Castle
Cromwell's Castle

St. Martin's

Bant's Carn Burial Chamber & Halangy Down Ancient Village

Innisidgen Burial Chambers

Hugh Town

Porth Hellick Down Burial Chamber

St. Mary's

Harry's Walls

Garrison Walls

5

Lundy Island

Ilfracombe

Lynton
Lynmouth

A39

Croyde

HARTLAND POINT

Barnstaple
A361

Bideford

South Molton

A39   A388   A377

D E V O N

KEY TO NUMBERED UNITARY AUTHORITIES
1 BRISTOL
2 SOUTH GLOUCESTERSHIRE
3 NORTH WEST SOMERSET
4 BATH & NORTH EAST SOMERSET

Hatherleigh
A3072

Bude
Holsworthy
Okehampton
Okehampton Castle

A39

Penhallam
Boscastle

A3079

Lydford Castles & Saxon Town

Grimspound

Tintagel Castle
Tintagel

Launceston Castle
Launceston

Merrivale Prehistoric Settlement

Hound Tor

Padstow

Tavistock

Ashburton

C O R N W A L L

Wadebridge

Hurlers Stone Circles

Dupath Well

Totnes

St Breock Downs Monolith

Bodmin

King Doniert's Stone

Upper Plym Valley

Totnes Castle

Newquay

A30

Restormel Castle

Liskeard

Trethevy Quoit
A38

PLYMOUTH

Perranporth

A3075

St. Austell

St Catherine's Castle

Looe

A387

TALLAND BAY

Leigh Barton

Fowey

Royal Citadel Plymouth

Kingsbridge

Chysauster Ancient Village

Truro
Redruth

St. Ives

Salcombe
A379

START POINT

Ballowall Barrow

St. Just
Penzance

Pendennis Castle

St. Mawes Castle

LAND'S END

Helston
Falmouth
St. Mawes

ENGLISH

Carn Euny Ancient Village

Tregiffian Burial Chamber

Halliggye Fogou

A3083

Lizard

LIZARD POINT

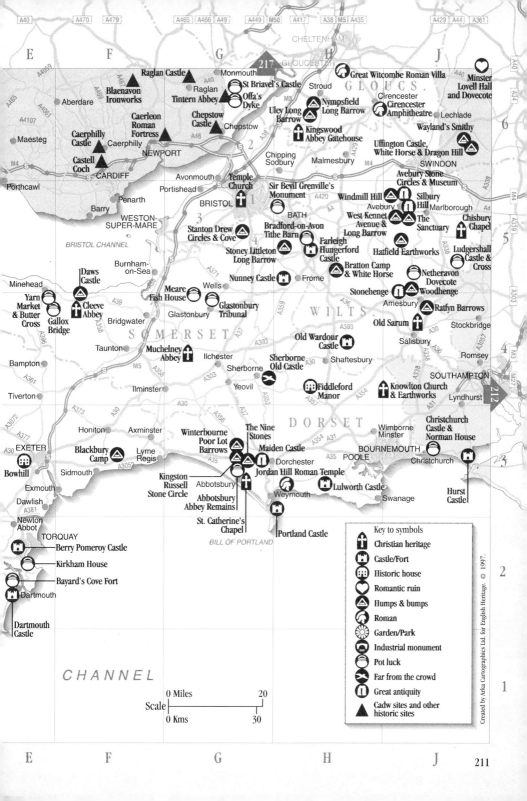

Key to symbols

- ✝ Christian heritage
- 🏰 Castle/Fort
- 🏛 Historic house
- ♥ Romantic ruin
- △ Humps & bumps
- ⌂ Roman
- ⊛ Garden/Park
- ⬤ Industrial monument
- ◖ Pot luck
- ◐ Far from the crowd
- ⊓ Great antiquity
- ▲ Cadw sites and other historic sites

Scale

0 Miles — 20
0 Kms — 30

Created by Arka Cartographics Ltd. for English Heritage. © 1997.

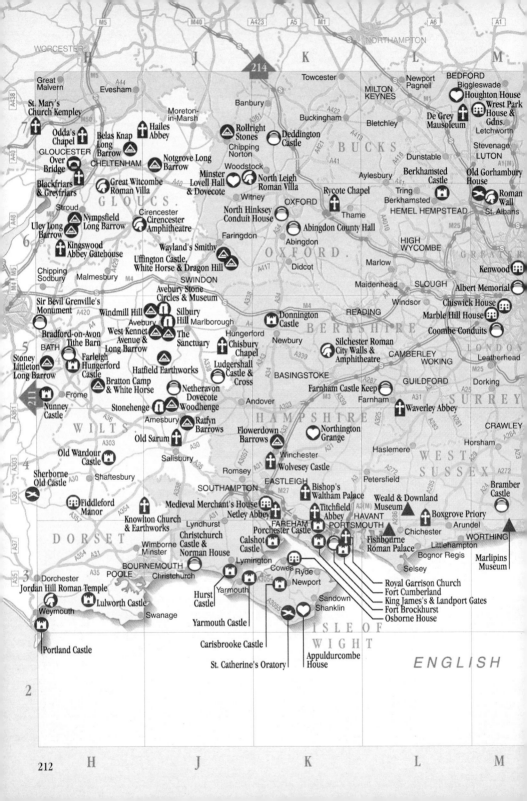

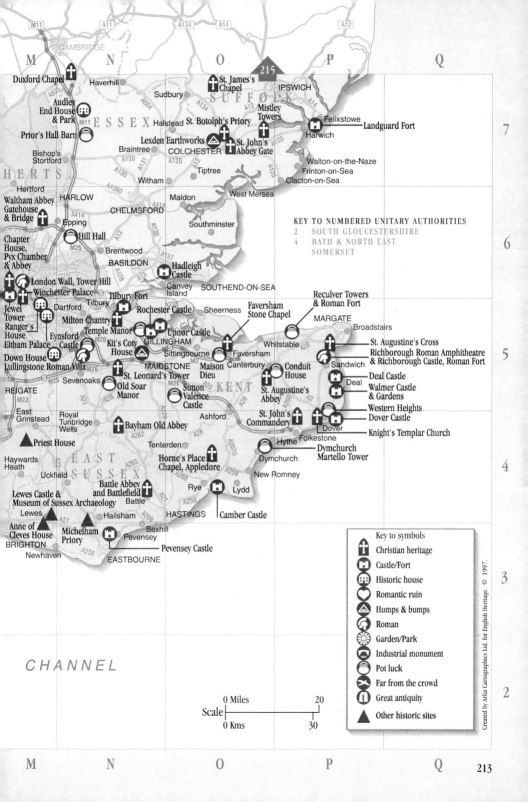

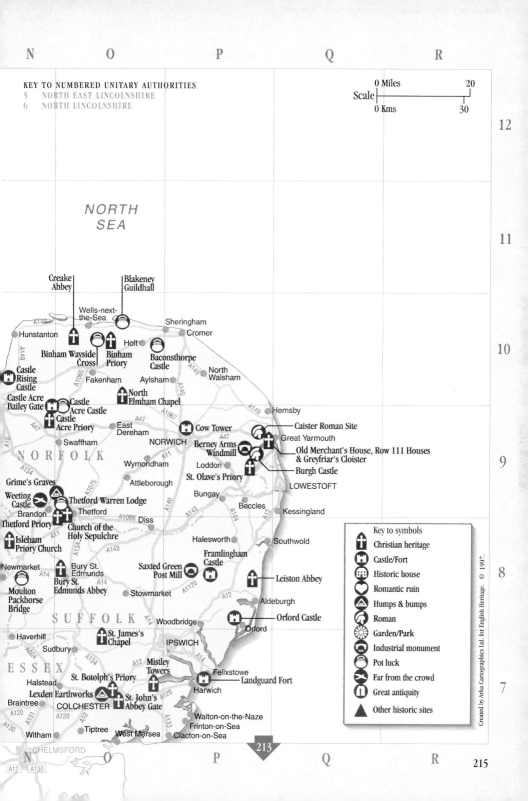

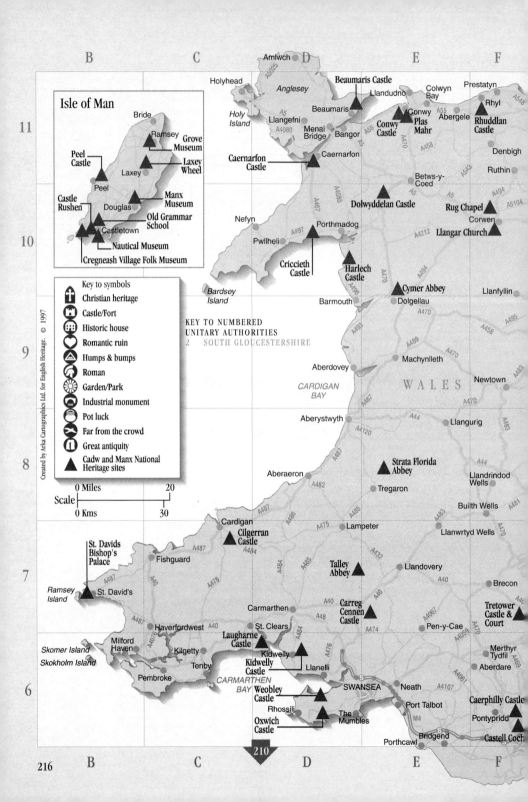

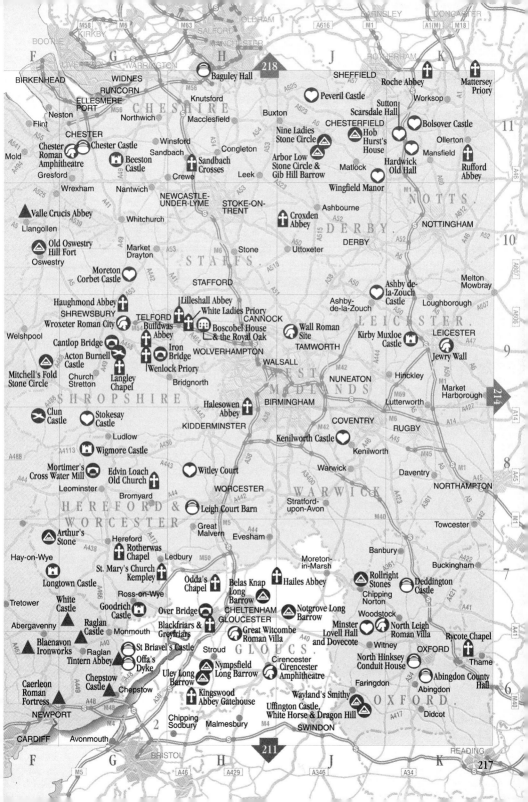

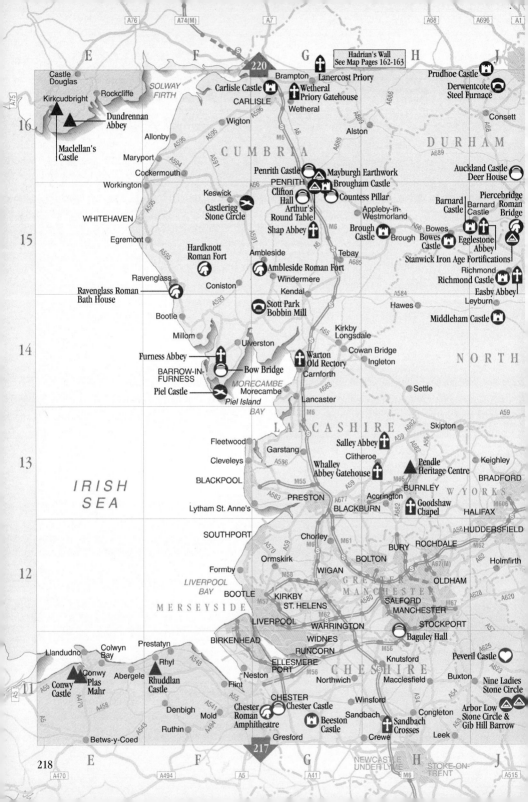

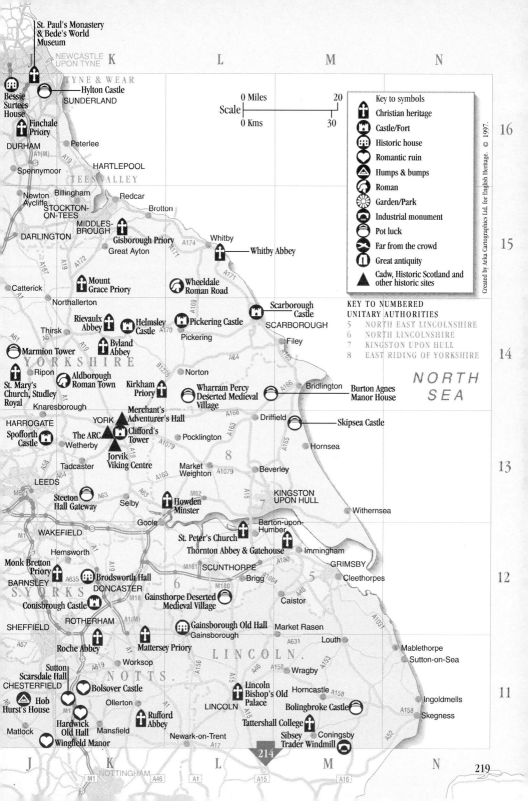

St. Paul's Monastery & Bede's World Museum

NEWCASTLE UPON TYNE

TYNE & WEAR

Hylton Castle

SUNDERLAND

Bessie Surtees House

Finchale Priory

DURHAM

Peterlee

Spennymoor

HARTLEPOOL

TEES VALLEY

Newton Aycliffe

Billingham

Redcar

STOCKTON-ON-TEES

Brotton

MIDDLES-BROUGH

Gisborough Priory

DARLINGTON

Great Ayton

Whitby

Whitby Abbey

Catterick

Northallerton

Mount Grace Priory

Wheeldale Roman Road

Rievaulx Abbey

Thirsk

Helmsley Castle

Pickering Castle

Scarborough Castle

SCARBOROUGH

Byland Abbey

Pickering

Filey

YORKSHIRE

Marmion Tower

Ripon

Aldborough Roman Town

Norton

St. Mary's Church, Studley Royal

Kirkham Priory

Wharram Percy Deserted Medieval Village

Bridlington

Burton Agnes Manor House

Knaresborough

HARROGATE

Spofforth Castle

Wetherby

YORK

Merchant's Adventurer's Hall

The ARC

Clifford's Tower

Driffield

Skipsea Castle

Pocklington

Hornsea

Jorvik Viking Centre

Tadcaster

Market Weighton

Beverley

LEEDS

Steeton Hall Gateway

Selby

Howden Minster

KINGSTON UPON HULL

WAKEFIELD

Goole

Barton-upon-Humber

Withernsea

Hemsworth

St. Peter's Church

Immingham

Monk Bretton Priory

Thornton Abbey & Gatehouse

GRIMSBY

BARNSLEY

Brodsworth Hall

DONCASTER

SCUNTHORPE

Brigg

Cleethorpes

S.YORKS

Conisbrough Castle

Gainsthorpe Deserted Medieval Village

Caistor

SHEFFIELD

ROTHERHAM

Gainsborough Old Hall

Market Rasen

Gainsborough

Louth

Roche Abbey

Mattersey Priory

LINCOLN.

Mablethorpe

Worksop

Wragby

Sutton-on-Sea

Sutton Scarsdale Hall

CHESTERFIELD

NOTTS.

Lincoln Bishop's Old Palace

Horncastle

Ingoldmells

Hob Hurst's House

Bolsover Castle

Ollerton

LINCOLN

Bolingbroke Castle

Skegness

Matlock

Rufford Abbey

Tattershall College

Hardwick Old Hall

Mansfield

Sibsey Trader Windmill

Coningsby

Wingfield Manor

Newark-on-Trent

NOTTINGHAM

NORTH SEA

Key to symbols

Christian heritage
Castle/Fort
Historic house
Romantic ruin
Humps & bumps
Roman
Garden/Park
Industrial monument
Pot luck
Far from the crowd
Great antiquity
Cadw, Historic Scotland and other historic sites

Created by Arka Cartographics Ltd. for English Heritage. © 1997.

KEY TO NUMBERED
UNITARY AUTHORITIES

5   NORTH EAST LINCOLNSHIRE
6   NORTH LINCOLNSHIRE
7   KINGSTON UPON HULL
8   EAST RIDING OF YORKSHIRE

Scale
0 Miles   20
0 Kms   30

214

219

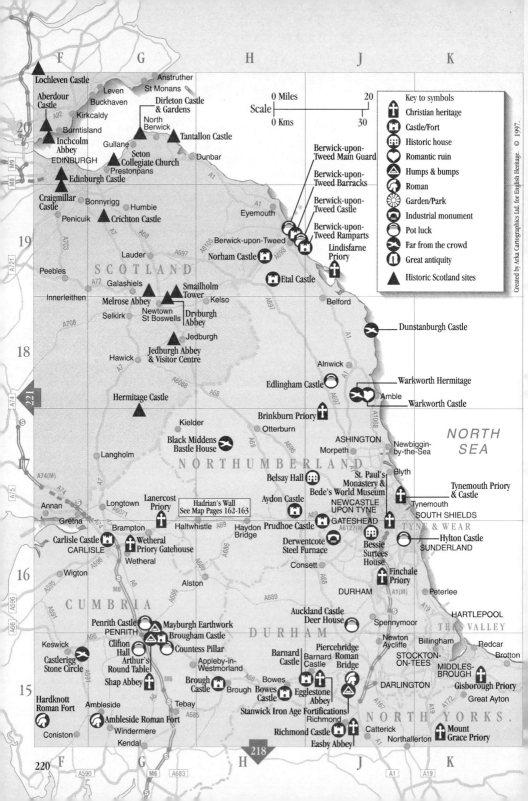

Key to symbols

- ♦ Christian heritage
- 🏰 Castle/Fort
- 🏛 Historic house
- ♥ Romantic ruin
- △ Humps & bumps
- ⊙ Roman
- ⊛ Garden/Park
- ⚙ Industrial monument
- ⚲ Pot luck
- ✈ Far from the crowd
- ⬤ Great antiquity
- ▲ Historic Scotland sites

Created by Arka Cartographics Ltd. for English Heritage. © 1997.

Scale
0 Miles 20
0 Kms 30

SCOTLAND

NORTHUMBERLAND

CUMBRIA

DURHAM

TYNE & WEAR

NORTH YORKS.

TEES VALLEY

NORTH SEA

Lochleven Castle
Aberdour Castle
Burntisland
Inchcolm Abbey
EDINBURGH
Edinburgh Castle
Craigmillar Castle
Crichton Castle
Leven
Buckhaven
Kirkcaldy
Anstruther
St Monans
Dirleton Castle & Gardens
North Berwick
Tantallon Castle
Gullane
Seton Collegiate Church
Prestonpans
Dunbar
Bonnyrigg
Humbie
Penicuik
Peebles
Innerleithen
Lauder
Galashiels
Eyemouth
Berwick-upon-Tweed Main Guard
Berwick-upon-Tweed Barracks
Berwick-upon-Tweed Castle
Berwick-upon-Tweed Ramparts
Berwick-upon-Tweed
Lindisfarne Priory
Norham Castle
Etal Castle
Smailholm Tower
Melrose Abbey
Newtown St Boswells
Dryburgh Abbey
Selkirk
Kelso
Belford
Jedburgh
Jedburgh Abbey & Visitor Centre
Hawick
Hermitage Castle
Kielder
Otterburn
Black Middens Bastle House
Langholm
Longtown
Brampton
Haltwhistle
Haydon Bridge
Lanercost Priory
Hadrian's Wall See Map Pages 162-163
Annan
Gretna
Carlisle Castle
CARLISLE
Wetheral Priory Gatehouse
Wetheral
Wigton
Alston
Keswick
Castlerigg Stone Circle
Penrith Castle
PENRITH
Mayburgh Earthwork
Clifton Hall
Brougham Castle
Countess Pillar
Arthur's Round Table
Shap Abbey
Appleby-in-Westmorland
Hardknott Roman Fort
Coniston
Ambleside
Ambleside Roman Fort
Windermere
Kendal
Tebay
Brough Castle
Brough
Bowes
Bowes Castle
Dunstanburgh Castle
Alnwick
Edlingham Castle
Warkworth Hermitage
Amble
Warkworth Castle
Brinkburn Priory
ASHINGTON
Morpeth
Newbiggin-by-the-Sea
Belsay Hall
Aydon Castle
St. Paul's Monastery & Bede's World Museum
NEWCASTLE UPON TYNE
GATESHEAD
Tynemouth Priory & Castle
Tynemouth
SOUTH SHIELDS
Prudhoe Castle
Derwentcote Steel Furnace
Consett
Bessie Surtees House
SUNDERLAND
Hylton Castle
Finchale Priory
DURHAM
Peterlee
HARTLEPOOL
Auckland Castle Deer House
Spennymoor
Newton Aycliffe
Billingham
Redcar
Brotton
STOCKTON-ON-TEES
MIDDLESBROUGH
DARLINGTON
Gisborough Priory
Great Ayton
Barnard Castle
Piercebridge
Barnard Castle
Roman Bridge
Egglestone Abbey
Stanwick Iron Age Fortifications
Richmond
Richmond Castle
Easby Abbey
Catterick
Northallerton
Mount Grace Priory

220

218

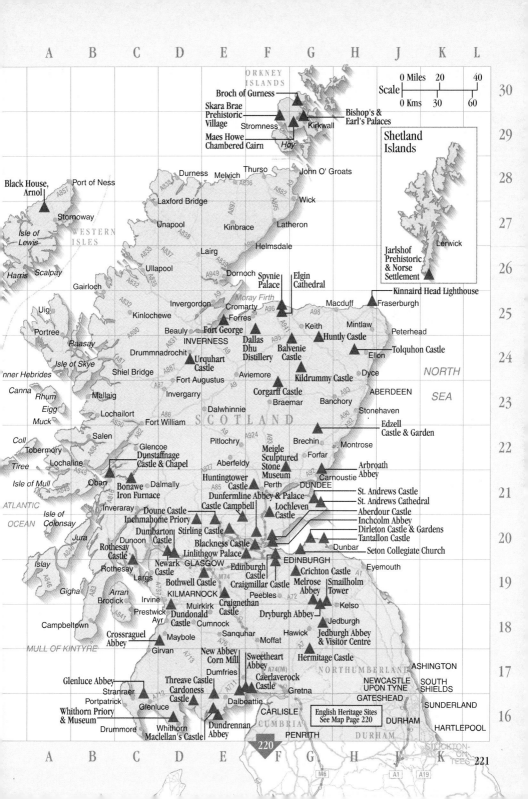

INDEX

INDEX

INDEX

Acknowledgements

Thanks are due to the following for permission to reproduce illustrations:

Sonia Halliday: 10 centre left.
Terry Ball: 10 bottom left, 158 bottom.
English Heritage/Skyscan: 19 top, 25 bottom, 27, 30 centre right, 35 centre right, 37, 38 top, 43 bottom right, 57 bottom right, 63, 72 bottom, 81 top left, 89 top, 106 top and middle right, 107, 109 bottom, 113 bottom left, 115 bottom left and right, 120 top, 142, 145 middle, 166 centre left, 178 top and bottom, 179 middle right, 186 bottom left, 188 bottom.
Salisbury and South Wiltshire Museum: 30 centre and bottom, 44 top.
By Courtesy of The National Portrait Gallery, London: 34 centre.
Wiltshire Archaeological & Natural History Society (Devizes Museum): 40 top, centre.
West Air Photography: 45 top left.
Wiltshire Archaeological & Natural History Society: 45 bottom left.
Michael Holford: 54/55 bottom.
British Library, London/Bridgeman Art Library, London: 52 top right, 154 top.
Carisbrooke Castle Museum: 56 inset, 58 top right and bottom.
Dover Museum (Ivan Lapper): 66 top.
Dover Museum: 67 top left.
The Hulton Deutsch Collection: 70 centre, 158 top.
The Darwin Museum: 74 top, 75 top, centre right, bottom right and bottom inset, 76 top and bottom, 77 bottom right.
The Royal Collection © Her Majesty The Queen: 82 top centre
The Royal Archives © Her Majesty The Queen: 83 bottom.
William Tomkins: 102 top.
Mansell Collection: 128 centre
Copyright British Museum: 162 top.
Carlisle City Museum and Art Gallery: 164 bottom left and inset.
Alan Sorrell: 171 top

The following original artworks have been based on illustrations from:

English Heritage/Skyscan: 31, 53, 57, 64, 82, 90, 99, 127, 144, 166, 172, 181, 187, 193.
Carlisle Museum and Art Gallery: 154, bottom left.
Radio Times Hulton Picture Library: 159 centre left.
Judith Dobie: 189 bottom right.
Karen Guffogg: 189 bottom left.